W9-AVJ-786

LEARNING TO FLY

LEARNING TO FLY

A Season with the Peregrine Falcon

by

P. H. Liotta

Algonquin Books of Chapel Hill   1989

Published by
Algonquin Books of Chapel Hill
Post Office Box 2225
Chapel Hill, North Carolina 27515-2225

a division of
Workman Publishing Company, Inc.
708 Broadway
New York, New York 10003

© 1989 by P. H. Liotta. All rights reserved.
Printed in the United States of America.

A portion of this book originally appeared in *Esquire.*

"Self/Landscape/Grid," by Terrence Des Pres appeared first in
New England Review/Bread Loaf Quarterly,
Vol. 5, No. 4, Summer 1983.

Material from *The Goshawk* by T. H. White was published by
The Putnam Publishing Group, © 1951, T. H. White.

Library of Congress Cataloging-in-Publication Data

Liotta, P. H.
Learning to fly.

Bibliography: p.
1. Peregrine falcon—New York (State)—Adirondack
Mountains.   2. Animal introduction—New York (State)—
Adirondack Mountains.   3. Liotta, P. H.   I. Title.
QL696.F34L57   1989   598'.918   88-35016
ISBN 0-945575-15-7

10 9 8 7 6 5 4 3 2 1

FIRST PRINTING

for Donna

The flowers on the wall spring alive.
—JORGE GUILLÉN

I will not be clapped in a hood,

Nor a cage, nor alight upon wrist,

Now I have learnt to be proud

Hovering over the wood

In the broken mist

Or tumbling cloud.

—W. B. YEATS, "The Hawk"

CONTENTS

PREFACE

At the end of my first year of graduate study at Cornell University, I received a phone call from Jack Shelley of the Peregrine Fund asking me to work as a hack site attendant for a peregrine recovery program at a new location in the Adirondacks.

The process of reintroducing raptors to their natural environment is difficult. Young chicks are raised by adult falcons until the third to fourth week of life, a period crucial for imprinting on parents. The nestlings, now able to tear and eat their own food, are then transferred to various release sites: tall buildings in urban locations (historically, peregrines lived and hunted in a number of eastern cities); man-made towers in flat marshlands; and cliff sites, in locations where many peregrines once maintained aëries. The young falcons, or eyasses, are kept in bar-fronted plywood boxes until approximately their sixth week of life, protected from predation while still able to observe their environment. During their sixth week, the bars are removed, and the birds are free to explore. The birds continue to return for food, which is provided daily using an ancient method known as hacking. In the absence of parents to drop live food from the air and initiate hunting forays, the young fledglings teach each other to survive.

My work at the hack site would involve eight weeks of twenty-four-hour-a-day care and observation. Without hesitation, without bothering to ask anyone for approval or advice, I accepted.

This book contains my own impressions and experiences. It is not a scientific treatise on peregrines. My observations in no way represent the official positions of any organization. It would be wrong, however, not to acknowledge the help and support of many people, whose names are changed in this manuscript, but who will nevertheless recognize the part they played in the falcon release at Fire Lake Mountain. I also owe thanks to Ken McClane, whose criticism and suggestions, as well as sense of humor, were extraordinary; to Robert Morgan and Jo Berryman, for their constant friendship and advice; to Stephen Jarosak, who first asked me to write down these notes; to John Pickering and Betsy Davidson, for their continuing faith; to Louis Rubin and Susan Ketchin, especially, for their stubborn refusal to allow me too quick satisfaction with what I had written.

Finally, I wish to thank ten peregrine fledglings, my "roommates" for the summer, without whom there would be no tale.

Some of the incidents, physical references and descriptions, and all identification markings have been intentionally distorted to protect the actual location of the site.

LEARNING TO FLY

THE BOXES

*To share fear is the greatest bond of all. The
hunter must become the thing he hunts.
What is, is now, must have the quivering
intensity of an arrow thudding into a tree.
Yesterday is dim and monochrome. A week
ago you were not born. Persist, endure,
follow, watch.*
—J. A. BAKER, *The Peregrine*

I am sitting on the edge of a thousand-foot cliff in the central Adirondacks, watching the hard disk of the moon, a white tabula rasa, rise from behind Blue Mountain, forty-five miles east.

After three days of cold and continuous rain, mist, and up-drafts of wind which shoot vertically up the sheer rock face, it's quiet. I fix my attention on the sharp outline of the half moon. If you stare at it long enough, as I am doing now, you can easily distinguish its perfect halves, the sharp line which separates the light from absence.

In the valley below, the twisting body of the Snake River Flow Area and the perfect geometry of Triangle Pond are easy to pick out; after a few minutes, the clouds disperse, allow the light to shiver down on Horseheads Lake. Legend claims that when a native tribe was slaughtered, the only survivors were small children found playing with the heads of horses which had been severed from the carcasses. Later inhabitants forgot the apostrophe when naming the lake, along of course with the sense that anyone had lived here previously. With that in mind, it's eerie to notice the formation of the lake. From this height it assumes the outline of a horse's head: small tributaries breaking off and feathered with pine in the place of a mane, a small island in the precise spot where the huge opaque eye should be.

One hundred and fifty yards below and to the northwest are two plywood boxes with green vinyl mesh fronts which, for the next ten days at least, will be the homes for ten peregrine falcon chicks, ranging in age from twenty-eight to thirty-four days. In the past week these chicks have had their fill of traumatic experi-ence. Due to a high mortality of offspring in the Peregrine Fund's breeding facility at Boise, Idaho, four of these young birds were donated by a private breeder in Sitka, Alaska. The chicks were flown from Boise to Ithaca, New York, taken to the Hawk Barn at Cornell's Sapsucker Woods, placed five to a cage in dog kennels, secured to the bed of a four-wheel-drive Ford pickup, and driven 250 miles to this remote location in the Adirondacks. Once here, they were welcomed yesterday afternoon by a crowd of "technicians" and observers from the Department of Environmental Conservation, each of whom looked either overly bored or overly concerned, each of whom I'm certain I will never see again.

The rain was still hitting hard. The mud along the trail to Camp Beaverkill spread rivulets; streams of flashing water ran on both sides of the road, and then rose above and joined in a flood.

Perhaps the most honest explanation for why these people were here is because a photographer and reporter from Syracuse also came along. Any and all media attention that's given to the release of peregrines will help keep the project alive; the New York State Return a Gift to Wildlife program helped fund this project. The publicity for the Department of Environmental Conservation, or "D-E-C" as I've learned to say with precision these days, hasn't hurt either. Curiously, the DEC's abundant literature on recovery programs never mentions the Peregrine Fund contributions.

My partner, Tom Peters, and I have the honor of carrying the first kennel of birds up Fire Lake Mountain, and of leading the entourage, collectively sliding and falling on earth that seems a living sponge. The trail follows the eroded path of a mountain stream, where new rivers and channels form each minute. There are four separate layers to the trail: a marshy flat bog nearly a mile across, with a mixed family of ferns, including elongated ostrich ferns; a steep rise over red maple and twisted growth, boulders scored with intensely green moss; and a forest of mountain paper birches in the shape of a forked tongue across the south face, which grew after the 1911 fire, started when stray sparks flew from the tracks of the now abandoned railroad. Finally, the trail levels near the summit to an open meadow where the light and mist spread through the trees, reminding me of the pure clear space of Tuolumne Meadows in Upper Yosemite. Crossing the meadow, we reach the peak, which narrows into a thin, knifelike plateau 400 yards long. After fifteen minutes of trekking through undergrowth and over rock, we reach the cliffs where we will spend the next seven weeks.

At the peak's crest, the photographer has us pose for some dramatic shots against the skyline and the frozen mist of the valley. I assume my best Jeremiah Johnson look of disdain. In the distance, fractured glimpses of Whiteface and the High Peaks appear north and east. We set the birds down on a flat rock shelf above the ledges where we've built the hack boxes. I leave Tom, two DEC officials, and the photographer, and go back to search for the others, wondering if anyone has taken a serious fall. The mountain narrows sharply as it approaches the northwest peak and there are sheer drop-offs on both sides.

I am easily visible, even in this weather. I am wearing a fluorescent orange, hooded hunting sweater, canary-yellow sweatshirt, and fire-engine-red sweatpants. "I like to blend with the natural colors of my environment," I explain to someone. The reporter dubs me a Gore-Tex caveman.

Twenty minutes later, the group is united and serves witness to the birds in their new home. The senior DEC representative excuses himself early, making a few quotable remarks for the media about the "important role the state of New York plays in the reintroduction of endangered species," how "it's an important chapter of your life, yes, but you do it and go on to other things." At the moment he has to go on to a reception for the Adirondacks Arts Festival. He smiles at me as he leaves, says, "Well, have a good time." I interpret his look to mean: "You have five hundred thousand dollars worth of birds in your hands. One mistake, you die."

"Hey, is it true what I've heard about Yeager?"

I look down in the direction of the sound, confused. George Gordon, who is the peregrine reintroduction specialist and is responsible for numerous other sites such as this one, is looking straight up at me from the hack boxes. He knows I dislike this circus; I have already said to him that if *they* really cared so much about this program, why is this the first time I've seen many of these people?

"Yeah, it's true," I call down. "My father knows him slightly . . . egotistical son-of-a-bitch. Great pilot. Second best fighter pilot in the world." My glasses are stained with rain.

"Well then, who's the best?"

"My father . . . or my brother. Depends on whom you ask."

"Well, I guess that's the way it works."

"Ay-uh." I nod in agreement, smile. "Hey, George, I really appreciate your letting me carry the birds up."

"What do you mean?" He throws up his arms in mock disbelief. "That's your duty."

"Well it meant a lot."

To be fair, I know I have removed myself from the events around me. I ignored all the bureaucratic coordination and political maneuvers required to set up this site at Fire Lake Mountain. I am an Air Force officer attending a civilian school who's been generously allowed to participate in a summer research project. This is all I pretend to know.

For the next seven weeks nothing else matters. All I truly care about are these birds, or so I think. Only one in three will survive their first year after release. And how many of those will mate and produce offspring? There are twenty-one birds planned for reintroduction in New York this summer. Ten of them are my responsibility.

Several people are pounding rocks on the upper shelf to produce gravel for the hack boxes. I've attached a flimsy rope to a birch and quasi-rappel the face; I'm carrying gravel fragments for the lower ledge in my backpack. Soon, the boxes look ready. George, a man eloquently lacking eloquence, proclaims: "Let's do it."

He takes the first chick, fluffy white and covered with soft down, and hands her to me to place in the box. I cover her near the wings, careful of her developing primary feathers, holding her gently. She is cacking: a short staccato burst of terrified air shoved from her lungs. The photographer pops up from behind some scrub pine and fires off a few rounds. I set her down inside the box and she runs to the far wall, turns and faces me. Her beak is open, her long thin tongue extended; too frightened to scream, all that comes out is a sharp hiss of air. The rain hits even harder and a white cloud shoots up the cliff, envelops us in fog. It's a wonderful moment.

This, as the Syracuse *North Country* Sunday edition will later describe it, is the Wilderness Experience.

MONDAY, 16 JUNE

I've strung a hammock up between a paper birch and a red spruce in time to watch the lightning. The hammock swings out over the cliff's edge. It gives the feel of weightlessness, as if I'm hovering in still air. If one of these knots slips, my attempt at free flight would be worthless. Perhaps a ledge would break the fall. Perhaps it would be better to die cleanly, falling the entire thousand feet to land in the thick forest. Besides the two of us, there is no living person for fifteen miles in any direction.

In the past few days, the birds have matured swiftly, steadily. In terms of size, they have already reached their full growth. At thirty-seven days, the oldest fledglings have begun to lose most of their down. Sharply rippled black and tan is visible on the breast; the intense dark mask of the peregrine is outlined on the head.

Most of the chicks are visible through peepholes in the boxes. In the near box, two birds have not yet left the "hide"—a diagonally cut space in the far corner designed for privacy and some protection from the weather. When they finally do appear, we name one Noah John Rondeau, in honor of the well-known Adirondack hermit. He's a young male, thirty days, still covered with down. The other is a small female. We christen her Anne LaBastille, after another local recluse who is also an extraordinary naturalist and field conservationist. When Anne sees the shape of my eyes through a peephole, she gives a sharp cack and runs back to the hide. I will not see either of them again for three days.

At this stage, the fledglings' bones are soft, still unformed. Many of the birds, particularly the larger females, will spend most of their time lying down in what seems a mock brooding position, looking like bowls of Jell-o with moving heads. Many field biologists, notoriously ignorant about raptors, have mistaken this condition for rickets.

Ignorance about raptors is fairly common. There really are no experts. I remember last Thursday when we set the birds inside the hack boxes, a biologist exclaiming, "Now they're imprinting on this area." Though we've no way of getting the fledglings' opinion on this statement, I think his proclamation is nonsense.

The birds, after all, are only prisoners. Until their release they have only a tunnel vision of how this valley really appears. For the next week, they'll see only a limited perspective of Horseheads Lake and the high peaks beyond. When they're released, when they learn to fly, they will either recognize this ledge as a place to return to feed, or they will starve. First they must learn to survive. Only after they're comfortable on the wing will they hone their techniques of the kill: stooping out of the sun at 200 miles an hour to snap a prey's neck with the slap of a talon and the bite of a razorlike beak. Their visual ability is estimated at eight times that of a human (and some owls have night vision a hundred times more powerful than ours)—able to see a beetle on the pavement from the sixth story of a building, or a mouse from a mile and a half away.

Living in a four-by-four-foot box is hardly a way to "imprint." Slaves of humanity, they must adapt to us; the hard part is up to them. There is absolutely nothing we can teach them.

Donna, my wife, has shared my fascination with raptors for over a decade. When we first met as cadets at the Air Force Academy, falcons and hawks were almost always attendant observers of our relationship. A prairie falcon would perch on a closet door or headboard whenever she came to my room; a red-tailed hawk would lean and balance in the back of my jeep whenever we climbed up the rough, four-wheel-drive path of Mount Herman to watch the sun sloping its pink light off the huge boulder formations at dawn.

The magic we shared then—and I think it's fair to call it that—was one of the reasons why we are still together. I was a senior, a firstclassman; she was a freshman: a fourthclassman, or "doolie" (from the Greek δουλοσ, meaning "slave"). Everything about the rules of order and discipline prevented our seeing each other; if we had been caught even visiting together, it could have meant my dismissal. Regulations on fraternization between upper- and lower-class cadets are strict.

I first saw her in Mitchell Hall. Perhaps the largest dining facility in the world, it accommodates up to four thousand people in a single seating. Fourthclassmen sit at the north end of squadron tables, and the hierarchy of rank and power moves away from them. I was commander of 157 cadets in 27th Squadron—

the Thunderbirds. A cadet lieutenant colonel, I was largely responsible for the academic, military, and athletic performance of each squadron member. I had probably more power and influence then, as a senior cadet, than I did as an aircraft commander.

Doolies must sit at attention at every meal in Mitchell Hall. They serve all other cadets at their table before, if they are lucky, they are allowed to eat. (Eating at mealtimes is not always a given. I lost over twenty-five pounds during basic cadet training because I hadn't learned that humility and discipline were key ingredients to getting food into your mouth.) Shoulders back and down, chin neatly tucked into the small of the throat, eyes straight ahead or down on the plate, a doolie doesn't really have much time to enjoy the Colorado landscape which occupies the entire plate-glass southern face of the dining hall.

As part of the traditional end of every meal, doolies are expected to "post"—they stand at attention and sing a catchy limerick which almost always attacks another branch of the military or ridicules a sister service academy. The first time I saw Donna, she was *performing* a "post." She was wearing regulation leather shoes, but she had attached metal taps on the toes. She was swinging her arms from side to side and singing in a clear, strong voice about the joys of military service. I had never actually seen a live tap-dance before, and here I was watching a fourth-classman perform it—brilliantly. My jaw dropped, and it stayed frozen in surprise.

This, I thought, *is really something.*

Once, after a squadron party, after having too much fun and too much beer, she returned from Woodland Park and began singing lines from Shakespearean plays to her roommates. Her voice carried down the corridors. I opened the door of her room, and she was visibly absent, though I could hear her voice, by then pouring out the music of *Twelfth Night.* I found her under her roommate's bed; in the shadows, she giggled and let out a *Hi there!* greeting for me.

At night, well after taps, I could hear tap-dancing in her room: her bright, metallic chorus of footsteps ringing the silence.

I began noticing her in the halls. Her right shoulder braced against the wall as she moved through the squadron area, her eyes staring at the distance in front of her, she would fire off a crisp "Good evening, Sir!" as I returned from library work every night. Her face was hard and indifferent to me. (Later she told me her roommates had decided that, as far as squadron commanders went, I was "a jerk.") After Christmas, though, her face looked drawn and tired. I learned that she had been secretly dating an upperclassman, and that he had promptly told her to "get lost" when the rapidly spreading news of their involvement threatened (should Academy officials discover) to kill his chances of winning a Guggenheim fellowship after graduation.

What I didn't, or couldn't, read in her look of tired despair was how desperately she wanted to leave. The demands on a cadet are intense, unrelenting; when she decided she no longer wanted to be there, her grades and her outlook began to plummet. It's something outsiders, especially close family members, simply cannot understand. Books, such as Truscott's *Dress Gray* and Webb's *A Sense of Honor* can give you the grisly images but cannot provide the *feel* of complete and desperate helplessness.

And most of us who did experience it would not want to do so a second time.

I called her in for counseling. When she began to speak, truly speak, I realized how entirely different she was from other cadets. She had her own ways of seeing, and of knowing, and the rigors and order of a military academy simply could not change her. It had changed me, I've no question of that. But it could not make her bend.

Without knowing it would happen, we devised ways of seeing each other in secret. After I stepped down as squadron commander at semester's end, I selected a dormitory room next to hers. I loosened the medicine cabinet in the wall separating our rooms so that, like Pyramus and Thisbe, we could speak through the crevice without others knowing. After a while, though, pulling the cabinet out became increasingly cumbersome and risky. I devised a way to jam my bedroom door so that a key, inserted from the outside, would not open the lock. But that, too, became suspicious.

During prisoner-of-war training, I learned the tap code method of sending messages through walls and I taught it to Donna; eventually, tap signals became our most effective method of communicating with each other in the dormitory.

But if we wanted to see each other, it had to be away from the campus. Sometimes she would visit me at the falcon mews, and we would spend time cleaning chambers and feeding birds. Sometimes we would hop in the jeep and climb up the rugged trails of the Front Range. And, always, there would be a raptor chaperone with us. With bright, shining eyes, our avatar bounced and twisted as the jeep churned up the mountainside, perched on the lip of a seat, watching and waiting.

The next bird we give some identity to (something slightly more personal than Federal Band Number of Male: 619-27536/ Left) is Figmo. Donna hiked up on Saturday to see the chicks and helped name him. We held back laughter seeing him perched on a rock, head covered with prickly down as if he were an old Marine drill sergeant sporting a sparse crew cut. His crop is full, gorged from the day's feeding of quail. His eyes look slightly crossed. He is resting on the base of his tail—huge, clumsy talons splayed out in front of him as though he's no idea what their use is.

Figmo looks quizzically at us, watching us watching him. He gives a soft cack, which sounds like a slow, satisfied burp. His condition reminds me of a personality dysfunction common among certain military members about to change duty stations, coasting along until the time comes to leave. "Figmo" is an acronym for "Fuck it, I've got my orders."

Since I became a pilot, my way of seeing the earth and atmospheric phenomena has changed. In Minot, North Dakota, where I was once stationed, a B-52 returned at dawn with its radome and radar partially fried. The entire nose section of the aircraft was missing, as well as some ailerons and a large chunk of the left wingtip. A five-by-eight-foot hole of open space, which was once metal, appeared in the tail. The plane had not, however, been hit by lightning; the damage was caused by electrostatic discharge when it passed between two opposite weather fronts.

On a flight in a KC-135 over the polar ice cap, my crew flew through the aurora borealis, a mass of phosphorescent green swirl which wrapped its arms around the skin of the ship.[1] From the cockpit, it seemed I was banking high and left and then diving into a whirlpool of brilliant green. I believed what I saw. Yet the artificial horizon, a bright orange delta like a bull's-eye at the center of the instrument panel, meant to represent the attitude and situation of the plane itself, showed the aircraft's wings to be straight, level: What my flight instruments told me was more *real* than what I saw. The gyroscopes whirred and turned continuously and self-corrected the instruments humming on the panel, a sound we could not hear beneath the dull drone of four rotating turbines. I had heard of the bizarre effects the northern lights produced on hand calculators; I pulled my calculator out of my flightsuit and watched a random number series being generated on the display screen. The calculator had been turned off when I had pulled it from my pocket; mysteriously, it was now on. A sequence of digits floated from right to left across the LCD panel; they would disappear and a new sequence would just as suddenly begin dancing in my hands. The huge swirling mass of green shimmered beneath us, and then around us. There at the top of the world, where the sun rises by falling south, we flew a single ship into the center of an element which no one knows the true composition of.[2] Holding tight to my geocentric view, I found it difficult to believe that charged particles, suddenly disturbed by the earth's magnetic field, could cause this rain of light which did not burn, this roiling sea of green in total darkness.

One night in North Dakota, while driving across the wide expanse of prairie emptiness, I looked up and saw the aurora consuming the inverted bowl of the sky. I stopped the car, killed the engine and the lights, and stepped out into a pure clear night of fifty degrees below zero, a windless night too cold for snow. I stared into a great beating atmosphere of grey, as if looking up into an obversed heart beating from the outside in, pulsing and glowing from a source which did not belong to the earth. The most beautiful description, one which matches perfectly what I saw, is to call its undulating motions a t'ai chi of the ionosphere, an atmospheric dance "graceful, in-ward turning, and protracted."[3] I have been told, or once read, stories of how, hours before the aurora would appear, compasses would spin wildly with an inner agitation—on board ships and planes, in desk drawers, in forgotten boxes, in the pockets of eager Boy Scouts, or sunk in the ground and lost for years, the axis of direction no longer certain. The story is a lie, but I could have easily believed it that night, as easily as I could believe that this glowing shadow produced what the Greeks called the music of the spheres. We flew at a distance so far north the magnetic compass turned aside, becoming worthless unless a compensation was made in grid navigation. Flying west, the compass had us flying east; flying north, south. The tiny core of its magnetic heart pointed its pin to the ore deposit at Magnetic North, above Resolute and Melville Sound, thousands of miles away. And nine hundred miles north of that, 90°00′ N and 00°00′ W: the Pole. But what lies north is not always true.

Last year on a return flight from Europe, we were three hours past the Azores when Saint Elmo's Fire engulfed us: a flashing, iridescent display. Trickles of light danced on our windows like small, hard tears. A green bolt of fire shot through my window and over my shoulder, and then flew towards the rear of the aircraft, finally striking the plane in the aft passenger section.

As we drifted high above the black Atlantic, my crew was silent. Our radio was intermittently operative; occasionally, we caught the scattered CB nonsense of truckers crossing Kansas but had no contact with any air traffic center. The only voice that touched me said, *When you die it will be like this.*

Tonight the lightning and rain are intense. A sharp flash from the north illuminates the hack boxes. The birds are quiet. Rain has a calming effect on them. During transportation, chicks are often "hosed down" in their travel boxes and will stay quiet for hours. But this is their first thunderstorm, a very different reality.

The rain is coming hard now. I fall back to the tent, settle into finishing Stephen King's "The Mist." While I read of people being consumed by grotesque abominations, the inside of my tent pounds like a swollen, arrhythmic heart. I wonder how long the stakes will hold before the wind rips them out of the soft, damp earth. I've tied most of the tent ropes to trees, so I've some solid foundation. I envy Tom's tent: a sleek, free-standing dome. The wind rails through my miserable mass of nylon and plastic. I feel the edges lifting. I crawl in the dark lit by a battery lantern, check to see that my books are safely sealed. I have a late nineteenth-century edition of Baudelaire; poems by Christianne Balk, William Carpenter, Cornelius Eady, Phyllis Janowitz; a copy of Frank Conroy's *Stop-Time*; two anthologies of English literature; translations of Rilke I've been working on for the past six months. The rain slams on the roof, its drops visible as they slip down the outer walls to flood my trench, moving at the direction of the wind.

I read on of the horrible fates of Mr. King's characters: innocent victims of the Arrowhead Project, a misguided apocalyptic failure of a militaristically motivated society. I hear them scream outside in the wind: *My God, there's something in the mist!*

The first lightning strike hits a few hundred yards south. Fifty million volts of energy slam into the mountain. Tomorrow I will find a birch cleaved perfectly in half. The second strike hits. I'm up instantly; I recognize its location: the northwest face, where the hack boxes are. I forget my flashlight and there's no moon to see by. I slip on a slab of granite; the tail of my spine slaps hard on rock. The pain will be a reminder in the coming weeks.

Gripping the thin stalks of trees, I find the observation point. A sudden flash lights up the outline of Horseheads Lake. I see the boxes. No damage. Boiled layers of clouds run for miles in all directions. The isolated peak of Whiteface, fifty miles away, is distinct. A perfect white vein of rock runs through its brow.

I return to my tent and find it collapsed; its wings flutter, as if wounded. I stumble to the supply tent and find the squirrel I attacked with an axe yesterday. He hides in a corner. Somehow, he has found a way inside the tent; he helps himself generously to our foodstuffs. Yesterday I chased him for thirty minutes, slicing a deep notch in the wooden cot, leaving thin cuts in the mosquito netting. Twice, he lunged at me with awesome speed, his teeth wanting the soft part of my neck. He seemed determined to make our sufferings equal. I pulled him off, terrified of death by rabid red squirrel.

And then I saw us from an outside view. A twinge of guilt reminded me of how, years before, during survival training at the Air Force Academy, my two companions and I jumped a ruffed grouse. We'd eaten nothing for three days; we were eager to eat the flesh raw, since building a fire was impossible (fire would be too obvious to the "enemy" searching for us). The look of desperation in the bird's eyes forced us to let her go. It was preferable to starve a while longer.

And so, tonight, I open the flap of the supply tent to set my squirrel free.

Held by the thread of fear and the need for shelter, he will not leave. I throw him a white slice of bread.

"Here, take this. And be quiet."

We're no longer enemies.

We spend the night together. Two lonely, wet companions.

THURSDAY, 19 JUNE

A spider reels up the length of her threaded line and hides under a leaf. Instinctively, she feels the coming rain; but I seem unsure if the clouds are even headed in our direction. I see virga to the west and south—streamers of rain at high altitude which dissipate before they reach the ground.

I'm sitting on a flat granite shelf on the back side of the mountain overlooking Fire Lake (which is the namesake for this peak), as well as Iron Pond, and Blueberry Lake, fifteen miles off. An A-10, an aircraft designed as a tank killer, rolls off the lip of a far peak and falls into its own shadow as it traces the outline of the landscape, flying just barely above the trees. It's an impressive plane, meant to take inordinate amounts of punishment and damage: the pilot is mounted in a tub of titanium which can withstand the impact of artillery fire; the high-mounted engines have self-sealing tanks which can swallow a huge number of bullets fired at, and meant to pierce, the aircraft's skin. Yet only a few years ago, a sparrow sucked into one of the engines could rupture the hydraulic lines, forcing the pilot to eject.

I hear the faint hum of the A-10's engines. Its camouflage paint scheme is a sharp contrast to the shagged green carpet of woods. The plane carries, aside from laser-guided bombs, an enormous Gatling gun, able to rotate and twist the entire airframe like a gyroscope at certain angles of attack. The plane is meant to give as well as take punishment. In pilot training, we half-seriously described the A-10 simulator as dropping a man in a dipsy-dumpster and stoning him with boulders.

The pilot turns west, perhaps heading for maneuvers at Fort Drum, a good sixty, seventy miles west. The first few days we were here, I believed there was seismic activity in the western Adirondacks. The ground shook at odd times and I heard the far-off rumbles of thunder; I believed the truth of Rip Van Winkle waking to the sound of strange little men bowling in the Catskills. Now, though, I know the distant rumbling is artillery rounds being fired at Fort Drum.

*　　*　　*

Earlier today, I hiked the ten miles out to Horseheads Lake to find my parked car hidden in a cluster of trees. It's two hours out and two and one-half to hike back in. My car could never make it through these rutted logging trails. I spent most of the day in the metropolis of Clear Lake, twelve hundred full-time residents. Haircut, laundry, food. At the laundromat a barefoot man is perched on the front steps smoking a cigarette. His hair is slicked with grease. A plastic garbage bag with all his worldly goods is at his side. I pause at the screen door. He looks up at me and smiles.

I must look far worse than he: no shave for nine days; a layer of dirt oiled in my palms; several hundred black fly bites generously spread over my flesh. Insect repellent, though it keeps away most common pests of the wilderness, does nothing to stop the black fly's vicious thirst; skin pores must be clogged to stop them from biting. (Tom has, until recently, been using a skin lotion called *Smooth as Silk:* it covers exposed pores and effectively stops black flies from biting. But it has its disadvantages, too. The lotion is sweetly perfumed: yesterday I watched Tom run by my tent and disappear in the thick wood, chased by an appreciative swarm of bees.)

We go inside, each keeping to himself. He lays out his possessions on a far table: five bottles of Brut, one nail clipper, two towels, three packs of Kent Menthols.

Most of the day I walk. Hiking back from Horseheads Lake, I read the *Canterbury Tales* out loud. By now I'm well into the rhythms of "The Miller's Tale." My Middle English is poor; it sounds like a bad Scotch brogue. Yet by the time I reach the climactic scene between Alison, the unfaithful wife; Nicholas, the clerk; and Absolon, the parish clergyman, the language has its own life. Branded in the "toute" by Absolon, Nicholas cries:

> That for the smert he wende for to die;
> As he were wood for wo he gan to crye,
> "Help! Water! Water! Help, for Goddes herte!"

I look up. A doe stands fifty feet from me, at the edge of a beaver pond. She's large, the biggest I've seen. She crouches for a moment, then realizes I'm aware of her. She snorts water in one huge blast: thick jets of spray flare from her nostrils. Her tail rises; her rear end jackknifes. White fur bobbing, she bounds through the marsh and into the trees. The woods swallow her sound.

A thick bandage of mist has settled over Fire Lake. A far section of the lake burns with the sun's failing light. Once, in the cadence and beauty of *Beowulf*, I read of this moment. But it was legend then, and the image was conjured in the realm of the ear. Now it is real:

> Hīe dȳgel lond
> warigeath, wulf-helothu, windige næssas,
> frēcne fen-glād, thær fyrgen-strēam
> under næssa genipu nither gewiteth,
> flōd under foldan. Nis thæt feor heonon
> mīl-gemearces, thæt se mere standeth
> ofer thæm hongiath hrinde bearwas,
> wudu wyrtum fæst wæter oferhelmath.
> Thǣr mæg nihta gehwæm nith-wundor sēon,
> fȳr on flōde.

> A secret land
> they guard, the high windy cliffs
> of wolf country, where a mountain stream
> pours down crags under darkness
> of hills, the flood under the earth. Not far
> from here, measured in miles, lies that lake
> hung with roots that sag and clutch,
> trees bound with frost, at the water's edge.
> Every night, there, a stranger wonder is seen:
> a lake of fire.[4]

The mist slides down from Iron Mountain. Often at sunrise I see similar fine layers of white cloud rise out of the knolls and graze the lee side of the peaks in the distance. It seems as if clouds are formed here and then rise slowly into the sky, pushed off by the wind. The wind moves again, an empty sound.

When the wind blows on this mountain, it's terrifying. It kisses the rock face and then slides against, rather than through, the trees. Sometimes it sounds as though air were being forced through empty space, as if there were nothing to stop it, no one to hear it.

The spider clings to the leaf. The wind shakes her. She is fat with eggs. She hangs on.

I hear the sharp crack of gunfire, followed by three more shots. Their sounds roll up the valley like waves, echoes, dissolving. I think of the doe feeding just before rainfall.

I pray with all the insufficient faith I have.

FRIDAY, 20 JUNE

Today, we hike the land west of Fire Lake Mountain, following the abandoned railroad tracks of the Adirondack Division. The forest presses against us from both sides; at times, the sharp drop-off of crushed rock is so steep we must walk on the warm ties. It's almost a perfect summer day. After a few hours, the only sound we feel is the rhythm of our feet on rusted metal, or the occasional shifting of rock if one of us slips. Years ago, when this land was as wild as it feels deserted now, native tribes worked from the northern railhead, and hired laborers, mostly blacks from Tennessee, formed the southern division which made possible this railroad line through a six-million-acre wilderness. They had to blast through rock, build bridges over empty space, and fill in with soil what was often completely swamp, had to endure constant exposure to fierce rains and subzero temperatures. When a man died, he became the earth. His body was dumped into the railbed and covered with metal and stone. Even now, as I walk, I wonder whose grave I step across.

> We do not ride on the railroad; it rides upon us. Did you ever think what those sleepers are that underlie the railroad? Each one is an Irishman, or a Yankee man. The rails are laid on them, and they are covered with sand, and the cars run smoothly over them. They are sound sleepers, I assure you. And every few years a new lot is laid down and run over; so that, if some have the pleasure of riding on a rail, others have the misfortune to be ridden upon. And when they run over a man that is walking in his sleep, a supernumerary sleeper in the wrong position, and wake him up, they suddenly stop that car, and make a hue and cry about it, as if this were an exception. I am glad to know that it takes a gang of men for every five miles to keep the sleepers down and level in their beds as it is, for this is a sign that they may sometime get up again.[5]

Near the eastern border of Fire Lake property we come across Dave, one of the two caretakers for the camp, on a road that intersects the line. He's responsible for the gunshots I heard yesterday at sunset. He patrols this land regularly; he stomps through the woods alone, with a six-gun strapped to his hip, the bottom of his holster lashed tight around his upper thigh.

I call him the sheriff of Camp Beaverkill.

I have been warned by those who left me here, and especially by George Gordon, to be considerate of the caretakers of this property. It would be bad publicity to develop poor relations with the owners. No need to be told that; Dave has a wild, more than half-demented look, and he seems eager to show us his proficiency with a pistol.

He wasn't, as I thought last night, shooting deer. Although if he had been picking off a few, no one would know. (No need to worry about jacklighting here.) Instead, he's been shooting beaver who are trying to complete their latest construction project along the south edge of Fire Lake.

This camp, which belongs to a cardinal from New York City and his immediate family, will be inhabited from July through September. Local rumor, dispatched by the inhabitants of Clear Lake who wonder what goes on out here, is that this property was a nudist colony before the cardinal's acquisition; the cardinal's niece is said to have been married here *à la mode*. The camp itself consists of twenty individual cabins and a 3,000-square-foot main lodge. In the sitting room there's a moose head perched above the fieldstone fireplace; the game room has two slate billiard tables and a bowling alley, and over another fieldstone fireplace ten different bear heads wear open, ferocious mouths and dark, glassy eyes. The kitchen has three gas stoves and a cast-iron antique stove for power failures. The dining room displays fifty fine bone china place settings; on top of one of the china cabinets is a stuffed great-horned owl, face frozen in confusion, as if he'd been "goosed" right at the moment of death. In the equipment room are enough fly fishing outfits to provide amusement for a small, independently financed army. Five separate docks provide guests easy access to fishing on Fire Lake, privately stocked with trout and landlocked salmon and continually fed by a waterfall bringing the runoff of fresh rain from the three surrounding mountains.

The first two nights we were on this property, Sandy, the head caretaker, allowed us to stay in one of the outer cabins. The rain had been hard and it was futile to set up camp on the site until the weather broke. Unpacking supplies dropped from a helicopter on a mountain fresh with rain was not an auspicious way to begin things. I remember the pilot disappearing in the dusk, the sound of the whipping blades above his head a dwindling blur. He must have been laughing to himself as he flew away from the rain clouds moving toward our mountain: his raised arm flared out of the cockpit and waved farewell forever to us.

That first night we lit a Coleman lantern and explored all the different rooms, our surprise growing at this empty paradise, as if we were the first to enter the City of the Dead. This property was originally owned, nominally at least, by Augustus Leer: several thousand acres from Horseheads Lake to twenty miles south. The cost to build this place, I'm sure, was immense.

And there is no one here.

"Don't get me wrong," says Dave. "I love animals."

He picks off another shot. A fat beaver flies straight up from the mound of an old logging pile. Dave's aim is good and he smiles with that kind of cold glee we seem afraid to find within us, reminding me how much "fun" people have shooting rats off the garbage heaps at the local dump.

"Can't stand beavers, though. Can't *stahnd* this *dawg*, neither." He swats a back hand into the maw of a bull mastiff tied to a rock in the bed of his pickup. The dog won't shut up. The froth at the bottom edge of his jaw bubbles. He's eager to take a finger, or two, off in one clean bite.

We've spent the past few days preparing the birds for release. Every third day, we clean the boxes, picking up, and sometimes scraping away, quail heads and chicken feet, wings, internal organs. At times, both Tom and I have climbed dangerously close to the edge of three different ledges to position poles, tall limbs, or dead trees for the birds to rest on after they're released. We will be able to clearly see all of these perch poles from the observation point. We've rigged thirty feet of PVC piping for a serviceable chute to drop food to the birds after release. Our intention is to use the chute as a surreptitious means of supplying food.

The fledglings must not make a connection between our presence and the presence of food. The goal is to provide them with enough to keep them healthy in the coming weeks, while keeping the source of the feed a secret. Ideally, we'll drop chicken and quail down the chute to land on the ledge by the boxes, and a peregrine perched nearby will turn and think to herself, *Ah, here's breakfast. . . .*

The pipe is set at a high angle of attack, running through the middle of scrub pine twisted and stunted from high winds. Some of the lighter quail will hit terminal velocity about halfway down the chute; they'll smash into the stone ledge with a satisfying plop. Any peregrine sitting there will be knocked unconscious if a quail bonks her on the head.

While rinsing off my plate with what little water I have, a voice behind me says, "You should boil the water before you do that. It helps sterilize 'em. . . . You don't know much about survival, do you?"

I am surprised at my sudden irritation with Tom's remarks. I suppose he is trying to be helpful, but his voice has the trace of finality only found in someone who is too certain of what he says. We have not been getting along well. When we speak, it's on a simple, necessary level: Have you checked the boxes? Do you need anything from town? We have not had a sustained conversation since we set up camp. I wonder if this is my fault, if I am intentionally condescending. And then, even now as I write this, what do I have to be condescending about?

The first night when I arrived at Horseheads Lake to load gear into the waiting helicopter, I wondered who my assistant would be. George Gordon walked to my car, stuck out his hand in greeting, and then said, "This is your partner for the project."

In the bed of the pickup a young kid sat with his eyes closed, hands crossed on his shallow chest. He looked no more than twelve years old. He opened one eye, waved, and mumbled, "Tom Peters. . . ." The look of disappointment on my face was obvious. How was I going to spend the summer with someone only half my age? Tom, it turned out, was twenty-two, a junior at Syracuse University, a local camp guide for the Boy Scouts, fairly knowledgeable about this section of the Adirondacks, and an Eagle Scout. When I learned this last nugget, especially, I was not happy: Eagle Scouts, from my experience, seem to believe that the woods will succumb to the superior knowledge and craft learned from years of wilderness experience. They're wrong.

The woods reveal or withhold whatever secrets there are for some reason other than the belief that answers might be found in a wilderness handbook. I know that simple truth from my own survival, evasion, resistance, and escape training. After three weeks in the Colorado Rockies with no food and no supplies, I quickly learned that ingenuity and need are the keys to survival. And hunger is a fairly strong motivator, too, gnawing away until it takes all sense but the sense that you have to continue. During my trek to the "partisan camp," a make-believe group of resistance fighters who would safely escort me to freedom, I learned how to sleep on the high branch of a tree, stumble through thick woods and fast-running mountain streams, and climb rock faces that even in a normal state of health I would think twice about. I knew I had to endure the trek. Finally, I didn't think whether what I did was right or not according to some instruction handbook. I did what I *knew* was right to survive. After hunger wore away my thought processes, after fatigue destroyed rationality, I felt what it would be like to be shot down behind enemy lines and try to make it back. Such foolishness and stubborn tenacity on my part, of course, could get me killed. But they could also be the only things to keep me alive.

"No, I guess I don't."

"Well I guess that's good for both of us. You know a lot about falcons and I know a lot about survival."

I don't know very much about falcons. No one does, and anyone who says he does is lying. But I say nothing.

I begin to boil water.

All of the birds have names; each is easily recognizable. The males, or tiercels (taken from the Latin; all male raptors are one-third smaller than females), have developed slightly faster. Shadowfax, a thirty-seven-day-old tiercel, is ready for release. There's not a single fleck of down on him. Most of the others spend their time cleaning the down from their bodies; the sharp, distinctive feathers of the peregrine are beginning to show underneath. At certain times of the day, the down drifts from the boxes and floats out across the valley.

Shadowfax has a dark mask which curves around his head and throat; his tight feathers' weave seems painted on. He's beginning to climb the front bars of his box, which means he's eager for release. His head-bob is instinctive when he notices something in the distance, a familiar sight to me from years ago when a falcon or goshawk, a fierce cast in the eyes, would bob a head at the sight of prey, an instant before flying from my fisted glove for the kill. Another memory, one not as welcome, is the falcon's awful, fetid breath from a diet of meat and blood.

When I was a cadet at the Academy, I named my favorite raptors after characters from Tolkien. A grey arctic gyrfalcon christened Gandalf was the first flyer I knew. He would test, eagerly and with malice, any human who flew a lure against him, tucking a yard-long wing forward to aim a sharp clip to the head as he zoomed past, or extending the rake of his talons to the falconer's face. Aragorn, a prairie falcon tiercel, was taken from the wild as a fledgling and never lost that edge of difference. His style, his complete technique of flying, was a world apart from our captive-bred falcons. From the moment he first flew, I realized how special he was.

The Academy has an extraordinary library of falconry manuscripts, some dating from before the seventeenth century. I spent long hours poring over techniques for training and flying; often, my methods met the ridicule of fellow falconers. (Some methods deserved ridicule: especially that of "seeling," still practiced in Arabia—the sewing closed of a bird's eyelids until accustomed to the touch and manner of the falconer.)[6] I would spend ten hours a day working with Aragorn. He slept on the headboard of my bed at night, waited on my fist as we watched afternoon formations and parades, and, hooded, perched patiently on my stereo during Saturday morning room inspections. Once, I received three demerits for "dust on falcon."

But Aragorn's unique flight style was not adaptable to flying exhibitions in crowded football stadiums for half-time entertainment. I taught him (or, more likely, he allowed me to pretend I taught him) to "wait on," a hunting method where the bird flies above the falconer's head, sometimes spiralling up a mile or more, often out of sight, until the game is flushed and the falconer calls the bird down for the kill. None of our birds, though, were taught to hunt game; instead, they flew to a winged lure with meat attached, either venison or chicken. The falconer would anticipate the flight path of the incoming raptor, holding the lure a few centimeters from the bird's face, and then loop the lure over the bird with an attached string. After a number of passes, the lure is thrown vertically, and the falcon pitches, thirty to fifty feet straight up, takes the lure in her talons and brings it to the ground. A game of catch.

Aragorn eventually developed the technique of making a tremendously high pitch when he "stooped" for the lure. I could hear the wind along the leading edge of his wings as he dove out of the sun, our eyes locked. In a steep dive, he reached speeds well over 150 miles an hour. My lure technique was more instinctive than calculated response. If I pulled the lure too quickly, he would lose interest. Not fast enough and he would seize the lure; by fair play, I would have to release the lure, admit my loss, and the session would be over. He became so accustomed to me in practice that he would wait on for thirty minutes and then fly over a hundred passes at the lure before release. (I once spent several lab sessions in Astronautical Engineering calculating the force response on his body coming out of a dive, when I should have been measuring the arc response of an incoming missile. My estimate was that from a steep dive, a falcon pulls 5 to 7 g's, a "g" being equal to one's own body mass against the gravitational pull of the earth. Fighter pilots, who pull 7 g's regularly, must practice special breath techniques and wear "jet jeans," canvaslike chaps with inflatable air pockets which push against the thighs and legs and constrict blood flow. If they don't follow these precautions, they suffer "g-blackout" and unconsciousness, as happened in one of the last F-20 crashes, before its contract terminated.)

Aragorn was once attacked by a wild prairie falcon, a female, perhaps looking for a mate. Though in theory he had no conception of the kill, he drove her easily off and returned to the lure, while I stood a helpless witness. A week later in New Orleans, a concerned citizens' group tried to prevent our falconry team from flying an exhibition in the Superdome, claiming that our birds would slaughter the feral pigeons roosting in the stadium. Finally, convinced that our falcons would not commit domestic violence to the delight or shock of the audience, we were allowed inside. Aragorn and I climbed a labyrinth of stairs until we reached the top. I slid/crawled on my stomach across a narrow catwalk, holding my left arm and Aragorn high above me, until I found an exit hatch, opened it, and unhooded Aragorn. He seemed mystified by the huge stadium beneath him. Confused, he turned and looked to me. His beak opened, and the sharp fork of his tongue stuck out. He looked down at the stadium, and then looked back to me. *You've got to be kidding,* he seemed to say. The sharp circular hole at the base of his tongue expanded; anxious and nervous, he panted in short, even spurts.

But then his head bobbed and he rolled off my glove, flying several hundred yards right before making his first stoop.

I hope the pigeons enjoyed his performance.

He grew increasingly wild. During halftime of the Air Force–Navy game, he took the lure in his talons and flew off. I pulled a second lure from my shoulder pouch as he climbed high into the blue west of the stadium. I continued to call him. The Annapolis marching band, ever punctual, marched onto the field. Their uniforms were an ugly, somber black; the only instruments I remember were the huge brass tubas. I refused to leave the field. The band refused to quit marching. They made a small compromise, however, by splitting off and parading around me as I stood in the center of the field, swinging my lure like an idiot, trying to call my falcon back. At that moment, I felt a keen sense of loss. I was certain I would lose him forever.

Nothing is more sure in the rules of falconry than the fact that many hours of training and frustration will often end up meaning nothing. A bird lives all too often by whim; a falcon lives according to a sense of wildness. As I stood there in the center of the stadium, ten thousand strangers watched my failure; I saw my greatest joy climb happily into the wild blue of the sky. Aragorn was fleeing because he no longer wanted to fly in performance: he wanted, simply, to fly. Yet I had committed the most mortal of sins: I had never taught him to kill. An eyass, or fledgling, in the wild, must be taught to kill by his parent. I was the surrogate parent, and I had refrained from instruction. I imagined, or believe now I imagined, that as I stood there, the bastard notes of Navy brass waving around me, I saw Aragorn caught by his jesses, hanging upside down from the high branch of a tree, a tiny mass of feather and bone caught by the wind, and swinging. Dead from starvation, and I had killed him.

Helplessness, guilt: I had condemned the thing I loved most in my life.

Finally, I gave up and walked defeated to the sidelines. Fortunately, Aragorn wore a telemetry band attached to the jess of his right leg. An hour later, and several miles north, I found him by means of a portable radar device, telemetry signal pinging wildly. I looked up and saw him perched on the high limb of a tree, gorged with a full crop. Fat, happy bird.

In Arizona for a week-long public relations tour, Aragorn decided to explore the landscape. Bored with our performance, he climbed high above the bleachers and soared out of the high school stadium, to the wild cheers and applause of a thousand students. I searched for the next three days. Bulletins were posted and broadcast by the state police. Reports poured in of a marauding wild bird, dive-bombing cars and small children on bicycles, reports of a "hawk" perched on telephone wires screaming with what sounded like hysterical laughter.

On Friday his tragic flaw undid him. Making a visit to the ranch of a retired Navy admiral who happened to raise chickens, Aragorn landed in the center of what for him was a gourmet's paradise. The admiral's wife, hearing the sudden shrieks, ran outside, saw the confusion, and responded immediately by throwing a raw beefsteak into the middle of the slaughter. Aragorn went for the steak. The admiral's wife then threw a laundry basket over him without, luckily, damaging his wing or tail feathers.

He was returned during halftime of the Air Force–ASU football game, which Air Force miraculously won. The head falconer accused me of using poor lure techniques, and though I argued against it, I admitted to myself that Aragorn was no longer fit for the limited spaces of exhibition flying.

Aragorn, that night, was close to death. Red, domestic meat, with marbled veins of fat rippling through the flesh, is too rich for raptors: it clogs the digestive tract. Hooded, Aragorn swayed drunkenly on his perch; every few minutes he would vomit a rich discharge, returning everything false he'd swallowed. Later, in my motel room, he had the odor of feculence and rotted apple must. Suffering for the sins of gluttony and lust.

The next day, during our return flight to Colorado, perched on the armrest of my aisle seat, his body swayed and pivoted like a gyroscope, exaggerating the accelerations and slow turns of the aircraft. Occasionally, he would spew a thick black bile into the center aisle, much to the horror of the flight attendants and passengers of United's friendly skies.

Anne LaBastille and Madonna are the most immature of the fledglings. Initially, I thought Madonna had given a virgin birth. To my embarrassment, inspection of the tiny oval I found her brooding on revealed that it was only a quail's egg.

Anne has ventured out of the hide now. Still fluffy with down, she often attacks the other birds, cacking and flashing her wings, or threatens me as I watch through the tiny peephole of the near box.

Kathleen and Tahawus (Native American for Cloud-Splitter) are the large dominant females of the far box. Tahawus prefers to seat herself on the comfortable perch rock near the front bars, where she has a commanding view of the valley. When her whim dominates, she flings her large mass across the box, sinking her talons into the back of any present occupant of *her* perch rock. Shadowfax challenges her; dwarfed by her size, he climbs up and butts the sharp keel of his breast against hers, vying for his share of the rock. Figmo screams constantly, living up to his name. He's a bit of a runt. Augustus Leer is his constant companion. He cacks whenever Figmo cacks, looks wherever Figmo looks.

In the near box, Rondeau is a quiet though large tiercel. His companion is Fuentes, named for Carlos Fuentes, with whom Donna and I took a seminar at Cornell. He has sharp, accusing eyes; he watches me constantly through the bars as if to say, "You will pay for your imperialist sins."

Belladonna is independent. She spends her time apart from the others, spreading her wings in mock flight, feeling the breeze touch her through the front bars of her prison.

I have named her for my wife, as well as for the strange, poisonous herb.

SATURDAY, 21 JUNE

I wash myself. I'm able now to bathe my body, shampoo my hair, brush my teeth, and shave in ten ounces of water. Water is the most precious thing we have here. The streams are mostly dry, despite the constant rain. We must backpack water in 100-pound containers every few days from a stream five miles down the mountain.

The blisters on my feet from hiking, and on my hands from using the axe, open and bleed. A black mold grows between my toes, which are cracked and red. Although it's a cliché, I can't help thinking that, even like this, I'm in a better state than over half the human race. I feel guilty every night, boiling water for my gourmet freeze-dried food.

I am grateful for the antibiotics Donna brought me last week. There are sores over my calves and ankles from insect bites; they ooze from constant scratching, which only spreads the infection. As I wash, I feel a tickle of pain in my leg. I look down.

A black fly sinks its head deep in my flesh.

"Eventually, all things merge into one," Norman Maclean once wrote, "and a river runs through it . . . runs over rocks from the basement of time. . . . Under the rocks are the words, and some of the words are theirs." For a long while, I tasted the strangeness of those words, and was uncertain. Now I still live in the air of their uncertainty, almost believing I know what their rhythms and phrasings mean. I couldn't, of course, tell you what they mean. But I know.

And some of the words are theirs.

Here at the northern edge of this mountain, which is no mountain by almost anyone's standard measure, which is, rather, a thickly treed hill of twenty-five hundred feet, I have found the kind of isolation I have been craving. I have books, words which represent the "greatest hits" of nearly a thousand years of literature. I have thoughts, ideas, the chance to dream of things which daily life makes almost impossible, impractical. I have the time to concentrate on living with these fledglings, while making my presence at best an absent one. Mostly, I have to live with myself. A difficult thing, really. Nearly impossible.

It's no wonder why Tom and I talk so little, even now, eleven days after our project officially began. We knew our responsibilities long before we arrived, and after the first day, after finding a site and setting up camp, there was little we had to share with each other, other than the tedium of routine. Tom needs, perhaps even craves, companionship. But he does not need me. I need to learn, to see: I have never been good at either. When I need thoughts, ideas, something beyond the fragile realm of my brain, I crack open a book. Reviewing my notes, I see how important, scarily so, these books are. Now they are part of the landscape. Now they are as real as the silence. It was Faulkner who said it, for me, most clearly, though at the time I thought he was being both pithy and quotable: *I prefer the silence to sound, and the image produced by words occurs in silence.*

Last night I stood at the edge of the cliff, after having read, for the first time, *Paradise Lost.* Until yesterday, I had thought much of Milton verbose, contrived. At the Academy, I had refused to read further than the opening and concluding lines of each of the twelve books. I had listened intently in class, had taken copious notes, pretended to pay attention to lectures, and received an A for the course. But I had cheated myself. Last night I stood at the lip of the observation point, feeling a sense of the rhythms and words pouring out. I had read the entire poem in a day, and by then, near dusk, I could no longer keep my mouth shut. I was singing the words, singing the lines to the absence, the shagged carpet of green in the valley, to Whiteface looming northeast. I was weeping.

No one saw me. Tom was off somewhere, busy trekking with a map and a compass. Shortly after dark, I heard the zipped flap of his tent open, heard him crawl in to sleep. My secret was safe. No one had to know what I knew. As I lay drifting toward sleep I shuddered: a sudden tremor pulsed with the sense that perhaps some words and ideas were, if not as important as life, sometimes the only things which made up a life and held it together.

Donna once told me that I was the only person she'd known who could be happiest alone. Her words stung because they were so true. Over the years I have lost most of my need for religion, so retreat to a monastery seemed somehow an admission that I could recover what I had lost—I was not willing to accept that. And though my situation is hardly so desperate, I realize I have been trained for the moments of confronting the self, for living with what might finally become the intolerable terror of one's thoughts. I have been taught to survive in the wild; to accept the chances of enemy capture; to learn, if only through a training program, how to endure as a prisoner of war. No one, I think, would easily admit to enjoying such training, but now I realize how valuable such training could be. The chances for capture, for imprisonment, are very real for any military pilot in times of conflict and war. In my experience, the phrase for confinement has been strangely transmuted to a morbid military euphemism: interment, the act of placing a dead body into a grave, from the Old French *enterrer.* The *correct* word for confinement (the one you will find in regulations and official handbooks) is intern- ment, yet I have repeatedly heard the word *interment* used in briefings and training sessions; I have often wondered how acci- dental the transmutation of the word was.

And yet what could be more perfectly accurate than to describe the experience of the prisoner of war as one of burial? My life on this mountaintop is simple and pleasant. Much of its simple pleasantness springs from the truth that I will one day return to the life about which I presently complain, observe, examine, deny, and refuse. For the prisoner of war, no such possibility exists. There is the belief, the arrogant and stubborn denial of your inter(n)ment, while at the same time there exists the reality *that you may never return.* Former prisoners of war have told me how they wrote novels in their head; designed and con- structed, stone by stone, homes they had dreamed of building; quoted passages from Shakespeare they had not heard in years— doing this in silence and in separate confinement, while knowing that no one, possibly, would ever hear them, while each day their captors stood at the crest of chancrous hill easily visible from each of their individual cells and threw—methodically and painfully slowly—all of their written letters back home into the crisp tongues of a burning fire.

It is a tribute to human persistence that those who returned *did* actually write their novels, build the homes which once existed only in the huge realm of their thoughts.

Interment. What better word could describe the loss of experi- ence, could take on the sense of demotic poetry, for those who were victims and witnesses to their own burials, never certain they would be found?

I have read of the ordeals of those lost at sea who cling to the most precious and simple thoughts to help keep them alive, which explains why so many powerful narratives, whether fic- tional or not, have sprung from immense isolation. In *Moby-*

Dick, Melville writes of the cabin boy, Pip, tossed from the whale boat and left to drift: "The intense concentration of self in the middle of such a heartless immensity, my God! who can tell it?"

My situation is hardly so desperate. My interment is something I have chosen. I crave isolation, though I'm not sure why. Before I return, and there will come a time when I must return, when at least some of these fledglings will survive and leave, I hope to discover why I crave separation, if only to understand some small part of the nature of being alone. Is it, I wonder, anything like the route of migration, when the peregrine, always fiercely independent and self-reliant, soars on the spirit of her own instinct in the awful and heartless immensity of air?

Pilot training consists of fifty weeks of intense concentration and study. The academic classes, although relatively simple, demanded immediate commitment to memory of technical facts, figures, emergency procedures; the flying, if there had been time to enjoy it, would have been wonderful. But pilot training was not meant to be fun.

It is divided into almost perfect halves. The first half of the course is spent flying the Cessna T-37: a safe, reliable, and painfully slow airplane (though, at the time, we thought it was incredible—we were actually flying an Air Force *jet*). The T-37 was designed to be a spin-recoverable aircraft; most aircraft are not. The purpose of its design was to build confidence in students, to show that a craft—sometimes inverted and falling at twenty thousand feet or more per minute back to an earth which seems to grab with two hungry talons wanting to pull you deeper and deeper into its body—could be recovered. I remember the first day I witnessed a spin: we flipped over a wing, the way a raptor arcs over a wing before the pitch, and fell back to the blurring whirlpool of ground. The tune of the emergency procedure sang in my brain: *throttles idle; stick neutral; determine direction of spin; apply full opposite rudder after one complete rotation; stick full forward; recover.* Hands and feet turned to ice; my bowels loosened; I was ready to void myself. My instructor, calmly sitting beside me, arms crossed on his chest, whispered through his oxygen mask and into my helmet: *Well, aren't you going to recover?*

It would be a great many spins later before I *would* successfully recover. But, eventually, I did learn to become proficient in spins, in aerobatics, in formation flying. Though for a while I was never quite sure: for a while, the only thing I was good at was projectile vomiting. Spin recoveries? That took some time.

But you had to learn to master it. If you didn't, you went no further in training. You *washed out*. A more popular term, probably because it indicated a self-initiated action, was to *punch*. "Punch," a peculiar military euphemism which describes the moment when a pilot ejects from a crippled aircraft: the moment when she or he can take no more. When students "punched," they simply separated from any further training.

One of the greatest joys of flight training was to go up solo. In those all too brief moments, when there was no instructor screaming in your ear, no sense of having to perform like a trained animal, you learned the secret that would help you survive: *Pilot training isn't supposed to be fun; you aren't supposed to enjoy it.* But flying solo *was* fun. During one of my first solos in the T-37, I was caught in a terrific headwind during my downwind leg of the traffic pattern. The runway supervisory unit told me on the radio that I should make a "full stop," a final landing, because the tailwinds on runway 30 were significant—measuring fifteen knots or greater. The normal traffic pattern is a simple rectangle: the downwind leg parallels the opposite direction of the runway; the base leg is the turn perpendicular to the runway; and the "final" is the turn to line the craft up for touchdown. Basically, the pattern looks like this:

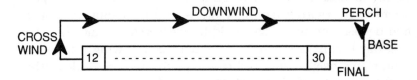

It is slightly different from the overhead pattern, a hard-breaking, fighter-type pattern designed for the rapid spacing and landing of aircraft, which looks like this:

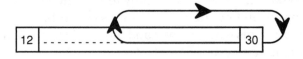

As I approached the "perch"—the point where procedure dictates you "drop" (lower) the landing gear and report on the radio your "callsign, gear down, base leg turn"—the wind at altitude was approaching fifty knots headwind. The tiny T-37 was struggling forward, yet it felt as if I were hovering in stillness. As I looked off the starboard wing, I saw a crow flying beside me. His mouth was open in surprise. His wings beat steadily, but he, like me, was caught at the perch, held in the headwind's stillness. Our eyes locked, both of us puzzled. Two figures frozen in the landscape of the air, strangers forever.

As I turned final and aligned with the runway, I felt the wind (now changed from headwind to tailwind) push me as easily as a leaf stirs in the breeze. I fought to control the plane, aiming for centerline. The VASI's, visual slope indicators, showed that I had a good visual glide slope for touchdown. What I didn't know was that the tailwind on the runway now exceeded twenty-five knots, which is far beyond the normal touchdown capabilities of the T-37. As I crossed over the threshold, I made a fatal mistake: I flew with my ego instead of my brains. I knew that instructors and other students were watching. After my touchdown, the active runway landing direction would be reversed. I touched down smoothly, and held the stick aft, keeping the nose of the aircraft off the runway as long as I could. This technique is called "air braking," and if I had been flying an F-106 or an F-15, aircraft with long noses and massive underframes which act as huge spoilers to slow the plane after touchdown, my use of the technique would have been effective. But the T-37 has a squat, ugly body: air braking does, essentially, nothing, though it looks impressive. My problem was that I was air braking with a tailwind pushing me rapidly down the runway, the way a hand gently guides the bowling ball down the alley. When I lowered the nose, it was too late. I was running out of runway. I smashed on the brakes; smoke poured from the undercarriage. With the kiss of black tires on burning pavement, I sailed off the runway and into the woods. Humiliated and certain that I would be washed out of pilot training, I keyed the microphone to declare "hot brakes" and ask for fire assistance. As I pressed the mike button, hearing the sound of my own breath on the airwaves, I thought, strangely and suddenly, of the crow back up at the perch, wondering if he was still frozen in air.

*   *   *

Thirteen years ago I was a senior in high school. I attended a Society of Friends preparatory school in Providence, Rhode Island: I was preparing myself for an Ivy League education. I did well academically; I was active in numerous activities; I was captain of the swim team, and a high school All-American. My family lived in Big Spring, Texas. In truth, there was no spring anywhere; the town grew out of the high mesa plateaus which sloped down into the vast and empty expanse of desert known as west-central Texas. My father was the wing commander of an undergraduate flying training unit. One day, in the late fall of that year, something happened that would change my life forever. One of my father's squadron commanders did something I have never forgotten. Safety investigation rules prevent me from saying his name; respect for his family forbids me to. His name is not important; whose names, after all, ever are? It is a life, if anything, and the actions of a life, which matter.

He was intelligent, articulate. An English professor and member of the faculty at the Academy, he had earned his doctorate from Yale, taught literature for several years, founded the cadet creative writing magazine *Icarus*. This last detail, especially: there is a beautiful irony in that. He was returning to a flying commitment as part of the normal duties of his career. He, like most pilots, did not fill the common expectations or role of a military officer.

The mission on that day was a standard aerobatic, commonly called "contact," ride. During the mission briefing he covered all the necessary details of the flight, outlined an energy profile for the consumption of fuel versus time in flight. He and his student planned to return early from the work airspace, fifty miles away from the field, to practice touch-and-go landings. The student had a check-ride coming up in the near future; he was anxious about his proficiency, or lack of it, in the traffic pattern. As instructors and students always do as part of their mission briefing, they carefully reviewed emergency procedures. One detail, particular to a design feature of the T-38, was covered clearly: ejection.

The T-38, unlike the T-37, is sleek, responsive, capable of astounding aerobatic maneuvers. Its nickname is the Sports Car of the Air Force. It's fast: the T-38, or more commonly the "thirty-eight," is the only plane I've broken the sound barrier in.

Successful mastering of basic flight techniques and maneuvers in the T-38 takes up much of the second half of pilot training. After the last formation flight, after the last engine shutdown in the "thirty-eight," successful students graduate and disperse over the globe to take up jobs flying a myriad of different military aircraft.

The T-38 has a reliable ejection seat (though hardly as efficient as the Aces Two, a system equipped with self-erecting gyros which can take a pilot—theoretically only 200 feet above the ground—ejecting from a flat inverted spin of sixty thousand feet per minute and upright the seat, fire rockets to shoot the pilot vertically up into the safe and high and distant air, and initiate the parachute release). T-38's have a zero-fifty capability: a pilot can successfully eject from the aircraft at ground level (zero) when the plane has achieved an airspeed of fifty knots or greater. This does not mean, though, that one can always successfully escape from a crippled plane when flying so close to the ground. There are specific phases, such as turning final from an overhead pattern (when the sink rate of the plane is twenty-five-hundred feet per minute), when it is not possible to eject safely. If you eject during one of these phases, your parachute will never deploy. You will die. You eject, as the phrase so chillingly describes it, outside the envelope.

The "thirty-eight" is a tandem jet; there are two individual cockpits. The instructor sits behind and slightly higher than the student; she or he cannot clearly see the student. Rather, the instructor monitors performance by the response of engine instruments and performance indicators. It is, I suppose, the purest form of instruction, one where student and teacher are visibly removed, one where the results of instruction, in this case the flying of a high-performance aircraft, are all that matters. There is a common expression in pilot training: *Fly the aircraft—or the aircraft flies you.*

One particular design feature of this jet's ejection system, though, might equally be called a flaw. Because it is a tandem jet, there is a specific sequence for ejection. Both pilots' seats have rocket packs under them. The backs of the seats are sloped with firing rails for a smooth, quick exit from the crippled plane. When one pilot lifts the ejection handles and pulls the trigger, he or she blows the canopy into the slipstream. Both pilot and seat are hurled from the aircraft; eventually, as part of the ejection sequence, pilot and seat will separate, the seat will fall back to earth, and the pilot will float downward in the same direction under the blossoming wealth of the parachute. (Sometimes, pilot and seat do *not* separate and the chances for a successful ejection then become very small.) It is, on the pages of technical manuals, an efficient system.

Normally, the instructor "punches" first. If the student, in the front seat, were to leave the aircraft first, the blast of the rocket sled would burn the hands and face of the instructor, and probably blind her or him as well. Only in an extreme emergency would the student "punch" first. The prospect of a blinded pilot hurled into the often unforgiving atmosphere is frightening: not knowing which way was up or in which direction your body was heading, you would grope through the hard and tearing open air, searching for the parachute automatic release cable, hoping it had fired, or feeling with freezing hands on your chest for the manual D-ring release, if it had not.

Both student and instructor knew this that day. They were both strong, capable pilots, though distanced by years of experience. The ejection sequence was part of their briefing. I, of course, can only guess what happened, yet I think my guess is accurate because I have experienced the same sensations, the same knowledge. He was a good instructor: patient and willing. He was not, as *my* T-38 instructor was, a "screamer." (My T-38 instructor, more than once, tried to kill me with his eagerness and anxiety. Routinely, he would take the plane from me on final approach, trying to show me a new and almost always asinine technique for landing. Once, during my early contact days, he hounded me so thoroughly and bitterly during a flight that I felt as if I was always behind, as if I would never catch up. During a hard break in the overhead pattern, while pulling 3 g's, I leaned the massive weight of my head down and saw that I had not strapped myself in during pre-flight. If I'd ejected I would have blown my remains across the wide expanse of western Oklahoma. I knew then that I would stop trying to please him, that I would start teaching myself to fly, and hope to learn. It sounds arrogant, I know: but when I started ignoring my instructor, I first felt that I was a pilot. Maybe, in a sense, I owe him a lot.)

Their pre-flight was normal. The student, naturally, would

make mistakes; the instructor, naturally, would correct them. Cleared for taxi, the student would nudge the twin throttles by his left knee gently forward. Firmly grabbing the control stick, he would press the red button on the front of the stick to control the plane's nose-wheel steering, and concentrate with fierce intensity on keeping the aircraft on the yellow centerline of the taxiway. His intensity would cause him always to veer away. Once cleared for takeoff, the student would verbally acknowledge to the instructor over the intercom that he was checking "*three green* lights for landing gear; *no red or amber* warning indications; ejection *pins pulled*; canopy *locked*; cabin *pressure up*; Master Caution *panel out.*"

The T-38 would lift from the runway; there would be a hard pull of afterburners and the pilots would lean back into their seats; the nozzles, compressing air and the blast of the engines, would light and send them climbing in rapid acceleration toward three hundred knots; the harsh smell of aviation fuel would drift across the field. Once in the areas, there would be a standard aerobatic profile. The purpose of these acrobatics was not for impressive display of aircraft capabilities; rather, it showed how well the student knew the limits and the limitations of the envelope. Aerobatics taught the student how to conserve energy, how to use altitude and airspeed and maneuvering to outwit an adversary. The instructor would listen, watch, correct. His constant refrain on the intercom became, for the student, a litany of patience: *No, this way. Follow me through.* Ten thousand feet for a loop. Barrel rolls around a specific, fixed target in the distance. Immelmanns. Chandelles. The always difficult lazy eight. There would be the dip of horizon, the flashing sun in their mirrors, the hard tug of the earth begging them back and the pulse of their beating hearts against it. There would be the measured rasp of the student's breath, and the instructor would listen to it. Sometimes, he could simply close his eyes and tell how well the student was flying by the sound of his breath. How well he breathed, how strong and confident and even, was how well the aircraft flew its slicing arcs of precision. *Fly the aircraft—or the aircraft flies you.*

This is what I do know happened: They returned to the field at Big Spring to practice touch-and-go landings. Shortly after they entered the traffic pattern, a Siberian crane hit the windscreen of the front cockpit at an altitude of four hundred feet. The Siberian crane: a species which migrates 7,000 miles each year from the Soviet Union to find a winter home in Big Spring, Texas. No one knows why. No one knows why this particular Siberian crane, on that day in early fall, had decided to permanently roost in that tiny desert town.

It whipped through the front cockpit. Feathers, guts, pieces of bone littered the instrument panel. The plexiglass canopy was blooded a dull, rich red. The mass of what once had been a bird smashed into the student's head, cracking his helmet visor, snapping though not breaking his neck. The rest of the body whipped through the cockpit, hurled toward the instructor at three hundred knots. It was as if student and instructor struck a wall head-on while traveling at three hundred and fifty miles per hour.

Both pilots were blinded with blood, confusion. The one radio call from their plane stated that they had a birdstrike, the aircraft was uncontrollable, they were going to eject. Pieces of the canopy which had splintered off, or pieces of the bird which hit them, caught in the turbines. The engines screamed; it's easy to believe they were in pain. The plane lost most of its lateral pitch control.

In the few seconds which became a lifetime, the instructor saw, as the plane rocked violently from side to side, that they were heading for a small housing area, a neighborhood not far from his own. Children standing in the street were pointing in awe at the crippled jet falling toward them. A few mothers scooped their children into their arms and, screaming together, they began to sprint for the open scrub of the desert.

A few seconds which became a lifetime. The instructor told the student to "punch." The student hesitated, said over the intercom that he wasn't going anywhere without him. The instructor's response was harsh: *Get out, you son of a bitch! Do it, do it now!* The instructor's response was simple, in those few seconds: *my life or theirs.* The blast of the front rocket sled slammed into him. He felt its heat, its fierce burning. He maneuvered the plane south, away from the houses, rapidly losing altitude. Years later, my father told me that his hands had been on the ejection handles, a hundred-hundredth of a moment from possible survival, when he hit the ground, when the T-38 exploded into flames.

He made his choice. I made my choice, too, I think on that day. I did not know how far it would take me then, thirteen years ago, that I myself would eventually become a pilot. But how many of us, given the chance to truly show what type of spirit hides within us in the space of an infinite moment—given no chance at all to think or consider, but only to respond with some sense of human caring—would have done what he did? Would I have done it, or will I one day have to make that choice?

All my life I will never know the answer to that question.

And some of the words are theirs.

I think of him often. I suppose in one sense I can never stop thinking of him whenever I climb inside a cockpit. As an aircraft commander, I most clearly remembered him on nights when my crew and I flew together in silence, when each of us knew our job and trusted each other, when the drone of our own four engines was the only lulling, irritating sound we knew. It was then, on nights when I was far from the sound of any human voice, I most clearly heard him say, *No, this way.* It was then, when I stared straight up through the pilot's number 4 window overhead into a universe in which over 90 percent of the stars are dead, searching for the light beyond the visible darkness, the light which would never reach me during my life, when I most became a history of other voices, other hands at the controls.

Evening.

Tom is spending the night at a guide's camp. Donna packed up the mountain this afternoon; she twisted her ankle after slipping on a sharp ledge. She rests on the flat shelf of the observation point. I clumsily prepare dinner, twice spilling food on the rock and then scooping the mixture back into the bowl. Burgundy beef with granite.

Our dogs have also made the hike. King, a ten-year-old Samoyed, almost too old for this trek, sleeps under scrub pine. Shakespeare, a young Siberian husky/Arctic wolf, crosses his forepaws and looks to the mountains beyond with pleasure: a born epicurean. One winter I flew back from Alaska with him, then a ten-day-old puppy, inside my flight jacket; he's retained his wildness. Eyes slightly closed, he lies on the edge of the cliff. His head cocks slightly when he hears the birds cack as they settle in for the evening. Master of all he surveys, he thrives on this moment's pure enjoyment.

At 2105, the full, orange moon rises from behind a far peak. Perhaps because of the refraction, it's huge, glowing with the sun's dying light. A Hunter's Moon on the night of the summer solstice. I am ecstatic, scrambling with ineptness as I focus the tripod-mounted camera. Even as I fumble with the open shutter, I tell myself I should leave it, that I should sit and watch with Donna, to let the moon rise alone, to let memory grant whatever gifts I will take away.

Five miles west on Horseheads Lake, a pair of loons begin a ghost song; they reel each other in, as if they both were lost.

Monday, 23 June

Six F-106 Delta Darts course over the mountaintop, dogfighting. They spiral downward, make sharp, intersecting turns as each tries to cut the other off. The dull thud of their punched after-burners echoes above me. I imagine the victor in his perfectly tuned machine, screaming, "Guns, Guns, Guns!" as he shoots down his adversary. In the place of a missile being fired, a camera shutter will open, centering the defeated pilot in the cross hairs of a gunsight.

This valley is not a Military Operating Area; I know these pilots are out of their airspace. Still, I see them as a good omen on the day that we are to release the birds, only three of whom may survive the next winter. In the moment more important than all others, whether peregrine or fighter pilot, the ability to kill is the only response.

I spend an hour watching the birds. I call to them with the coo of a mourning dove. In unison they turn towards my peep-hole; they twist their heads sideways, quizzical, fascinated. Belladonna spreads her wings, ready to fly.

As I lie in the hammock taking notes, I hear a red-tailed hawk—a chicken hawk—cry above. Hawks and great-horned owls, especially, are natural enemies of young fledglings. They often kill for intrusion on territory, seeing falcons as competitors for mutual prey: kill without eating the body. I have seen the body of a young peregrine, killed by a great-horned owl, perfectly preserved save for the absence of a head.

But fledglings are tough. Last year in Baltimore, a twenty-eight-day-old chick fell off a thirty-story building and was unharmed. The chick was two weeks away from taking her first flight.

The hawk's cry is shrill and unmistakable. *Keeeeeearrrr.*

Terrence Des Pres once ended a letter to me by saying, "poetry won't save us, but meanwhile it can help us endure." I suppose that nothing can save us but a few precious thoughts and ideas we grip on to, as if they were magic. Somehow, their pleasure is a form of salvation. And when the magic is gone, there is nothing.

> Over my head, I see the bronze butterfly,
> Asleep on the black trunk,
> Blowing like a leaf in green shadow.
> Down the ravine behind the empty house,
> The cowbells follow one another
> Into the distances of the afternoon.
> To my right,
> In a field of sunlight between two pines,
> The droppings of last year's horses
> Blaze up into golden stones.
> I lean back, as the evening darkens and comes on.
> A chicken hawk floats over, looking for home.
> I have wasted my life.[7]

A small tuft of peregrine down peaks up the cliff, floats softly by my face, and heads west.

RELEASE

*And there is a Catskill eagle in some souls
that can alike dive down into the blackest
gorges, and soar out of them again and
become invisible in the sunny spaces. And
even if he for ever flies within the gorge, that
gorge is in the mountains; so that even in
his lowest swoop the mountain eagle is still
higher than the other birds upon the plain,
even though they soar.*
—HERMAN MELVILLE, *Moby-Dick*

THURSDAY, 26 JUNE

Shadowfax and Fuentes are perched contentedly seventy feet beneath the hack boxes. Rondeau seems to have spent the night on the southeast face of the cliff. Since dawn, he has been trying to return to the hack boxes, though still unsure of his flying or landing ability. He has smashed into solid rock face and been pulled out of the air by tree limbs in his attempts to return.

Kathleen "took the dive," though a brief one, shortly after sunrise. Her wings high and outstretched, she ran off the edge of a downsloping ledge. She flew less than ten seconds, turning back toward the cliff immediately.

Most of the other birds gather on a perch ledge to the left of the far hack box, puzzled by this new trick called "flight." If I lift my head too quickly, though I'm watching from 500 feet away, Figmo begins to cack, a harsh bantering. The other birds move away, ignore him. Yesterday, shortly after release, he was ostracized as soon as the birds left the boxes. Perched at the edge of a cliff, he screamed as the others huddled close together and apart from him.

What we had anticipated as an early release on Monday was delayed until yesterday morning. Jack Shelley, a specialist with the Peregrine Fund, missed his return flight to Ithaca from Boise. A high wind developed Tuesday as I hiked down to meet him and Kathy O'Heir, a DEC worker. The wind brought rain, which considerably slowed our hike back up. By the time we reached the hack boxes the visibility, which had been greater than sixty miles two hours before, was now a hundred feet.

Both Tom and I had considered the fledglings' release. We spoke carefully about what we hoped would happen when the bars were removed, weighed the possibilities and what we would do in each instance. Though disappointed by the delay, we realized that it was best to wait. I had read and reread (and reread) the Peregrine Fund's book *Hacking*, paying attention to the "Release" section, preparing myself for what to expect.

Release is the "single most critical aspect of the hacking procedure."[8] An overwhelming number of factors might predicate failure. The specific age of each peregrine must be considered. The optimum age for release is between forty-two and forty-five days: if released too early, the birds may not fly at all; too late, a fledgling could fly off and never return. Males, because they are smaller and therefore develop faster, usually are ready to try flight first. The winds and the accompanying strong updrafts on the cliff here will stimulate their first attempts, as Gilbert White pronounces it, "to make wing." If the winds are too strong, though, it will blow the novice solo away from the mountain, never to return. In the wild (or perhaps, a more appropriate way of saying it is "in the natural state"—these peregrines, after all, are in the wild, too) an eyass would leave the ledge on foot and might not fly for several days, and when she did, two parents would be watching over and accompanying her. The ability to fly, and the timing for when it is best to first make wing, depend directly on each bird's maturity.

Another problem, and one thankfully we won't see, is the buzzing, interfering human presence, the humming of public relations officials and clapping shutters of photographers. The booklet *Hacking* makes its position clear: "A picture of a young peregrine frightened off into flying away to starvation is not worth much." But, despite my aversion to humans and our presence here, we have our part to perform. It is critical that no one be standing near the vinyl mesh fronts when they are removed: this can often make a falcon bolt and fly immediately out of sight. The fewer people near the boxes, the better all of our chances.

We had cleaned the boxes, taken away all scraps of bones, legs, feathers, and dried internal organs, and withheld food. We fed the fledglings a final supply of quail and chicken on Sunday afternoon. We could only hope that the eyasses would be eager for food and fun. Since we do not have telemetry transmitters to track and locate fledglings once they are free to roam, it is critical that we be as quick, secretive, and quiet as possible.

On Tuesday night, the temperature dropped. I had nothing to counter the sudden fall below freezing; I piled on layers of clothing, which did no good. We spent several hours standing under a wet tarp—our kitchen area. The Primus stove sputtered its last asthmatic breath to the wind. It was cold.

We told stories and lies about falconry. Lies, because each new story we told became slightly more exaggerated while it became better. As fishermen tell of the one that always got away, so falconers tell stories always slightly more refined, more impressive each time each new tale represents the truth inside the fiction. Jack described how a young fledgling fell off a 300-foot cliff last week, during the banding of a wild nest. The chick was not hurt. His mother had flown down from the cliff and fed him before humans found the fledgling in the brush and returned him to the nest. Then he told us of one night last summer in a New Jersey salt marsh, when the ocean rose and met the bay. Waking inside a trailer rapidly filling with water, he and his partner ran out into the storm to save the live quail population, quail they had been raising as feed for the young peregrines. A third of them had already drowned. During much of that night, Jack was hand-drying quail, wrapping them in aluminum-foil space blankets for warmth.

I told of berkutes: eagles used in the Crimea and sections of south-central Russia to hunt deer and wolf. A large, wooden T-pole is strapped upright to the side of a horse from which the berkute, far too large to be held on the hunter's arm, can perch. If the eagle tenses, even momentarily, the talons could snap a man's forearm as easily you could break a twig. Recently we visited a friend in Maine, and when I told him of the berkutes he returned the story to me:

The Hunting Eagles of Afghanistan

That morning, because we had drunk till two in a
                                        Venetian bar
where the waiter kept offering us octopus and eggs from
a glass bowl, you were still sleeping; and though I pulled
open the shutters to the sound of the boat bringing
                                        vegetables
and the men haggling over profit and loss, the sound of
piledrivers shoring up the ruined palace across the canal,
                                        you
tightened your mouth and I could see the dream follow
itself under your eyelids like someone reading a
                                        newspaper

or magazine furiously in the dark. How could I wake
you and say there are no headlines about the dead, that
the city, the apartment poised over the wrought-iron
                                                    bridge,
these things already were further from ourselves than we
could reach? Once, a man visited in winter with two dogs
from Alaska that were half-wolf, more than half maybe,
                                                      with
their white eyes and the way they ran down the rabbit
                                          in the snow.
We found each other without looking. And yet the
                                      hunting eagles
of Afghanistan wear hoods over their huge eyes right to
                                                     the
last moment, when the deer are cornered, exhausted,
                                          and, crazy
with discipline or hunger, they are allowed to fly.[9]

Perhaps the most disturbing image humans have of falconry
is this: the sport of kings, like all forms of hunting, results in
the death of living things. Yet the terms between hunter and
bird are obviously more equal when a falconer must spend hours
training a bird to kill and hunt than when a hunter plunges
into the thick wood, weapon at his side. It is far more difficult
to cast a falcon off against flying prey than it is to squeeze the
trigger of a loaded gun as the target edges by overhead. There
is a more natural selection of game taken by falconers than by
those who amble into the woods with a rifle at the ready. The
falconer must devote many hours of preparation, patience, and
attention to a bird before she successfully takes prey. What would
be a natural, instinctive act in the wild must be redefined by a
man: now, she must share the joy of her kill with him.

What grew to be a refined art in medieval Europe was practiced
only by a small and leisured class. Mounted on horseback, hunting parties strayed carelessly over fields, through glen and woods
(which they often owned), to find a site where prey could easily
be taken. Today, the restrictions on the practice of falconry are
numerous, making it difficult for novices to acquire licenses,
and almost impossible for outsiders to gain any familiarity with
the sport. Contemporary falconers, as all hunters, must deal
with lands privately owned, with seeking permission to enter
separate parcels of property. Yet unlike the common hunter, who
does not have to worry about the path of his bullet, the falconer

must closely follow his bird as she pursues and perhaps takes down prey. Unlike the accipiter—goshawk, Cooper's Hawk, Sharp-Shin—whose flight, spurred by an explosion of adrenaline and incredible energy, is a blinding bullet of stealth and speed over a short line of distance, the hunt of a falcon often covers a large and rough terrain: over irrigation ditches, thick woods, stretches of open space. (I recall bounding across the flat expanse of Wyoming prairie in a four-wheel-drive government truck at sixty miles or more per hour, once again chasing Aragorn. Bored as always with halftime performances, he decided to leave the scene of an Air Force–Wyoming game—which resulted in a 0–0 tie. I was thankful for the tiny telemetry band pinging on his leg. I remember leaning out of the bouncing, jaw-loosening cabin, the wind slapping my face, the radar unit searching out my falcon as he soared off into whatever distance he hoped we could not find him in, for a while.)

The flight of the raptor in pursuit is intense, unrelenting. F. W. Remmler, a handler and trainer of eagles, has written of how Louhi, one of his most prized birds, followed rabbits on foot into thick brush, unwilling to admit that her prey might be lost. Jack Shelley once told me that he witnessed a peregrine, pursued and badgered by sparrows wanting to drive the falcon from their nest, suddenly flip over a wing in the air, extend a talon and pluck the tiny mass of a screeching sparrow from the swirling whirlpool of black about her, and sever the spinal cord with her beak. It was a warning; the sparrows apparently understood, and quickly disbanded.

Louis Agassiz Fuertes, distinguished naturalist and Cornell professor, wrote in the December, 1920 edition of *National Geographic* an extensive and passionate article about the spectacle of watching sacres (sakirs), "desert falcons," engage in aerial pursuit and combat with kites, thousands of feet above the earth, their ranging battle often finally invisible to the naked eye. Sakirs have also been used, in Arabia and India, to hunt gazelles. The pursuit of game ranges far over rocky, and at times dangerous, terrain. Five hawks are released to take down the leaping antelope with her huge, lustrous eyes. Fuertes notes: "There is great danger that the hawks may be impaled on the horns of the gazelle."

The most fierce and relentless of all raptors, though, is the goshawk: a machine full of fury (whose talons are "engines of death," writes Fuertes). The short, swift explosion of the goshawk is strikingly different from the graceful hunt on the wing of a falcon. The goshawk kills prey by clutching and driving her talons into a victim's vital organs. Lascelles describes witnessing his hawk miss on her first strike at a rabbit, who leapt four feet in the air to avoid the killing stroke of the raptor; the goshawk turned over, flew underneath and caught the rabbit in the air, "rolling afterward down a steep bank head over heels, but never leaving go her hold."[10] One goshawk killed twenty-four rabbits in a day. Others were perfectly willing to follow a rabbit into a burrow. Both raptor and prey would disappear; the goshawk would always emerge clutching the rabbit in her foot.

Falconry is the oldest persisting "sport" in the world; its origin is unknown. The first contact between man and falcon probably occurred in ancient Egypt, perhaps as early as 2000 B.C. Numerous Egyptian and Persian frescoes and sculptures and the ruins of Babylon (now in northern Iraq) hold images of falconry. Years ago, I saw in Iran (my family's home during my last three years at the Academy) an impression of a royal figure holding a hawk on his uplifted arm to the rising, eternal sun. The figure is nearly 3,000 years old; he slowly crumbles back to dust among the ruins of what had once been the springtime capital of ancient Persia in its greatness: Takhte Jamshid, perhaps better known as Persepolis—the great city destroyed by Alexander.

References to falcons and hawks used for hunting are found in early books of England, France, northern Africa, Holland, Italy, Spain, India, China, Russia, and Japan. Although the ancient Greeks apparently knew nothing of the practice, the Lombards, who settled in northern Italy about 560, did. By 875 falconry was widely practiced throughout western Europe and Saxon England. The advent of the gun and rifle made hunting an easier (and more accessible) practice; falconry, however, never fully disappeared. With the introduction of firearms, falconry dwindled in western Europe, though austringers and falconers of Scotland continued to perpetuate the "Noble Art."[11]

Today in the United States there are only a few thousand licensed falconers. No one knows how many practice the sport without sanction, who, left to their own devices and sometimes brutally bizarre ideas, secretly harbor a hawk or two of their own, away from the sight of other humans.

Abuses, naturally, occur. Fledglings are stolen from wild nests. The black-market price for a peregrine can be thousands of dollars. Those who choose to practice falconry away from the sight of others often care little whether what they do is legal. Perhaps, ironically, this may be the safest thing to do. The more quietly the falconer practices the sport, the safer the bird remains. During legal hunting season, many rifle-bearing "sportsmen" shoot hawks, eagles, falcons from the sky, considering them vermin and threats to their own taking of game. I have heard of those seeking to protect the lives of wild pigeons actually dynamiting cliffs where peregrines nested. The twisted reasoning behind this brutal act seems to suggest that it is better to protect the species one loves to kill from the threat of another species which kills to survive.[12]

Falconry is commonly regarded as an archaic, perhaps even cruel, practice. It requires time, patience, and even love to share in its pleasures. Few are willing or able to participate in its joys. Yet all true falconers possess an intimate and enduring knowledge of raptors.

The art of hawking is an individual and very private act which takes place between hunter and bird of prey, and one other, the always unwilling participant, the quarry. Only one in two thousand people has ever seen a trained raptor fly, and much of the dubious credit for what few opportunities there are goes to Academy falconers who fly their birds at halftime performances, sometimes snatched at by the curious cameras of network television and broadcast on the airwaves as another military anomaly, sometimes seen high above the grandstand seats of so many stadiums by audiences waiting for halftime to end, for the "good stuff" to begin again.[13]

It would seem logical that state wildlife departments would welcome a sport that required a practiced knowledge on the hunter's part, that left no prey crippled and bleeding to death as it struggled off to escape and die, that posed no threat to other humans or animals. Such logic, of course, is not present. Those few game departments which issue permits for falconers make it extremely difficult to obtain them: potential licensees must build mews, or sleeping chambers, for their birds and have them inspected; they must also pass exams which test their knowledge of various diseases, but which ask nothing about their knowledge of the practical application of hunting with raptors. Yet, after issuing a permit, departments rarely follow up to see if licensees are even giving proper care to the birds which, more than likely, they have trapped in the wild.

The best falconers I've known were those who cared little about taking game, about drawing attention to their involvement in a rarely practiced sport. They were quiet, self-possessed people who held inside a deep admiration for the courage and strength of raptors. They were most often people who no longer practiced the sport itself: not because time and other restraints stopped them from it; rather, there was something stronger and purer to be found in all too rarely seeing on a far horizon a falcon fall from the sun to take prey for herself. The heart of the passion for falcons lies in knowing how exceptional, solitary, and unlike any other species they are. It is no accident, I think, that the people I most admire in the Peregrine Fund—Shelley, Gordon, Keats—were all once active falconers, and now have withdrawn. Occasionally, while nursing a bird taken to the mews at Sapsucker Woods, they will fly a recovering falcon to the lure, and think of what they once practiced.

I will not make a plea for the sport of falconry. There are too many compelling arguments against it. For example, there are those who claim that keeping a bird in captivity is wrong and cruel. One need only visit the nearest zoo to see the miserable condition of the animals in cages, and the often bizarre and miserable behavior of the humans who view them. Keeping a falcon in a mews is not the same type of captivity. She has the option to escape, to return to the wild, whenever she flies, and eventually one out of three falcons will make that choice. And I should mention that those who have made the most significant advances in protecting and recovering endangered raptors have not been ecologists, not wildlife managers, not animal-rescue organizations, but falconers. Sometimes—I think T. J. Cade is the perfect example—they are both scholars and hunters.[14]

Yet, I cannot make a plea for the end of man's participation in the hunt, either. Certainly, there is a belief that humans act as predators by hunting and so renew their own affirmation of life, retrace their own origins and achieve a proximity to the primal need to survive. Certainly, the pure moment of the falcon's hunt achieves a communion few will experience, few could think possible. The falconer cannot know the falcon's rage, hunger, agony, and fear: centuries of civilization have taken the primitive away. The falconer cannot partake in the actual kill; it is vicarious: there is an inseparable bond between human and raptor and victim. It is heightened awareness, the perfect Zen-like sense of *satori*. The falcon, in the long spiral of flight, is familiar, sorcerer, shaman.

The magic is not in the man.

I believed, because I was told it would happen, that Aragorn was released into the wild when I left the Academy. I was assured he would be trained to kill and not fly to the lure, and thus would no longer be fit for demonstration flying. He was independent. He had his own personality and style, and did little to adapt toward pleasing others. He would fly only for me, though I'm not sure if he was doing me a favor; of course, he only flew superbly for me when there were no others around. I often imagine him finally released from the fist of a falconer, climbing high over the front range of the just beginning Rockies to the west of the Academy boundaries, peaking the snow-tipped mountains as he soared into the wild blue of the Continental Divide. It would be a happy circumstance (and I would be lying if I claim that I never dreamed of it) if one day, as I sat idly by a window staring at distance and recovering the past, there came a crisp pecking at the sill and I would look to see Aragorn with his mate, proud and dominating and yet nuzzling shyly by his side, and a slew of tiny fledglings, cacking and insistent as they lined up beside him at the window. . . .

I could imagine the fierce pride of his eyes, the swell of his breast. If Aragorn could speak, he would say, *I was always meant to be free. I never belonged to you. But I think you understood. . . .*

Such things never happen in this world of chance.

And, fearing the answer I might receive, after I left the Academy I never asked about Aragorn. I never asked.

> Winter. Morning.
> I kick and slide down the slope.
> My breath forms crystals in the fog.
> Beneath blue pines
> I secret the path.
>
> In the mews he shifts and mutters on his perch:
> Grey gyr, a tiercel. The others,

In separate pens, each on leg supported,
Ruffled in sleep, still.
Dried flecks of blood on his talons.

In the clearing I see him: face
Pressed against black bars.
Inside, he flings to my arm, head bent,
Waiting the hood. Our last season,
The final weeks of imprisonment.

These same talons once pierced my hand: foreclaw
Poking through flesh between thumb and index.
Now, he learns what I replaced, unlearns
The whorish attraction of the lure. Kills, makes
This blood his own, he's learned what I can't.

Unhood: one green eye stares, blinks, head bobs.
I cast him off toward where I think the sun must be.
He flaps, arches, gone. I crouch in white
Snow, breathing fog, making fog. Woodpecker
Drums an echo. In an open

Meadow, a young hare tears through.
I whistle, know he's there:
Over my shoulder, at five hundred feet,
Hangs the grey gyr: waiting on the kill.
Flying out of the darkness I've kept him in.[15]

When Bill Carpenter came to Cornell a few months ago to give
a reading, he handed me a copy of his poem, "The Hunting
Eagles of Afghanistan," and diffidently muttered, "Here, I think
you might like this." I did more than just like it. I thought of
what it implied and, as all poems do, failed to say directly in
those few brief lines. I thought of Afghani falconers, huge eagles
by their sides, as they rode across the level plains at high eleva-
tions. The image seemed a perfect symbol for freedom and release
in a country where freedom and release have always been elu-
sive. From Alexander to the British, and then the Soviets: it is
a country of loosely connected clans which have always been
forced to repel foreign invaders.

Extending the image, I recalled how nomadic tribesmen from

the Kirghiz steppe had trained berkutes to kill wolves, as well as deer. Berkutes, as with all eagles, will drive a wolf from an animal's carcass, but do not seek wolves, naturally, as quarry. The wolf, like the raptor, lives to kill. Robinson Jeffers once wrote: "What but the wolf's teeth whittled so fine / The fleet limbs of the antelope." Wolves, most perfectly created for the role of communal predators, vulnerable it would seem only to men of the Kirghiz, became prey for a bird which weighed at most no more than twelve pounds.

Yet there is an incredible strength of physical mass as the eagle slams into its prey, a ton of crushing force in the palm of each talon. Paralyzed, the wolves would lie helpless beneath the berkute, a distant and smaller cousin of the golden eagle. The berkute would bind the spine of the wolf, or, as the wolf turned to bite back with its teeth, bind the nose of the victim, suffocating it.[16]

In the *Journal of the American Falconers' Association*, two decades ago, F. W. Remmler wrote a lengthy account of his experience adapting the methods of these tribesmen to train berkutes to kill wolves. What seemed an act pure and solitary and free in south-central Russia became, for me, a slightly bizarre practice, but a practice I suppose no more bizarre than hunting game from the open bay of helicopter or aircraft, or through the open window of a roving automobile. Yet Remmler distended the strangeness of human behavior by first training his eagles to hunt large moving objects by turning them loose on children, covered with protective leather, clothed in wolf skin, with raw meat (used as bait) strapped to their backs. Here, the cliché is reversed—the lambs are dressed in wolf skin. Once the eagles successfully knocked the children to earth, Remmler moved on to the real target of his desire: wolves. Confined to a large caged enclosure, it took Remmler's eagles several days to learn how to kill the wolves which were penned in with them. After they had mastered this stage, Remmler released both wolves and eagles on an island. The experiment was successful: Remmler writes of Louhi, his favorite hunter, having killed two wolves in ten minutes. One night, as they gathered around the fire, Remmler and his friends heard the howling of a mournful wolfpack: "It may be that I had drunk too much . . . but the horror that filled me was very real. If I could have given the two dead wolves their lives back I would have done it immediately."[17]

I cannot excuse myself from such behavior; on one occasion, at least, I participated in training a prairie falcon to do something that was as abnormal, though far less brutal, than Remmler's experiment. While still an apprentice falconer, I helped teach one of our prairie falcons to stoop on an effigy of the West Point mule. We had crudely painted the image of the mule on one side of a white sheet and draped it over the balance of a sawhorse; toward the lip of the balance, I had drawn a bright red bull's-eye on the high end of the mule's rump: five concentric rings narrowing to a ground zero where we attached a piece of chicken. The sawhorse was placed in the center of the intramural playing fields. On a far hill, over a half mile away, a cadet with his back toward us unhooded his bird and then turned toward the fields. The falcon, rustling her feathers, suddenly stood straight, her feathers sliding back to glistening sheen along her body. Her eyes gleamed. Seeing the meat on the sawhorse, her head bobbed twice, and she cast off. During the first days of practicing this bizarre lure technique, she veered off from the sawhorse, afraid of its size. Then, later, she would land on the top edge of the sawhorse as if she were landing on the tail of the mule, lean over and delicately pluck the chicken from the bull's-eye. Eventually, though, she began to enjoy this routine and became so fierce that one day she knocked over the sawhorse after her steep pitch from the sky.

On the day of the Army–Air Force game, she was ready for prey. She had weighed in earlier that morning at slightly under her normal flying weight. The scales could discriminate fractions of an ounce, which was critically important. (The difference of an ounce or two, for a bird that weighed slightly more than a pound, could tell whether a falcon was ready for flight, could explain a sudden change in a prairie falcon's always temperamental mood.) I remember her dancing from my fist onto the scale, like a prizefighter ready for action. I was happy just to be handling her, and the weigh-in was one of my few chances as an apprentice to have a bird on my fist. She looked from the scale and then to me and then back to the scale, emitting a tiny cack of delight at what it seemed she could recognize on its intricate balance. As I rubbed the front of her breast, she eagerly pushed the sharp keel of bone vertically bisecting her body into my fingers, showing me the thin tissue of muscle under her flesh, the absence of fat. She was, as falconers, or for that matter, prizefighters, would call it, "keen."

I no longer recall the score of the game at the second quarter. Nor do I remember the long introductory spiel from the announcer on behalf of the Academy falconers. I do remember looking up into the high sun from my seat in the grandstands (as apprentices, we were not allowed to participate in performances—as with all things military, and otherwise, one has to prove oneself first) and seeing the falconer lean down to loosen the leather ties of her hood with his teeth, softly shielding the falcon against his body with his free hand, and then turning and lifting her high above him. I could not see, but imagined I could see, her sharp, instinctive head-bob as she looked down to the center of the playing field toward the falconer there. He, however, stopped reeling his lure and brought it back in, as the falcon cast off from the tower. She rose high over the stadium, climbing. No one seemed to notice the falconer. She rose, turned a half circle, and then seeing her quarry, stooped almost vertically toward the drowsing, disinterested mule on the sidelines. He screamed: a high wail of pain and terror as she smashed into him, as her talons furrowed the rear of his back. Both sides of the stadium went wild: visiting Air Force cadets poured out of the stands from the east; Army cadets from the west. Pieces of uniforms, the blue and the grey, flew by: hats, shoes, shoulderboards and rank insignia. Officers who tried to intercede became part of the brawl as well; their sharply pressed uniforms were ripped and torn, their faces blooded by random fists. Milton first penned the word in *Paradise Lost* which perfectly describes that day on the banks of the Upper Hudson: pandæmonium.

All except for the single falconer who stood in the center of the carnage, pulled out his lure, called down his bird, and calmly walked off the field.

We lost the football game, but won the halftime. West Point, after all, is an awful place: two centuries of tradition unhampered by progress.

Tradition. Even as I write this, there are hunters on horseback crossing the Kirghiz steppe, berkutes at their sides, dogs trailing at their heels.

And so I return the story in kind.

The Hunting Eagles of Afghanistan

Once, near winter, I visited a man who lived alone.
As he stood, waving from his porch, I set my two dogs
from Alaska (half-wolf, with their white eyes that ran
down the rabbit in the snow) free to chase whatever
cravings their noses questioned in the woods.
Here, come to the window and look, he called,
motioning me to the dead expanse across Penobscot Bay.
A skein of geese was turning south
as our shadows locked like joining hands.
The only faith I have, he whispered, mostly
to himself, *is in how little there is some
men will not do . . . I have no faith.*
And it was something in the wild blue
of his eyes, the way they stared past anything
as if they were following the outline
of a wave breaking underneath the eyelids
in a dream from which he could not wake,
that showed the secret secret
only in tradition handed from the father to
the son, from the Kirghiz Steppe
and then across the Caspian to the
Hindu Kush to prove dominion over life,
or death, and Remmler, fifty years ago
discovered it, when he trained his eagles
to hunt wolves by first loosing them
on his children dressed in wolf skin,
the raw meat strapped to their backs, when
he later saw his berkute bind the spine of a wolf
with the ton of force behind the crushing
talon, when another wolf was found
cornered and exhausted, and another
hunting eagle of Afghanistan, hooded right
until the final moment, and crazed
with discipline and hunger,
was allowed to fly.

On Wednesday, yesterday, Jack and I entered different hack
boxes to bring the birds back into the hide, while Kathy and
Tom removed the front bars. We cut fifteen chickens, a two-day
supply, into sections and scattered them around the boxes and
on the cliff ledge.

I had difficulty herding the birds back to the hide. Augustus
fell on his back, his wings splayed and talons footing the tendons
of my right hand. I cupped his small body from behind, careful

not to damage any of his primary or tail feathers. I wet the birds down with a solar shower, a collapsible black plastic container with an attached nozzlehead which heats water naturally from the sun. As I held the nozzle above the terrified eyasses, I thought how both Tom and I could have used this same device each day to keep clean. When packing for the wilderness, there's always something you forget.

The shower immediately calmed the chicks, though I'm not sure they appreciated it. Holding a flat rectangle of cardboard in front of the hide, I waited for Jack to do the same thing in the near box. Kathy and Tom signalled from the observation point.

We pulled our cardboard shields and ran. Hoping to get quickly out of sight, we scrambled up the rock above us, knelt in the brush, and waited.

Condemned prisoners freed from incarceration, they stumbled out into the light. Shadowfax fledged almost immediately, flying straight out from the cliff and over the valley. He spent the next six hours soaring above us and along the cliffs, occasionally pausing to rest, sometimes less than twenty feet from where we sat on the observation point. Head tilted slightly, he looked both perplexed and ecstatic. When he returned to the boxes, the other eyasses arched their wings, as humans greeting the sun would raise their arms, and ran to Shadowfax, surrounding him with what seemed congratulatory joy. Then they became submissive, instinctively reacting to Shadowfax as a superior, a *flying* falcon, one who returned with food to feed them all.

Fuentes and Rondeau flew shortly after. Fuentes spent the night roosting on a ledge a hundred feet below the boxes. Rondeau perched on a rock a quarter-mile behind us, cacking, and unsure of how to return to the boxes. Even now, he looks toward me as I zero in with my binoculars: afraid to leave, afraid to stay.

And Figmo, the great explorer, has flown twenty feet up the cliff, thrown a condescending look down to his nonflying companions, and sauntered off into the unknown wood.

Friday, 27 June

The wind hits the cliff at almost forty knots. My fingers, my brain, are numb. Waiting, hoping for the sun to rise over the far clouds. I have seen eight birds so far, though identifying the bright-colored leg band markers, even with the sighting scope, is difficult. They roost on an exposed ledge, feathers fluffed and raised against the wind—five tiny falcons huddled close near the far box.

All of the eyasses have flown. Anne and Madonna took wing at dusk last night. Belladonna has discovered the perch poles. She stretches her wings, up and wide; her feathers ripple as she rouses in the rhythm of the breathing air.

Figmo has become more independent. Three hours after his trek into the forest, he returns to his siblings. His bearing is more confident, as it seems with all the birds after their first flight. But his walk is ludicrous, the waddle-shuffle of a drunk duck. Though all peregrines are capable of astounding aerial stunts, able to flip over on the back, twist and maneuver with enormous sureness, grace and agility are lost on the ground. They stumble, run with short, thin legs. Figmo imitates Chaplin's tramp.

Shadowfax, Rondeau, and Fuentes began tail-chasing yesterday. They stream past us in a surrealistic dogfight, twisting in the spiralling gyre of wind, trying to shake each other off. They let the wind take them out beyond the north face, away from my view. Mock combat. They are at play, but it is play with a murderous intent.

Each of these peregrines must kill to survive. Play always precedes the hunt. Sometimes, a peregrine will stoop into a flock of birds for the joy of sensation. The falcon has no desire to attack, only to fall, fascinated, through the drifting and rising and pouring of bodies in flight, only to be driven off by a flurry of black figures, rising like smoke, in defense. Fledglings, especially, love to chase anything that moves: witnesses have seen eyasses chase white-tailed deer through open fields. They will attack branches, falling leaves, insects, drifting feathers. Practice, endless practice.

Instinctively, the peregrine is born for pursuit, for speed, for seeking the death of prey which lie in the path of a blinding bullet of light. Young fledglings, even before leaving the nest, know how to use their beaks in defense, or to bite into the neck of prey.[18]

A peregrine is emotionless; she has no thought in the way we know it, other than the kill. She strikes with a fury of folded wings, biting into the cervical vertebrae of quarry, snapping the spine with an audible crack. Unlike accipiters, the peregrine will not chase game on the ground or pursue it under cover of brush or wood.

She is the perfect predator: her very being is meant to destroy. But it is destruction both reasoned and natural. Her head is rounded, moves smoothly through the slipstream. She has tomial teeth on the cutting edge of the hooked upper bill, which fits into a corresponding notch on the lower one, and uses these teeth, by a slight twist of pressure, to sever the spinal cord. Her relatively short bill, powered by strong jaw muscles, can easily grasp and strip flesh from the bone. She has twin sets of baffled nostrils, conchlike passages in the nasal cavity, though their purpose is unclear. Some have suggested that these baffles relieve pressure during stoops; others propose that a falcon uses these nasal passages as airspeed indicators by sensing changes in temperature and pressure during high-velocity flight.[19] Her tail is squared and narrow, aimed for speed. The tarsi are thick, muscular and long. Three anterior toes, and an undercurving hind toe, bear powerful, sharp claws; each toe has proportionately spaced bumps underneath to help grip a victim. The breast is wide and strong; the sternum has a deep keel which projects forward, layered on either side with fibrous tissue. The pectoral muscles, when well developed, help power the network of wings in long flights of endurance, as well as in rapid flashes of speed. The eyes are huge, well-developed, phenomenally acute. The dark, feathered mask absorbs light. The rufous coloring and design of her feathers are camouflage in the air. She excretes electrolytes and sodium through her nasal glands. Unlike owls, the falcon has a crop, a saclike extension of the esophagus, which stores food before passing it on to the stomach: thus, she can consume up to a third of her body weight at a time and eat large prey after a kill, as well as survive a week or longer when food is scarce. She regularly sheds the koilin inner lining of her muscular stomach, perhaps to remove grease and mucous from her digestive tract.[20]

Her most distinctive features, though, are the fingers of her streamlined wings. Long and pointed, slender and delicate, they hold the key to her mystery. The primaries are designed for speed; the secondaries for stability and strength, for carrying weight in her talons. The quills are stiff. The wing-loading areas, like the chord, camber, and internal spars of an aircraft wing, withstand tremendous pressure.

The peregrine seeks out the anomaly, the aberration. The sick and diseased fall victim to the plummeting shock wave which falls like an avenging Harpy. Riding above the shifting quilted pattern of a flock, she finds the sudden hesitation in motion, the slightest physical weakness or difference, and seeks to erase it from the mass of identical wings in flight. The slightest shade of plumage, movement, shifting dance of sudden beating arms will drive her mad with a sudden love to kill, as if she *must* kill the thing she loves. The prey will flail, look for escape, want desperately to save itself from death. But it is a moment pre-destined. And hunger is only part of the equation. It is the beauty and the blossoming of violence.

Figmo screams as I stand to put on gloves. I nod and smile. He keeps a close watch on me.

Earlier this morning, he tried to land on a nearly vertical cliff face. Wings mantled, talons digging into rock, he looked like a bat. Confused, he glared up at the others, hoping they did not see his predicament. Last night he tried to roost in one of the hack boxes. He stepped out once, cacking for the others to join him. Finally, he left the box and joined the rest, lonely for companionship.

I begin to notice the different voices of birds. Till now, I could only recognize the shrill call of the raptor, the percussive echo of the barred owl. Now each dawn I single out a song, as if learning to sight-read: hermit thrush, cedar waxwing, bluebird, junco. I hear the white-throated sparrow echo the opening section of Mendelssohn's Wedding March from *A Midsummer Night's Dream,* or Dvořák's *New World Symphony,* or Tchaikovsky's *Dirge of the Damned.*

Saturday, 28 June   0600.

A dense fog, swirling up, consuming the cliff. The spotting scope is worthless; condensation forms a dull sweat on the lens.

I recognize Figmo's screams through the mist. He is sensitive to every word I write. *He* has no difficulty seeing *me.* If I lift my head to watch, he screams; if I return to my notes, he screams.

A sufferer of "constant cack attack," he screams even as he flies. Perhaps he should be the first recipient of a falcon muzzle.

Shadowfax was perched on the observation point, almost seeming to wait for us to arrive this morning. His dexterity is amazing. Yesterday he had no problems maneuvering in the wind. He made several beautiful landings on the perch-pole ledge. He continued tail-chasing Fuentes and Rondeau, twisting his body and attacking from below. Raising a wing and rolling over a shoulder, he made his first attempt at a stoop, a steep dive he finally pulled out of, unsure of what he'd accomplished. Belladonna dived on him from above, sinking her talons into his back. Both Tom and I were disappointed. A young Ace brought down in the prime of his career.

As I crawled through the wood for a closer view of their ledges, he flew up, warning the others. He found me hiding behind a paper birch, and dove to within ten feet of me. His face had the sharp, confident look of a falcon in flight.

A year from now, Shadowfax will be able to perform maneuvers that no human pilot, even at the controls of an X-30, could possibly duplicate.

He will be able to: if he survives.

I never planned on becoming a pilot. It was an accident. My eyes were 20/200. As a cadet, I was not eligible to be even a navigator (and given the opportunity, I would have declined). I had selected a special intelligence field during my senior year at the Academy. I had chosen Crete for a location to pursue my new job.

Two days before graduation, I received a message from the Surgeon General of the Air Force that I would be given the chance to attend pilot training, if I wanted to. The news was a shock, something I never considered as a possibility. I was given three and a half hours to decide. I stood in a whirlpool of confusion, holding the now silent phone in my hands. It was the longest afternoon of my life.

But I said yes. I've never known if I made the right choice; in more ways than one, it no longer matters. It happened.

In one way I could say it was because of an accident that I am still a pilot.

*   *   *

Tom and I rarely talk. I suppose we share little. He loves these mountains; I love these birds. We split the tasks of feeding, packing in water and quail, and making observation notes. I hope our tenuous relationship can last.

I came here for solitude, wanting to be as far as possible from human contact. Donna, I think, understands this. Certainly, it must be a relief to be rid of me for a short while. Even this void of writing notes ("the exquisite whiteness of the page," is that what Baudelaire called it?) conveys little of this open space I live in now. Being here reminds me of my time in Alaska, where the people are proud of their separation at the edge of the world, disdainful of the "commoners" who reside in the "lower 48."

The mist grows thicker, begins to merge with this white page.

The falcons are quiet. I can only hope they stay in place and return to the ledge when the fog lifts. On days like this, fledglings have been lost trying to find their way back, only to become disoriented and starve. This morning the fine spray of mist keeps even Figmo calm. Belladonna sleeps on a high perch-pole, head tucked under a wing.

I can only hope. As always, there's little I can ever do.

0903.

Tom has left the mountain for the next few days. I thought I was alone, but I was wrong.

A buck and two does stroll onto the observation point, eyeing me vaguely. The buck's horns are just beginning to show; he has a puerile, innocent look. A whirl of black flies around their heads, around mine.

I half believe, as the fog drifts on the rock, that they can *will* a transformation into fauns and satyr. Sometimes I wake to hear their muffled, distant celebrations, as they drink to the long-dead Bacchus, dance in the circle of a godless night.

The four of us, figures in the gathering mist, share the private joy of seeing falcons stream out from the boxes, exhilarated as they pass in and out of cloud and head for the north cliff. Now, they are gone.

The white tails of the deer flick. I slap at the fly drinking at my neck. The deer turn to the trees. The buck pauses, calmly looking back. Unafraid, as if his hide bore the imprimatur: *Noli me tangere quia Caesaris sum.*

Touch me not, for I am Caesar's.

Ten years ago I visited my family in Tehran. This was a short while before the revolution. Roaming the streets, I stared in amazement at the reverence that people gave to falcons and hawks. I saw hooded raptors ride on the backs of bicycles through traffic, turning and bending their bodies automatically. Years later in Riyadh, I saw calm hawks carried in crowded bazaars, and the sakir falcon emblazoned on advertisements for Air Saudia.

There, the image of horsemen crossing the desert in search of ibis or other low-flying game is as fresh today as hundreds of years ago.

An Arab prince once offered an enormous amount for Baffin, the Academy's mascot, a white Arctic gyrfalcon. Gyrfalcons were once held as the highest falcons, fit only for royalty.

The prince was not pleased by the refusal.

In Atlantic City, at one of the larger gambling casinos, the management recently built a nesting box adjacent to the ledge of the $750-a-night penthouse, in an effort to encourage a pair of wild peregrines to call the casino rooftop "home." Although more than willing to support the project, the owners would occasionally be upset by the stray deposit of a blue jay or woodpecker head on the sill of the panoramic window which overlooked the ocean.

A frequent guest of royal Arabic lineage spent much of his time watching the falcons, while the rest of his party gambled in the casino below.

He was delighted with them. Above his head, in the incandescent swirls and Gothic flourishes of T's and O's which spell out the casino's logo, seen from miles away, the falcons neatly cached side-by-side their private food collection (like a fine wine cellar), having separate levels for the common sea gull, or the occasional arctic tern, the woodpecker, jay, pigeon, and the finest gourmet treat for any peregrine: the mallard duck.

The huge letters of the casino burn all night, every night.

SUNDAY, 29 JUNE

Donna left early this afternoon. She plans to spend the next three weeks in New York City. She seems overly concerned about me. Perhaps she's right. In the short time here I've grown irritated with the habits and rituals of humans, including myself.

On Saturday, we ate lunch at a saloon in Clear Lake. We heard the plastered voices of those around the pool table and over the bar, drunk and stunned before noon, the monotone of some sports event humming from the television on the wall. It could have been anywhere: Chicago; Brooklyn; Minot, North Dakota. The voices were softer than they would be at night, muffled in the glare of solid light outside.

At the local ski slope, where 10,000 trees have been harvested, golfers were spending their day tracing the arc of a ball in the vaulting wind. Donna considered them with disgust. Quizzical, intrigued, I watched with fascination. Shakespeare barked from the window of our truck.

Donna is afraid I'm losing it, that I'm going as George Gordon calls it, "shack wacky." It's true. During the day we spent together, I was a pain in the ass. She endured a six-hour drive from Ithaca only to hear my semi-coherent grumblings. CBC broadcast a segment on peregrine fledgling releases in Saskatoon. I began to criticize their methods.

Donna told me, rightly, to shut up.

I wonder what my visits to Clear Lake are doing. I live either in isolation or out of it. I'm able to spend long hours without a human voice. Yet I wonder why I feel so comfortable, here, in the absence of human company. I think, not that my thoughts may be right or true ones, my need to escape to the peak of this tiny mountain has much more to it than a need to escape the often needlessly pretentious ritual of life at Cornell, the voices of too many graduate students who believe they carry deep in the core of the inner self the strength of certainty and conviction. All too often, everything I've heard, and everything I say, turns out wrongly. I came here because of a wild sense of caring for a way of life I once had. When I was a cadet, my closest friends—before I met Donna—were falcons. Creatures who cared little more for me than as one who supplied food, who released them from the bounds of a chamber and from the falconer's fist to let them soar in distance for a few short moments. This summer was a time I had waited for a long while, had known was coming in the same way some strange and beautiful words of writers lovingly tell why they left their homes, why they had to leave.

I thought I could speak with a sure touch and knowledge of the season and the sounds and sensations, as purely as Isak Dinesen did when she wrote: *I had a farm in Africa, at the foot of the Ngong Hills.* I am here writing on the granite ledge of this thousand-foot rock for a few weeks. I will return, I know. Everything has changed since my days of first learning falconry. There can be no intimacy now between myself and these peregrines. For this project to be successful, I must keep my distance. In the years since knowing Aragorn, I traded the unruliness of a falcon for the unruly character of high-performance jets and a life of procedure and checklists in refueling aircraft. I have felt the pure rush of exhilaration of popping through the sound barrier; seen the pitot-static instruments, altimeter, and vertical velocity indicators suddenly reverse themselves at the sudden moment when the air rushes in to fill the spaces where the aircraft has been; I've been released in the pull of afterburners that took me into the high, still silence of the black atmosphere ten miles above the earth, where the air is so thin one tiny crack in the pressurization system could crush the canopy, send the package of bone, guts, dangling tissue, and whatever remains of me into the absent provinces of altitude.

Now I know that I cannot recover the past. But this is a good place to live. I have the silence, the intricate beauty of the landscape, the unsure wisdom of my own vision. For now I live here, on Fire Lake Mountain, and I can pour my spirit into its waiting presence, and the mountain can hold it there forever.

To escape the screams of falcons overhead, I become absorbed in simple, mundane events. My mind is consumed by trivia: another word for reality. I hear lecture notes by Jon Stallworthy on Yeats, and William Morris, "happiest of the poets." Or, worse, the incredible, tenacious jingles of advertising, phrases I've not heard in years. *Com' an' listen to mah story 'bout a man named. . . . Take Sominex tonight and sleep. . . .*

I make three packing trips up Fire Lake mountain. Donna has spent seventy dollars on four bags of groceries: small insignificants which will mean everything in the next few weeks. I argued with her for her considerateness; a stupid thing to do, I realize, long after she is gone.

My knees ache with the weight—150 pounds of water (we've found a running stream three miles from the peak), 50 pounds of chicken, my own supplies. On my second trip down, I meet the caretaker's sister and her daughters. She's brought four ice-cold beers. I laugh, tell her I forgot what beer looks like.

We set up the spotting scope for viewing. They ask the obvious questions. The girls are most interested in the names of each bird.

Shadowfax circles high, drops out of the sun, diving on us. He flies by repeatedly, as close as five feet from our heads, screaming. His face is sharp, his eyes angry. For the first time, I notice the whitewash of falcon mutes around us and realize that the observation point, the highest elevation on this mountain, is no longer mine.

A hard rain lasts for three hours. Brilliant arcs of lightning strike around us. Near sunset, the rain stops and we are enveloped in a living cloud, moving over the cliff and rippling through the lower marshes. All of the birds have been sighted, huddled near the boxes.

Sunlight slips through a grove of maple over my left shoulder, forming the impression of a Celtic cross in breathing mist. When I look again, the image is gone.

In its place is a corona with the sun at its core. At the edges, a soft prism of color describes the circle.

Monday, 30 June

At six o'clock, I send ten chickens down the food chute. Though gassed in a relatively painless way, they thaw in grotesque figures of suffering. A face, set in its grimace of discomfort, is wrapped around a foot as it tumbles through the tunnel of white, turning as it falls. The last three chickens stick in the pipe; gravity will not free them. I find a dead limb, use it like a plumber's john to flush the carcasses, and end up flushing all the falcons from the boxes. Three of them try to dive on me, finally turning away within thirty yards, still afraid. I inspect the boxes, the first close view I've had since release. I see half-eaten chickens, covered with moss and dust and feathers, strewn on the ledge. Falcon mutes decorate the granite.

At 0918 a turkey vulture strays through the valley. Immediately,

Rondeau launches. What at first seems mock combat, which the birds have been practicing in groups of three to five all morning, becomes battle. The vulture's wing span is huge, over six feet; he turns well for his size. But Rondeau continues to find sharp updrafts of air, and using that advantage thermals up and pitches on the vulture from above. He flies through the tail of the larger bird, unaware that he must strike at the head for a kill. (When a falcon kills, it is not by the strength of talons, which cannot, usually, pierce and kill prey in the air. Rather, she relies on her jaw muscles and sharp, razor-like beak to strike a victim's neck.)

It's an impressive display. After ten minutes, the vulture curves low through the trees, knowing he has little hope for escape through open air. Rondeau returns to his companions on the cliff.

Without a parent's care and concern, without being allowed the normally slow, cautious process of learning to hunt, these fledglings are willing to dare: they know no other way. They are teaching themselves, and each other.

TUESDAY, 1 JULY   *1200.*

Rondeau thermals high into the perfect circle of the sun. A few minutes ago he flew by the observation point, eying us, and then caught the first rising draft of warm air. Instinctively, he turns and lifts in the widening gyre, faintly beats his wings, and rises higher on the quilted heat until he is invisible in the cerulean sky.

I hear Rondeau's faint cack as a C-130 Hercules air transport passes overhead at 8,000 feet, probably well below Rondeau. If the pilots could see him, they would stare up in amazement as he stares down at them. A slow, lumbering machine with wings forcing its way through the currents of air, while above a peregrine fledgling floats on the lifting palms of a thermal.

Rondeau's tiny lungs can carry him high above the surface of the earth. When he hones his skills and participates in the hunt which will range far over the landscape, he will climb a mile or more into the air for advantage and perspective.

In the Himalayas, there is a species of crow that inhabits the thin realm of the atmosphere above 18,000 feet.[21] In my altitude chamber training, I am told that the time of useful consciousness at such an altitude is no more than thirty minutes. I know that this is not entirely true. In the early sixties, for example, four American climbers were trapped at 27,000 feet in darkness, after having descended too late in the day from the peak of Mt. Everest. Air Force studies, a few years earlier, had predicted that humans could survive no longer than three hours at that altitude without oxygen. The climbers, however, had by that time spent many weeks in the high mountain altitudes. They huddled together on a small ledge on a fortunately windless night in the relative warmth of twenty below zero. They stayed at that altitude for over eighteen hours. Although two of the climbers lost most of their toes and fingers to frostbite, they all survived. A British team on a subsequent expedition was trapped at 28,700, just below the summit of Everest, for almost nine hours.

In 1978, Peter Habeler and Reinhold Messner successfully climbed Mt. Everest without oxygen equipment; a few years after that, Messner climbed Everest solo, again without oxygen. But the performance of such an amazing feat is supreme: it requires women and men of perfect physical condition and determination. The risks are equally supreme: in the "death zone" above 27,000 feet, blood vessels in the eyes burst, frostbite is likely, logical and coherent thought processes die, and oxygen deprivation will cause pulmonary and cerebral edema if you remain too long. In the 700 feet which separate the peaks of K2 and Everest, there is a third less oxygen available. Messner was warned before his ascent: *You will go up a sane man, and come down a madman.*

The adaptability of birds for high-altitude flight is all the more astonishing: the respiratory pigments of hemoglobin adjust to the decrease in oxygen and efficiently combine oxygen and iron atoms in the lungs, which are carried to the capillaries and exchanged for carbon dioxide. Birds' performance at high altitude, unlike that of humans, is still effective.

Ten years ago, I climbed an extinct volcano 19,000 feet high on the border of the Soviet Union. My guide, who did not speak English, left me. I passed out at the summit, woke, and, because I had eaten no solid food in the previous twenty hours, began vomiting blood in dry heaves. Because the Air Force was both smart and kind enough to drop me in an altitude chamber on my eighteenth birthday as part of my flight training, I recognized my personal hypoxia symptoms. I found a glacial slope, and slid 4,000 feet down to where I could breathe again. I had ascended too quickly (three days from sea level to high altitude), and had not allowed sufficient time to adjust to the effects. I was close, very close, to killing myself.

Every three years, when I repeat my training in the altitude chamber, I think of the possibility of losing pressurization at altitude, of feeling the cold rush of air as my lungs and internal organs explode with the loss of pressure in the sudden thin realm of the air at 35,000 feet. The possibility is real, and I know several crewmembers who have experienced it. If it is a slow loss of pressure, inattentiveness can cause the crew to experience oxygen starvation and, most likely, eventually pass out before recognizing the insidious onset of hypoxia. (Last year one of the aircrews in my squadron had a rapid depressurization over Greenland. The navigator told me that his most vivid memory, aside from the sudden rush of ambient air into the crew compartment, was seeing their crew chief, who had been joking and laughing a moment before, suddenly fall to the floor as though he were dead.)

Every three years, my refresher training reminds me how important the oxygen mask that rests by my shoulder in flight is. Part of the profile for altitude training involves a sudden loss of pressure at altitude; the chamber mists with a sudden fog, and then it's a rush to get on oxygen and stay there. Another part of the training requires an uncomfortable cruise without oxygen at an altitude of 25,000 feet. Sitting in the cramped and claustrophobic chamber, waiting each time to recognize my personal hypoxia symptoms (which usually are seeing my fingernails turn purple and feeling my brain, starved for oxygen, swell with a sudden overconfidence), I hear a tape played over the intercom system: the last flight of Phantom 392. Each time I hear that tape, I realize how fragile the human body is; how, in order to climb into the high atmosphere, we must wrap ourselves in breathing equipment and pressurized design systems.

Flight 392 was an experimental test flight for spin training in an F-4 Phantom. Shortly before takeoff, the pilot reported on the radio that he was having problems closing his canopy. He eventually found a harness line that was caught in the rigging of the canopy rail, removed it, and reported ready for takeoff. His wingman joined him shortly after he lifted from the runway and climbed with him to altitude. The 392 test pilot failed, however, to check both his cabin pressurization system and his oxygen supply. Neither was working. Task-saturated with the mission ahead, he failed to check the most simple items of his flight routine. Although he was wearing an oxygen mask, his master control lever had been set inadvertently to OFF. As he climbed to altitude, he was, in effect, breathing the thin and rapidly decreasing oxygen of the outside atmosphere.

Eleven minutes and forty-nine seconds after takeoff, the pilot of 392 made his last radio call: a garbled and confused transmission that everything was "OK." Both his wingman and the radio control monitors failed to recognize that he had already succumbed to hypoxia. Passing 30,000 feet, the aircraft entered the first of over twenty tight, spiralling turns as it fell back to the earth. Because the F-4 had been trimmed for a specific airspeed, the plane would at times level out for a short while, fly straight and level, and everything would indeed seem to be OK. The wingman would call on the radio and report that although 392's pilot wasn't responding to radio calls, it seemed he had worked out his problems. The assumption was that he must have had a radio failure.

And then it would begin again. The F-4 would enter another steep, diving turn. Even if the Phantom pilot had been conscious, and it seems merciful that he was not, he would have been helpless. The long line of his descent and the tight turns of his spin would have prevented him from doing anything. His eyes would be open in the white shock of terror, and his hands would lie like massive boulders at his sides: estimates predict he was pulling up to thirty-three transverse g's in each spiral. Trapped in a metal coffin, he fell.

Below 10,000 feet, the wingman became frantic. His voice on the radio, which had been confident and cocky, was now frenzied: *Pull your nose up, John! Pull your nose up!* His calls on the emergency guard frequency, to the pilot and to the control center: *He's wrapping it up! He's wrapping it up, tighter and tighter. . . . He's not gonna make it!* It took eight minutes from the time he first nosed over from altitude until impact. The people who listened and watched could do nothing. From the moment the pilot of 392 lit his afterburners for his takeoff roll, he was already dead.

Rondeau soars with a mysterious instinct.

This is the first warm day we've had. Already I feel the thick pockets of air forming that will lift these falcons high into the sky.

Each day I am astounded by what I witness. These falcons have extraordinary intelligence; they're learning at an incredible rate. Belladonna circles overhead, and then thermals up, disappears. Figmo, tired of combat, practices steep dives on us. As he skims the cliff, Tom and I hear the flutter of air over his body and his incessant cack. He's rapidly discovering how to stoop. Tucking his wings into his streamlined frame, he looks like an extended bullet. He picks up speed and then pulls out, afraid of what he's found.

The immense speed that an adult peregrine achieves during the stoop is accomplished by smoothing her wings into a deltalike arc and falling head first toward prey well beneath; manipulation of the alulae and slight adjustment of the wings help control steering.[22] How fast can a peregrine fly? A pilot in a 1930 pursuit plane once dived on a flock of ducks for practice and claimed that he saw a peregrine stoop past him at twice his speed, which was 280 kilometers per hour (173 miles per hour). In 1975, terminal velocity calculations placed the rate of a peregrine's stoop at 228 to 238 miles per hour.[23] It will be a long while, though, before these fledglings are able to perform such impressive feats. They will have lost their immature plumage of dusty brown and gained the sharp grey, black, and navy blue colors of the adult, before they will be able to fall out of the sky like living missiles. For now, they are having fun. Learning new things of the air, of this thing I call flight. Figmo's first attempt at a stoop was not meant as a fall from high pitch to catch prey: it seemed the easiest way to get down from the height he'd attained.

The hack boxes are empty. I unearth the cooler—which I've buried in earth to help prevent the food supply from spoiling— take out ten chickens to thaw. They fall like stones down the food pipe. The ledges are still empty, so I decide to climb down and clean out the mostly consumed carcasses. It seems best to bury the remains rather than leave an open food source for scavengers—squirrel or bear.

What I find on the ledges is a shock. Millions of flies feed on the chicken. The bright ringing noise of their swarm envelops me as I pick up a body. Turning over the bubbling grey flesh, I find a wealth of maggots, some nearly an inch long, writhing in the agony of sunlight.

I vomit over the ledge.

Panicked, I begin throwing remains—heads, feet, whole bodies —off the cliff as a sliver of fear uncoils inside me. It's an obvious clue to raccoon or fox (which can climb a vertical face to obtain food): an easy meal. But I can't take climbing back up to bury these remains; I can't have them strapped on my backpack, feel them against my skin.

I wake. The rain slaps my tent and the pine's limbs drip water on my head.

In the dream I am perched on the cliff; I watch through the spotting scope. The ringing begins, volubly increasing.

Huge greenhead and black flies, gold faces and looming eyes, visible teeth, rise up from the cliff face and swallow me.

WEDNESDAY, 2 JULY

Reviewing the previous year's report on peregrine releases, I find a subsection on owl control in Minnesota. It mentions the great-horned owl's threat to eyasses.

I read of two researchers who flush a great-horned from a cluster of pines east of the hack site. They pursue with shotguns, firing rounds to frighten him off. A young peregrine decides to join the hunt by driving the owl to the ground after repeated "stoops," once forcing him to land in a stream. After reaching a cover of oaks near the water, the owl is then twice knocked to the ground by a female Cooper's hawk, angered by the invasion of her nesting space.

At that particular site, four owls were shot. Although it is not a common occurrence to flush and kill great-horns, I feel a sharp regret. Palestinians of the raptor world.

Taughannock Falls lies a few miles north from our home in

Enfield. It is one of the most beautiful gorges in our area, rivalling the steeper and longer gorges of Watkins Glen. The waterfall itself is the tallest fall east of the Mississippi. The plummeting water drops from the precipice and flows into Lake Cayuga.

Shakespeare, King, Donna, and I would often hike the rim of the gorge or explore the paths leading up to the waterfall. Each season, the scene would change. Always we would witness something new, something we had not noticed before. In summer, the water would dwindle to a trickle of wetness against the face of the cliff. In autumn, the trees would explode in a hundred shades of gold. In winter, the small basin at the base of the falls would freeze, form into a green mass of ice. The water would rush under the ice and pour out to the lake. The mist would rise from the cracks in the snow and float over the gorge, misting our eyes and our lips. Recently, we learned that the sharp rising V's of the gorge had once been a popular nesting site for peregrines. Louis Agassiz Fuertes took his most beautiful photographs of peregrines, "the most cosmopolitan of birds," "the falcon of falcons," often perched on a branch over the edge of the cascade of blue and, varying by season, green water.

> A pair whose eyrie I watched on a 400-foot cliff near my home one July day had three young on the wing. During the middle of the day there was little activity and all the birds sat quietly pluming and resting; but for the first three hours in the morning and the last three in the afternoon, one old bird or the other returned about every twenty minutes with a pigeon. On that one day sixteen pigeons were brought to the young.[24]

Those days are gone forever. When reintroduction efforts were first made by the Peregrine Fund, Taughannock was the first site chosen to hack a brood of fledglings. First, because it was a historic aërie; second, because of its close proximity to Cornell. A large, elaborate hack box was built and lowered from the edge of the cliff. Bolts were sunk into the soft shale of the rock, and the box was secured. A twenty-five-foot food chute was rigged from the cliff down to the box, allowing hack site attendants the chance to feed the eyasses without being seen.

Hacking, at one time, was the first step in training a bird for falconry. (The most popular birds were called *passagers*, those trapped during the autumn migration. The Dutch village of Valkenswaarde—even the name betrays its revenue and commerce—became the most popular site for trapping falcons. Thousands of passage birds, followed by falcons which preyed on them, flew over the open moor near the village during each autumn migration. Some claim that master falconers used shrikes, often called butcher birds, to warn of a falcon's approach. Upon hearing the cry of alarm and confusion, the falconer would hide in a turf-covered trench, leaving a tied pigeon as quarry. When the falcon struck, the falconer pulled both falcon and prey back into the trap. Falcons were then brought to an auction, where emissaries from each court, duchy, and province of Europe gathered to bid on the raptors. The Möllens family of Valkenswaarde was considered for many generations the most skilled trappers, handlers, and trainers of falcons.) Haggards, or passagers, once arrived at a destination, would be allowed to roam free in the area near their hack box. Food would daily be placed on a board, until the bird learned to take prey for her or his own. The wider the bird ranged the better, that is, as long as she returned to the hack area for rest and the daily supply of food. Often, a bird would be left at the hack for several weeks until it was evident she was taking game. She would then be "caught up," and next came the long, arduous task of manning the falcon and training the bird to the lure. Falcon and falconer entered a relationship as partners, or equal victims.

The same plan was used for the reintroduction of the peregrine, with the one exception that once the bird was taking game, the feeding would stop, and the falcon, in theory at least, would be free.

Now, as we walk the trails along Taughannock, Donna and I look up to the hack box sunk into the high cliff. It is crumbling slowly; the seasons' rains are rotting the wood; the food chute has fallen and, held by a few remaining supports, dangles in the air. In the years since the disappearance of peregrines from the east, a new predator came to inhabit the gorge: a pair of great-horned owls. No one had known they were there. But the owls, sensing a threat by the fledglings, killed all of them. Each separate body was found at the base of the gorge.

*   *   *

1000.

Mist. Rain all night. Tahawus, the Cloud-Splitter (a name also given by white settlers to one of the notable peaks here), sails low beneath us. She returns, turning her head to watch as she passes by. She skims a scrub pine, glides back to her ledge. The boxes disappear in fog. Her wings flare and her tail splays wide as she prepares to land and then vanishes. Silence.

I cannot make a picture of this with a camera. Her movements are too swift and unpredictable to zoom the focus of the telephoto from infinity to specific distance. What I see lies beyond the borders of frame.

This has to do with my obsession with time, particularly now as I feel the air on the rocks, can see only fifty feet in any direction, hear the occasional, contented chirp of an eyass. *Remember this.*

The more miserable the weather, the happier they seem. This morning, I heard them arguing as they jockeyed for position on the observation point.

This afternoon, Tom and I have our first real conversation. The tension between us is obvious. Reviewing my notes, I see my refusal to acknowledge him in the fact of his absence from much of my writing. (As if I could erase the fact of his presence by refusing to mention him.) We do small favors for each other: because I rise at dawn each morning to make notes, I leave the coffee warming for him on the stove; he'll tighten the tension on one of our tents when he sees a slack line. But we never talk. And when we do, it becomes so clear how different the environments we live in are. I wonder if it's because of my limited background; after all, I've been in the military since I was seventeen, since 5 June 1974, the day I dropped my bags at the bottom of the overshadowing BRING ME MEN ramp at the Air Force Academy and learned the five responses I would be allowed to make during the next year ("Yes, Sir"; "No, Sir"; "Sir, may I make a statement?"; "Sir, may I ask a question?"; and, my personal favorite, the only response to a why question: "No excuse, Sir"— did Wordsworth stand above the river Wye at Tintern Abbey and sing his "no excuse" lines to the wind and world in general?). On that day things changed forever. *The military is my life; it's all I know,* I once told someone, and then, on saying that,

I became overwhelmingly depressed because it was something I had never realized until that utterance.

So, as we sat on the observation point, I asked Tom about his plans, about what he was going to do in the future. To my surprise, he told me he had dropped out of Syracuse last semester. He wanted to go west, maybe look for work in wildlife jobs. "I hear there's a lot of beautiful spots out there, like the Grand Canyon, Yellowstone, Yosemite. I know they're not as beautiful as here, but I want to go there and prove it to myself." I pictured him standing at the base of Bridalveil Falls in Yosemite or Ragged Falls in Yellowstone, beneath the plummeting cascade of mist, and hearing his thoughts: *Back home, the waterfalls are taller, purer, whiter.* No one really does that, do they? No one stands in the meadows of thousands of wildflowers in the Maroon Bells–Snowmass Wilderness and thinks only of the flowers which grow in the open meadows of home?

To my further surprise, Tom tells me that he wants to find a job working with raptors. I think of saying that he probably won't want work which involves field notes and observations and tedious routine, but I hold back. I say only that, if he is able to find such work, it should be challenging. Tom then asks if I mind if he takes the next few days off, if he could spend time working with the local scout camp. It's amazing: as soon as he returns to the mountain, he wants to leave again. "No, that's fine," I say. *And don't come back,* I think.

I once thought it would be simple to spend two years, two months, and two days living in a small cabin at the edge of Walden Pond, or spending my time romping through the fields and woods around Tinker Creek, making observations and notes and witnessing the small everyday miracles unfolding before me which I had never seen before, which my ordinary life would prevent me from seeing: the widening spiral of a hawk lifting into a sky which can barely endure its own blueness; the pilgrimage of an insect, ant or spider, across the vast expanse of my back porch; the running of wild turkeys through the acres of scrub brush in our fifty-acre backyard; the families of deer—bucks, does, fawn—outside our bedroom each morning, lifting their heads from the mist to stare at us with only slightly fascinated wonder. It's difficult not to see these things now, almost impossible to witness what must be the most common occurrences.

But I am learning to see; it has taken time, silence, isolation. Job, school, routine, schedule, life: they stun me from amazement. Pressures of humanity keep me from my humanness.

My thoughts, I fear, are not the normal ones. When I told friends I had the chance to spend the summer working in the Adirondacks, most looked at me as though I were insane. Their looks of puzzlement almost mirror the looks of people who discover I am in the military, after learning I am also a writer, *But how can you write? What about your own freedom? I mean, you can't say what you really feel, can you?*

The answer is that there is no answer. It just happened. I have no apology or defense; I would not seek one. In the course of these notes, I have tried to preserve a unity which interweaves my observations with the daily lives of these fledglings, even as I know I must separate myself from them, even as they must separate themselves from each other. But knowing that is not enough. I witness their natural progression. I have wanted to be honest and true in my observation, though realizing that what I see may not be as it is: their actions are as strange to me as my presence is to their routine. I see with the knowledge of what I have learned and gathered: it is never enough. I see through the emotions and thoughts and behavior of the watcher himself. These are, perhaps more than anything, the true facts of my existence, and I must record them.

I believe that everyone should spend some time alone in the wilderness, alone with her or his own thoughts, until some peace of mind gives birth to itself. An impossible thing, I know, and so I throw out my belief knowing its impossibility makes it so easy to dream of. I believe it so deeply because in these past weeks I only now have had the opportunity to confront the silence, to listen to whatever absence needs to speak. The wilderness is not the long valley which stretches out to north and west. The wilderness was born in my refusal to listen to the silence. Maybe it's not so wrong to question the reasons for one's existence; truthfully, I see a lot of merit in questioning. We live as victims in a world we barely understand. We live as blind witnesses to the disappearing of a natural order we never knew existed. Yet what other way is there to see, other than through the knowledge of one's own life?

Maybe I have the wrong perspective. Maybe when Donna told

me it was OK to spend the summer away from her, she too was thinking, *And don't come back.*

Near dusk, what I thought was a commercial airliner flew over. Focusing through the spotting scope I saw the unmistakable wings of the refueling boom tucked under the tail. KC-135, my old "bird." I felt strange, as if my days as a pilot were another life. I miss flying, it's true. I don't miss, though, the constant stress of being away.

Two years ago, I was gone from home 264 days out of 365. But the constantly changing missions were, in their way, exciting. The thought of taking a ten-million-dollar airplane—you and three other people—and flying it around the world must seem outrageous. Military flying is nothing like airline or civilian flying.

The time spent on the ground was often as diverse as in the air. The streets of downtown Cairo are as different from New York City as they are from Riyadh. The people are different. In Saudi Arabia one night, my boom operator[25] and I were passing through endless corridors and around corners of an old bazaar, where the wealth and the poverty seemed almost coincident, the smells as richly distinct and different as the absent sterility of an American shopping mall is familiar. Then, rising above the maze of faces crusted with age, I saw, turning from the edges of the shadows, two robed figures who called to us: *Yankees, where are you going? We can take you there.* We looked quickly to each other, each of our faces saying, *Well, you decide.* Neither of us decided, so we got in their car while one of the figures held an open door for us. Both of them wore cream-colored gowns made of fabric that must have been silk by the way it shone in the light of the dim street. Both wore identical, tightly knotted gold-banded headdresses (which I later learned signified position in the royal family—and which then, of course, I didn't know). They drove a sophisticated white Toyota, huge and rambling, a type not available in the United States. On the instrument dash, a panel was flashing warning signals for at least five different types of problems with the car, from broken headlamps to a leaking fuel tank. But the flashing signals didn't seem to bother them—why should it bother us? Our two friendly guides quickly asked where we were headed. I replied *the Al Yamama.*

The look that crossed their faces as they glanced at each other did not escape us: they had no idea where the Al Yamama was. We drove slowly toward the edge of the limits of Riyadh; we were heading for the desert. They asked us two questions, constantly: *What are you doing in our country? Do you not love our country—is it not beautiful?* Their English seemed limited to these questions; our Arabic, unfortunately, was about as good as it was going to get. We were heading west; the Al Yamama was to the north. As they slowed near a corner, I gripped the handle of my door. Glen, my boom operator, looked to me and nodded. We were ready to jump. A few broken bones, cracked ribs. What did it matter? At least, we wouldn't be kidnapped.

But we did not jump. We did not move. Our two friends merely circled the perimeter of the city, wanting to show us the wondrous pleasures of Riyadh at night, before we returned to our hotel. The next night we launched on a refueling mission. As we lifted smoothly from the runway, engines roaring as we climbed across a desert in which there was nothing visible but the tiny sentinels of the burning oil fields to the north, I saw Ursa Major standing on end, the Great Bear rearing. We were far away.

Images and ideas: even as I write this down, there comes the sudden unfolding of memory. How can I tell you of the solitary emptiness I saw outside the cockpit window at twenty-five thousand feet, a barren landscape of Greenland where, like etched highways on a road map, the cracked blue veins in ice splintered off towards each horizon? There, as we hung in the tiny pocket of space, I knew how small we were; as I looked beyond the wing, and the frost-tipped lip of the nacelle which held our port outboard engine, I saw massive icebergs, floating in a fiercely proud and barren waste beneath, icebergs broken and separating from once solid earth, towering cathedrals of crystal drifting on black as if they wanted only to assert their domination, to have only their solitariness. Some rose to the shape of individual peaks: here, Machhupuchare, the earth's most magnificent and sacred peak rising to greet the sunrise; here, K2; here, Annapurna; here, a tiny Everest imitation of several hundred feet proudly cast in the sea. In Antarctica, where Mt. Markham rises to over fourteen thousand feet, the mountains of ice are so desolate and numerous you can name your own peak merely by setting eyes on it. There, a C-141 Starlifter can remain on the surface of the earth for less than thirty minutes before the instruments begin to seize with numbing cold, the frozen gyros start to tumble.

As a pilot, my way of seeing the earth has changed forever. There is a truth beneath the almost simple, meaningless claim of saying that my duty in the military is to serve my country: my duty—or if one is uncomfortable with the ambiguity of the noun, my role, my job—is to protect life, and paradoxically, that may mean I have to destroy it. Yeats knew this perfectly when he made his Irish Airman speak: "Those that I guard I do not love, / Those that I fight I do not hate." I think I understand why people seem so puzzled when they learn what it is I do. I work, or try to work, with language—and it is an opening out, an expansion of the small web of thoughts which so rarely reveals itself. The military seems a tool to describe specific boundaries, to close itself in societal restraints. Yet if there is any resolution in this intersecting grid of conflict, it is in knowing how every poem and every society must attempt to resolve the concepts of freedom and order, while realizing how imperfect such resolution will be; to find whatever there is of worth in each glorious failure, what becomes the worthwhile failure of our lives.

So. I believe in words. Not a particularly grand statement, I realize. But a frightening one, perhaps because by claiming this, by believing this, I stake my life on their worth. Emerson saw poets as more than makers of verse: he saw them as emancipators of the human spirit. Stevens thought he could refine this grand and lofty idea by envisioning poetry, the words themselves, as the resource for ordering and redeeming the world.

I have no grand claims. One solitary singer. One solitary listener. The maker and the reader: sometimes, often, when the sense of the music in words is working well, there is little difference. I have no illusions about how few people read anything at all, much less poetry, in our tiny universe.

My life in the military has also meant a brush with sudden death, and though I have tried to write of it I know how little I have been able to recover, of losing those once close to me: of Scott, crashing in a thick wooded forest, the oxygen mask melting his skin—grafted to black flesh when they found him, a human voice; of Jim, failed parachute, earth swelling beneath him like a net; of Chad, leader of an air demonstration team, taking himself and his wingman into the ground; of Gus, the whine of engines saying *something's wrong* as he lifts from the runway and then flips on his back, the way a hand slaps hard on pavement; of Susan, six months into pilot training, the stabilizer separating, she falling hopelessly through air; of John, caught by power lines, the sudden brilliant flash exploding night, his dog tags the only part of him we ever found; of Mark, deadlocked eyes on target, unable to turn or look away.

Years ago, Terrence Des Pres wrote a strong, articulate essay which seemed, for me and for many others, to clearly show the problem of the age and spirit of desolation in which we live. His essay begins:

> —I live in upstate New York, rural countryside and lovely hills, a place my neighbors like to call the "village." It's small, quiet, great for raising kids. Forty miles north, however, lies Griffiss Airforce [sic] Base, known locally as Rome, because Rome is the town the base uses. Out of there fly the B-52's that control our part of the sky. There too the Pentagon keeps its brood of cruise missiles.[26]

The aim of his essay was not just to critique the nuclear arsenal inside the base and carried in the planes which daily crisscrossed the sky overhead his house, "half a hemisphere ahead of their thunder." Rather, the essay questioned how in the past, in times of concern, people turned to literature, especially poetry; yet in our time they largely ignore words. In our time, Des Pres claimed, poets have become increasingly solipsistic, each relying on an inner and private landscape:

> . . . our poetry grows increasingly claustrophobic and small-themed, it contracts its domain, it retires still further into the narrow chamber of the self; and we see in this not only the exhaustion of a mode and a tradition, but also the spectacle of spirit cowed and retreating.

While the crews in the planes overhead are bored, those on the ground seem oblivious to both their existence and the reason for their existence. Yet the individual, the landscape, the natural world exist as acceptable losses in the nuclear age. Among American writers, poets, there was and is a refusal to acknowledge his claims—that "the will to greatness is absent"; that poets continue to write "celebrating small moments of the human spectacle." What struck me about his claims was how deeply they affected my way of seeing, my way of life. I wrote to him: a brief, immature letter which only touched on what I wanted to say, but which was a beginning of my own feelings of why poetry, and for that matter, how we live our lives in this country, no longer makes any impression on anyone. We have no one with the voice of Whitman because no one is here to listen. Part of my letter read:

> People still want to hear what little pockets of hope exist in the tiny threads of being which hold us together. It does not have to mean: *We're living at the edge of destruction*; words sometimes only have to say *there's something about your life, and maybe mine, that matters.* Perhaps there are reasons for our failure to respond.
>
> Your own home may be only forty miles away from Griffiss; you may escape the detonation. But those upstate hills will do little to stop the 500 knot tailwind pouring away from ground zero. Those B-52's crisscrossing the sky with their payloads are part of a reality we must acknowledge. It is a reality which now has become part of our environment. The B-52's, the fighter jets, the missile silos are no longer alien elements; now they lie irrevocably within the Emersonian landscape.
>
> No one wants destruction. No one wants it less than those who spend their daily lives with nuclear weapons. They are intimately aware of a vast destructive potential. The B-52 crew is not a pack of bored airmen boring holes through the sky. They live under an intense and unrelenting pressure. They know what the end result of their mission training may one day cost. They have their own lives, homes, families; they are not bent on destruction.
>
> I tell you this because I am myself a SAC crewmember. Although I fly the KC-135, and not the B-52, I must be, at least to the world at large, guilty by association. Yet I agree with the premise of your essay. I see how we live in an age of closeness, unable to confront whatever messages we should make in a dark time. . . .
>
> This is my personal response. . . . I know how serious what I do is. I don't desire to see the world end in a firestorm. But it's also misleading, a fault of a lie made to seem the truth, to believe that we continually improve our weapons so that we might "try them out" on someone. (You did not write this, but you know whose words they are.)
>
> . . . Shortly after my return from Bread Loaf [Writers'

Conference], a colleague, genuinely interested in my work, asked a number of questions about contemporary poetry and writing. Another innocently asked if poetry was merely a hobby for most writers. Bristling, I replied "No, it's a serious academic discipline."

A serious academic discipline—rarely have I regretted a statement more. If that is all poetry and its intent may be limited to in the future, then words will have no meaning, freedom of choice will mean limited imprisonment, and destruction will be inevitable, if not welcome. There will be no future.

Now as I look at my response to Terrence Des Pres, it seems like so much egotistical whining. Trying to elevate the worth of my position, while wanting, on the surface, to be filled with humility. Perhaps I should have said that I would be happiest if I were out of a job, if there were no need for a military or the means to wage war. But everything about existence would prove me wrong. The long path of civilization has been threaded by the supreme efforts of humans doing their best to kill each other. *Homo* is the only genus capable—and willing, it seems at times—of genocide. The business of history is blood.

I never told him, and now I think perhaps I should have, of a claim a missile officer once made. We shared a table during night education classes, both of us working toward a master's degree. During the days we shared little in common: my job was air refueling in the skies over the western half of the United States; his job took him below the earth to a chair in a cramped control room, to practice constant procedure and vigilance for a day that may, may not occur. Life in a missile silo.

One night, during a break in a three-hour class, during a week in which a semester-long course was smashed into thirty-five hours of instruction, he told me without my really asking that he had no hesitation about performing the final, and in some ways the only, task his job required: turning the key to launch a missile toward a target another world away. But once he had done that, once his grim role was fulfilled, he had no reason to live. He knew, he said, that on the surface, on what little remained of the surface above, his family, his wife and two daughters would be dead, already caught by the response of an enemy missile. Calmly, he told me he would take the elevator back to the earth to join his family.

Heartbreaking, yes. But I do not know if he was being truthful or maudlin; I will never know. Perhaps I should have mentioned in my letter how confused roles often become. A few years ago a B-52 launched from a base in North Dakota; under the huge, mantling wings of the plane, a B-52G model, was a cruise missile. The mission was to fly north and west to a strategic test site in Canada, to deploy the missile for the first time, to test its effective range and limitations. Greenpeace actively and loudly protested this missile test; there is no reason why they should not have. If their mission is to protect the environment and to prevent actions which they feel threaten the environment and the survival of species, Greenpeace did what they needed to do. Taking an adversary position, they launched metallic weather balloons in an attempt to divert the path of the fired missile. The balloons rose into the atmosphere and exploded; the missile hit its target. The radar navigator on board the B-52, himself a Greenpeace member, directed the flight path of his crew home.

In reply to my letter, Terrence Des Pres wrote:

> It *is* hard to tell people why poetry is important. . . . If people can see how much we live by words—and die by words—then language can come to seem more powerful in our/their lives . . . in times of crisis and deep emotion— births, deaths, great sadness or great joy—we go instinctively to poetry, in the Bible, in famous sayings, any utterance deep enough and expansive enough to allow what we feel to be said and thereby realized.

Terrence Des Pres died last November.

He was an influence. An influence in the sense of what he saw, and what he saw I believed; an influence in the way that a man who died with his aircraft thirteen years ago was an influence, who took his life so that he would not take others'. They hold an irredeemable, relentless, mysterious force. There is a term, taken from navigation, which embodies their hold and their power: dead reckoning. Among pilots, sailors, marine or air navigators, it is a term which defines the calculation of a ship's position without observation of the sun, stars, or heavenly bodies; the prediction of a craft's position, based on direction and speed, from a previous known position. But in another sense, one slightly more ambiguous and therefore richer, dead reckoning suggests the strength and the knowledge of the "dead," both judging and accounting for those of us alive. The power and the force of the metaphor are frightening. They no longer see; I can see only with the help of their eyes.

Words—the incidents are what we make of them—words are how we possess our lives. All my life I have wanted to see through what I know, to make even knowledge transparent. I see—and know—that cannot happen now; I, like anyone else, am limited only by that which I can say. It is the words we use, finally, that matter.

> Of all the quilled creatures which nature in her plethora of species had reared to sing and to prey over the fields of England, and the prairies of America . . . Gos was one, as was I one of the other: so insignificant as to be significant, so transitory as to be eternal, so finite as to be infinite and a part of the Becoming. How should we feel fear and impatience, being so large and small?[27]

The tanker, the "one-thirty-five," flew by. My days as a pilot *are* another life.

I have never believed, as some have while growing nostalgic about fieldwork, that I could vicariously share a falcon's gifts. Nor have I wanted, despite my amusement with their personalities, to ascribe human characteristics to them. We have given them names, yes, but all names are rote; each of them equally exists as Pink/Left, Blue/Right. When I identify them, it's something in me I recognize.

It is somehow strange and humorous to realize that all the former falconers involved in this reintroduction program, those who no longer practice the sport, have themselves learned to fly. Gordon is an instructor pilot at Tompkins County airport; Shelley and several others have reached the point where they are ready to solo. The normal, easterly traffic pattern of the airport has a downwind leg over the Hawk Barn in Sapsucker Woods. Though we never talked of it, I wonder if Gordon, as he flew overhead with his new and struggling student, had ever thought of dipping his wings in salute to the few remaining hawks and falcons in the mews below him?

> Pinto saw the peregrines sitting on their wooden blocks in the small paddock by the house, and he circled after dropping to a thousand feet, peering down at the birds, and wondering to himself why they did not fly up to him.

> *Chek-chek* he called several times, and one of the falcons
> flew again and again to the full length of its chain,
> screaming loudly, and then fell helplessly to the ground.[28]

I have had an easier time of it, and a harder time. I have not
had to pay for a moment of instruction. I spent a year in pilot
training where all I needed to do was live, breathe, and think
flying. It seemed such a waste then that all I could do was not
think about flying: I resisted every impulse to learn, fought each
new phase of training. Only when I was a copilot in the "one-
thirty-five," after the Air Force had poured several million dollars
into my training, did I really feel I was learning, I was flying.
I came from a family of fighter "jocks"; the last thing I wanted to
fly was a fighter. For some, it should seem natural that I would
want a fighter out of pilot training. But somewhere in the heaven
of pulling g's, I came to realize that I was only a man inside a
machine, and I would always be that. Sometimes, in the purest
moments, I could forget that difference, and sometimes in those
moments the sheerest enjoyment and skill and ability came
through. But those moments were rare; perhaps, for others,
they were not. I knew I was never suited for high-performance
flying; I could never erase the difference, or the knowledge, that
my power and performance would always be less than the most
natural flight of a raptor.

Gordon and Shelley do not understand this. They assume that
because I was an Air Force pilot I flew the fastest, newest, most
expensive, most dangerous machine available. The KC-135 was
none of these. It is, though, a reliable and practical aircraft. In
many ways, it reminds me of the multiple roles and functional
uses which the DC-3 once had. Some of the tankers I flew were
as old as I was. Most of the tanker fleet, after the reskinning of
their wings and after the re-engining program, are projected to
remain in the operational fleet until the year 2059. My great-
grandchildren, or yours, could be flying one-hundred-year-old
airplanes.

During our first few days on the mountain, during pack-in
and supply, Gordon, Shelley, and I spent long hours trekking up
and down the mountain, talking about flying. Poor Tom and
Kathy O'Heir trailed at our heels, along with Gordon's dog, convinced we were speaking some foreign language: backcourse
ILS's, the best visual glide path after an instrument approach,

microwave landing systems, astral trackers. The only common awareness we could share was the vacuous, cultural wilderness of *Top Gun*: we spent a long time talking of the flying sequences in the film. I was on firmer ground than I normally would be: the Russian MIG's in the movie were actually T-38's, and since I had several hundred hours in the "thirty-eight" I could provide some comment that was not a complete lie.

During one of those long afternoon treks, Gordon sheepishly admitted that he had recently done something foolish. Three weeks before he had flown out to a potential peregrine site at a high notch in the Green Mountains of Vermont. On his return flight, he ran into a strong, impassable weather front. The surprise of the weather, after taking off from a runway under blue and cloudless skies, hit hard; he had failed to check the weather in front of his flight path for the return trip. His tiny plane had little hope of negotiating the storm and he would be even more a fool if he had tried. He was also not currently checked out for his instrument rating. He flew over a thick forest and found the trail of a highway which snaked alongside the shadow of the mountains. When he found a suitable stretch, straight and long enough, he set the aircraft down on the road. He continued to taxi along the empty highway until he found a log cabin. There were a few cars on the lawn, electrical and phone cables overhead. He taxied the plane up the driveway, kicked in the rudder—which did little—tapped a brake and used opposite throttle to turn the plane around, and then shut down his engines. He sheepishly popped out of the cockpit, and said hello to the confused family staring at him from their porch. He asked, if it wasn't too much trouble, to use their phone to call back to the Peregrine Fund with a report.

Through the spotting scope I find Gus and Anne sitting on a ledge shaped like the prow of a ship, socializing with two cedar waxwings. None of them consider this strange. A week from now, these eyasses may be feeding on waxwings, jays, other small prey.

Figmo dives on Belladonna and together they fall from the cliff. They disappear to my right. Figmo's silence is unnerving. I hear a rustle of air, turn and see him heading straight for me across the flat ledge of the observation point. I bring the camera up, focus, and his body floods the lens.

*   *   *

We are inside the mist. I pick up *King Lear* and begin. A good day for light reading. *Never, never, never, never, never.*

THURSDAY, 3 JULY

The rain continues. Sightings are impossible.

Tom left yesterday to spend time with his family in Ottawa. Strangely, I feel relieved, happy that I will not see another human for a week.

Early this morning, I slide down a muddy slope to find the cooler. I pluck slugs from ten blood-soaked chickens and toss their fat bodies into the woods. Because I can't see more than a hundred feet, I flush eight falcons from the perch poles and boxes. Angry, they zoom past, cacking. I wait until they're out of view and send the chickens down to the ledge. One slides on slick granite, falls off the cliff.

I stand back from the ledge, puzzled. I focus the camera on eyasses swinging overhead, tracing the paths of swift flight. I am dizzy, feel as though I will fall.

I sit beneath the dripping tarp in the kitchen area. My tri-legged stool sinks in the mud. Last night the rain filled one of my trenches and water snaked its way through my "waterproof" tent, destroying half my food supply. I'll make it, though. I have to. My car, eight miles from here, has, aside from the cracked muffler and flattened shock absorbers, a split distributor cap. The engine will not start in the presence of visible moisture. I'm here for the duration.

There is no sound but rain slapping the tent, which breathes with the motion of wind. I think of the night before release, when Jack Shelley slept beside me in the tent, watching the far wall move like an aspirating lung as it expanded and then enveloped his face, a thin membrane over his skin, never interrupting his snores.

I feel sorry for myself, and then grow disgusted with my sorrow. I have as much reading material as I can afford. I pile on clothes, a living advertisement for army surplus. The temperature spirals down. This isolation is nothing. *I can handle it.*

I'm angry that I can't see the birds, angry that I can't know what they are doing, helpless to know if they are lost in this weather.

To cheer myself, I recite poetry, singing my lines to the mist:

A man on skies stops at the edge
of a forest. It is a clear,
cloudless night and above him the chipped
bone of the moon is a cold and distant
face he imagines smiling, like the face
of a man who knows he is dying,
who has no hope.

Not very cheery. Switching to Baudelaire doesn't improve much.

C'est l'Ennui!—l'oeil chargé d'un pleur involontaire
Il rêve d'échafauds en fumant son houka.
Tu le connais, lecteur, ce monstre délicat,
—Hypocrite lecteur,—mon semblable,—mon frére!

Hypocrite reader: Hypocrite writer. Brother, I am my own likeness.

I store urine in a water bottle under my clothes to stop shivering. The warmth lasts for a long while. Still, I shake with the cold around me. I try to remember the symptoms of hypothermia.

Yesterday at noon, the weather lifted for an hour and, conveniently, a representative of the DEC Endangered Species Unit and three regional personnel show up as I am relieving myself in the woods. We rarely have visitors, but when we do, we're either bare-assed changing clothes, or in the bushes. We've both agreed that every time we drop our pants, we should check to see who's dropped in for a visit.

My relationship with DEC personnel has been something slightly better than lousy. The regional director, whom I have dubbed The Faceless Wonder (because his rugged yet always carefully groomed appearance and disarming personality seem so perfect he remains anonymous), happens to be leading this entourage. Watching them pop out of the wood and slowly stroll across the observation point, I feel as if I don't exist, or, if I do, I am at best invisible.

They don't murmur acknowledgment; they don't even look at me. They talk softly among themselves. The Faceless Wonder holds up a pair of binoculars and I wonder if they are equipped with some new and sophisticated technology: visibility, in the last few hours, has risen to 300 feet. He drops his cloud-piercing spectacles; they dangle from a cord around his neck. He looks in my general direction, and then seems slightly startled, as if he's just now finally realized I was there. The one word which issues from his surprised mouth is "Well . . ." punctuated at the end with a perfectly rising "?".

"?"—I ask myself.

I did not think I would be this angry at seeing him return. But I am. I was mad enough on the first day when we placed the chicks in the hack boxes: he didn't bother to help anyone; he stood by making pithy remarks for the Syracuse paper, looking tanned and handsome, sporting his perfectly groomed beard. Then he shot me a conspiratorial wink, said, "Well, have a good time," and disappeared. That was over three weeks ago.

But there is something else to my anger: thanks to the Faceless Wonder, my mother-in-law, Virginia, may never speak to me again. There was a slight misunderstanding between Virginia and myself as to when exactly I would begin work on the project at Camp Beaverkill. Somehow she had thought I would start during the last weekend in May; in truth, Donna and I had simply driven up to the site to survey the local area and spent the day with the dogs at Horseheads Lake. We drove home early Sunday and spent the entire day fishing on Lake Cayuga.

Because King, our Samoyed, starts running for cover whenever he hears the sound of a fishing reel unwinding, we decided to leave him at home in Enfield. Shakespeare, however, *loves* fishing. Donna caught a long, silvery, landlocked salmon which glittered and shook in its arc as she lifted it from the slate grey of the lake. Shakespeare became so excited he leaned far out over the edge of the dock and fell into the lake. Swimming toward shore, he tried to retain his dignity, but our laughter soon overwhelmed him.

We returned home late Sunday, well after dark. Our house was surrounded by five police cars. I expected the worst, and the cold chill of fear inside seemed to confirm it: *someone's been murdered; we've been robbed; we're under siege.*

We walked around to the back porch and saw King sitting uncomfortably on the couch. A flashlight illuminated his face: he seemed like an accidental tour guide, his face full of friendly hope and certain terror. When we opened the screen door, the uniformed officer whipped back to face us. The flashlight blinded us both. "Who are you?" the hard voice demanded.

"Sheriff Howard?" I asked, putting my hand up to shield off the light.

"Pete . . . is that you?"

"Yeah. What the hell's going on here?"

What was going on was that Virginia had expected Donna back in Ithaca by late Saturday night, and because Donna hadn't answered the phone, or even turned off the answering machine, Virginia went into shock. She had alerted her son and daughter-in-law, her ex-husband, and the New York state troopers. A search was under way in the Adirondacks for both of our bodies.

I couldn't believe it. Sheriff Howard, fortunately, was also our landlord; after we explained, he seemed to laugh the situation away. When we walked up the dark stairs to the bedroom, we played back messages from every known relative asking Donna *for God's sake, please call home!*

Neither Donna nor I knew what to say. Like an idiot, I held up our yellow bucket to show off our catch.

"Isn't that a beautiful fish?" I weakly asked.

"Yeah, it's real nice," said Sheriff Howard.

We later learned that Virginia, before calling the state police to begin their search and rescue mission, had called out to the DEC offices in Inferno. As bad luck would have it, she had the misfortune to speak directly with The Faceless Wonder, whose reasoned and thoughtful reply was *Gee, I don't know, Mrs. Jarosak. Maybe he's run off with some local wood nymphs. . . .*

The birds respond to our guests by strafing the observation point, performing dogfights overhead. I explain that two of the birds are of the *anatum* subspecies: the continental peregrine; heavy dark crown, distinctive black molar stripe like a huge sideburn, rufous overwash on the head and breast. One of them is particularly recognizable since he never keeps his beak shut: Figmo.

The regional personnel say nothing. They look condescendingly at me. Figmo flies over, dives and clips one of them on the head. His cack sounds like insane laughter. I cannot hold back laughing, either.

Fuentes, Figmo, and Gus tangle off the ledge fifty feet from us, turning and pivoting, falling and rising as they slash each other with talons.

"I'd like to see one of your fighter jocks do that," says Kathy O'Heir. I want to explain that what she's seeing is exactly the principle behind the X-30, the Advanced Technology Fighter: the more unstable a flying platform is, the more maneuverable; the ATF is so unstable that if just one of thirty onboard computers fails, the plane will destroy itself in one-tenth of a second.

Instead, I just reply, "Maybe if they had flexible wings."

The weather turns poor once again, and they decide to leave. "Do you need anything?" I'm asked. "Yes," I answer. "I think you should think about getting us an emergency radio. I don't care if it's just single-band transmission on Channel 9. Just something so we can reach the state police in Clear Lake. If we have to.

"This trail is too steep to make it down in the dark, especially if one of us has a compound fracture. We'd be covering ourselves with a radio. We need it."

The Faceless Wonder turns to me, seemingly without even thinking, and fires off: "You see your paycheck getting any bigger?"

"No," I reply. I smile grimly.

As they disappear into the trees, he turns and yells back, "Hey, you know it's supposed to snow tonight?"

I make another cup of coffee, sit smoking, and realize now if anything happens, I will have to find my own way out. If I break a leg, I've got to splint it and wait until Tom gets back next week. If I fall off a ledge, I hope the birds have already learned to kill so they don't have to depend on me for food.

I plow my way through John Foxe's *Acts and Monuments*, perhaps better known as "The Book of Martyrs," convinced that a New Jerusalem will rise somewhere in England, that eternal damnation for Roman Catholics is inevitable. Captain of my Destiny, I resign myself to Fate.

My left thigh cramps from cold; the quadriceps knots and flares with pain.

I soon put "The Book of Martyrs" down. Something else has taken hold of me and I must pay attention. I no longer see or know what it is Foxe is writing of; I hear only the screams of martyrs, the image of them writhing at a burning stake. For a moment, I am beyond words. I do not know of their existence.

I am drifting.

Once, long ago, when I trained and flew falcons of my own, I thought there could be a relationship, a bond, between us. It was a majestic sense of self-importance, as if I could look up and see something of my own presence in a corner of the sun, see it fall in the plummeting shock wave of a falcon from the high perch of the sky. I could have believed, then, that in training a falcon I was affecting the whole tenor of my life: so much time had been diligently and patiently spent in the company of a wild being, it was my own sense I eventually trained. I was not forming a creature of my own making; I was making myself.

When I cast a falcon into the air, it was myself I thought I had set loose. I was releasing something so indefinable and solitary and beautiful that it would be impossible to explain the special bond which existed between falconer and falcon. But I could just as well have stared into the sun, believing I could finally see the light behind it, until I became blind, until the retinas burned through the film of their own ignorance.

Finally, I would lose my sight to realize that my seeking dominion over the air through a falcon was a way of seeking domination over the bird herself. There was a bond between me and each of my falcons, it's true; once, with Aragorn, I thought it was a bond of friendship and even a wild form of love. Once I thought that every hawk or falcon I saw on the currents of air was trying to teach me; now I know that if they had been *trying* to teach, I was a poor pupil. I was, always, full of a sense of myself, ignorant that my understanding and beliefs should have been the first things to go.

Rousseau claimed, in his *Social Contract*, that in our move from a natural to a civil state we have substituted justice—and following the orders and laws of society—for instinct. He suggests that this is both right and good. But Rousseau was wrong. Humans seem to have gained intelligence at the expense of intuition; we cannot understand without becoming lost in logical connection, reasoned thought.

It seems ironic that so many pilots I have known have died because of this loss of intuition and instinct. A recent safety study indicated that 84 percent of high-performance aircraft mishaps result from "human factors" (what was once called "pilot error"): disorientation, vertigo, task saturation. A few years ago, an F-4 Phantom caught fire during its takeoff run. The pilot set the aircraft back down into a three-point attitude and ran off the overrun and into the desert. His one radio call over the intercom was *egress the aircraft*. But the navigator either did not hear him, or did not understand him: he initiated a dual seat ejection. (The Martin-Baker system allows an F-4 backseater to initiate ejection for both pilot and navigator.) The pilot, in the front cockpit, had one leg over the port railing; he was ready to jump from the burning plane. The force of the exploding rocket sled split him like a wishbone. Half of his body flew into the air; half of his body fell to the ground. Why did this happen? Safety investigators and accident review panels could argue and argue until the point became moot, and the words an exercise in tautology. But the disturbing truth lies in how the navigator reacted to an emergency condition: what may, at first, have seemed an instinctive response became, finally, a conditioned response without thought, without reason, based solely on fear, the need to escape. It happened in the space of a moment. Years of training and checklist discipline (themselves laws of survival and rules of order in the small universe—or civil state—known as military flying) did not allow for analysis. He was not *thinking*, thinking, that is, in the way we commonly regard thought: there was no time or space for analysis, no methodical decision. He acted only on response which told him that the safest way to exit an airplane was to eject. Conditioned instinct killed both of them: after shooting into the sky, the navigator's parachute safely deployed and then the raging fireball sucked him back down into the wrecked carcass of the aircraft from which he had ejected.

One of the keys to survival in an aircraft is *not* to trust your senses, not to fly "by the seat of your pants," for example, in deteriorating weather. What were natural and relatively easy methods of learning to fly in a low-performance Cessna or Cherokee propeller-driven aircraft often became the very things which would kill you in flying a high-performance jet. Learning to fly then means having an uncanny ability to ignore what the equilibrium of your inner ear tells you; it means being able to see with your eyes what your instruments defiantly tell you. I have lost a number of friends to accidents and malfunctions. Many of them died because they obeyed what their senses told them: suffering from immense vertigo, they became nauseated and physically blind—no longer able to even *see* their instrument panel—falling back to earth, victims to the whirlpool of coriolis in their inner ears, an equilibrium which had meaning on the ground but killed them in the air.

Sometimes I wonder if men have built into their machines the same kind of sadness, the same kind of flaws they have in themselves. Raptors have several advantages over humans in the realm of the air: extraordinary vision; adaptability to high altitude; hollow support structures in the tiny fibers of bone (similar to the internal spars of aircraft); furled leading edges of their wings, which deaden the sound of their flight. Though humans and raptors now occupy the same airspace, we are, to each other, always foreign.

Now as I wait and observe, I see how closely these fledglings depend on each other. A strange, mysterious, and instinctive sense is unfolding in each of them. Each day their behavior becomes gradually more aggressive. Their play becomes practice for killing. I feel a bond with them, but it is a bond of distance. I was never foolish enough to believe, in training a falcon, that I *owned* a domesticated animal. A falcon is a bird of the wild; for a short while, she shares a common sense of hunting prey and seeking quarry with a falconer. That is all there is.

Yet even knowing that, even knowing that now I am a distant witness, I feel closer to these fledglings than I have been to most humans. When referring to them, I always use the relative pronoun "who," as if they *were* human. Each of them has a separate identity; I could close my eyes and hear their cacking screams and know who was speaking to me. I could never refer to Figmo, for example, as "It."

They are more real to me than most humans; they have more personality; they have a sense of themselves.

Now I know that as I witness them I witness a sense of understanding about who, or what, I am. Now I see that the single figure who has stayed mostly out of these notes, other than a simple surface presence, has not been Tom, but Donna. It's incredible, somehow, to think that after all the years we've been married, all the years I spent flying and doing what seemed my best to absent myself, the first summer we would ever spend together would be the time I would choose once again to disappear. I have thought of her often—no, constantly—these last few weeks. I have, intentionally it seems, kept her presence out of these pages. But the thought of her, of some sort of reuniting, continues to occupy my thoughts, and my fears. The large fact of my failing to mention her indicates, probably, how simply I can manage and manipulate words on a sheet of blankness, and not reveal what's inside my brain, or my heart.

But it's something I have to face, to deal with directly. I, fool that I was and am, ran off to spend a summer alone; she, fool that she will always be, let me do it. She remains constant and loyal and loving, and I constantly step on her faith. She is a gifted teacher and writer, has a true sense of spirit and self. I wonder if I step aside from her because I see in her things which I most want, or crave, to be? She has a passionate, inquiring mind; she's generous, honest—everyone who has ever known her well has said that. To live with someone like that can be difficult; to live with me, I suspect, is nearly impossible. At times, I found her perfect honesty to admit to her imperfections maddening. I would lock myself in the study, struggle with ideas and words as if it were her I was attacking. At times, all too often, I left on "temporary" duty; sometimes I was gone for months at a time. And all through those times, and these, she's never lost faith that someday I might grow into something larger than the bastard I've almost always been. We love each other, there's no question of that; but love, as she often reminds me, has little importance when compared to reality. Now, the fact that I'm writing about her, finally, gives the hint of a promise that the person I am who is going to return is not the person I was who left her behind. What a surprise that would be.

I have been here less than a month. Already I have grown into a recluse, unwilling to think of a world beyond the realm of my sight. But knowing that other world exists, I must accept its presence.

I have grown into these mountains. My breath, a fog of my lungs, swirls in the beckoning cold of an Adirondacks summer. I have closed into a vast space and silence, hoping to withdraw.

I can feel the energy of the rock beneath me. I have come to the simple reality of living—the cries of the wood, the whitewash of falcon shit on the cliffs, eyasses climbing and diving in the clarion air, the touch of wind, the constant turn for the worse of the weather. My mind, I sense, is gradually emptying itself of sense. I rarely speak; I have no one to speak to. I am never lonely. I could almost believe that I could stay here forever, perched at the lip of the observation point, and overlook the rest of my life.

I have turned into myself.

The sun breaks in late afternoon. I run to the observation point and fledge six falcons. Anne, perched on a ledge, is confused, and stares at me and the birds overhead.

I dance naked on the cliff. Feet sleeved in mud, I shout and curse the sky. Something in the air heads toward me. I squint, make out Figmo's eyes heading for the target: me. Wings tucked halfway to his body, he's flying around eighty knots.

I scream in joy at seeing the first real stoop by an eyass. "Nice! Very nice!" I yell. "Get those wings in, mister!" He breaks sharp and to the right, pulsing by me. Convinced I'm insane.

Shack wacky.

FRIDAY, 4 JULY

While setting up the image in one of my cameras, I see something horrible: whirring wings, grotesque face, ommatidia filling the specular glass. I pull back to see a yellow-striped fly inches from my eye, like the huge beast in Poe's infamous tale. The fly lands on my wrist and I pull it close to hear its high whine. It probes my flesh, examines me.

Figmo has refined his stoop; he hones his skills on me. I feel as if I am flying a bird to the lure again; at times, he makes twenty, thirty passes, taunting me. The difference now is I cradle a camera instead of the winged effigy of the lure, and Figmo is more interested in slicing off a piece of my face. His talons, fully extended in front of his plummeting body, seem grossly out of proportion. They are still open as he passes. I know that he resents my occupying the observation point, a popular perch.

Kathleen and Figmo have developed an antagonistic relationship. Perhaps this is natural. When they feed together, each eyes the other's meat as being more tender, more worth having. Each grabs hold of the same chicken with a talon. Each tries to pull the carcass from the other. They do a rhythmic push me—pull you foxtrot across the ledge, while still managing to eat and look fierce. They decorate the cliff with organs and blood.

Two nights back, Kathy lunged at Figmo's dinner and pushed him off the cliff. He refused to relinquish his meal and they flew north and south along the mountain for an hour: Kathy pursuing and screaming; Figmo, carrying a chicken half his body weight, cacking and still able to outmaneuver her. Great exercise for the wings. Now Figmo is perched beside Kathy as she eats. His crop is full; he doesn't seem particularly hungry. He turns his back to her, lifts his tail, and sends a generous spray of falcon squat into the center of her main course. She responds by finishing her meal, then flinging herself straight up and dropping, sinking her talons into his back. She flies off. Figmo maintains composure.

Anne lands on a low ledge, opens her beak as if to disgorge a cast, and instead yawns. She stretches her beak wide, perhaps relieving barometric pressure.

Madonna begins to slide off the ledge as she greedily swallows a chicken head. She rides on top of the white carcass, its soft body acting like a sled. Her slow glide is stopped by Belladonna, perched at the lip of the cliff. Madonna uses the other falcon's body as though it were a feeding station; delicately and methodically, she lays entrails across Belladonna's splayed tail, and sucks them up like soft pasta. A junco lands beside them, watching the feast.

Fuentes and Rondeau tumble overhead, trying to knock each other back to earth. The wind is strong, over twenty knots. The headwinds and tailwinds are difficult to fly in. Kathy launches from the north cliff and heads south. But the wind catches her and she is frozen in midair, five feet from me. She opens her beak in surprise but nothing comes.

A gust of wind rolls up the rock face. Seconds later, I watch its shock wave through their feathers. Anne lies on the low ledge of the ship prow. Her thick outer eyelids close in sleep. Her wings rise up and behind her plump body like delta shapes. She is a black swan riding the crests of air.

I say: remember this moment, remember.

SATURDAY, 5 JULY

In May, when I accepted my position to work with the Peregrine Fund, Donna and I took a tour of the Hawk Barn in Ithaca. Now that the breeding chambers and most of the support facilities are in Boise, Idaho, the facility at Ithaca holds more than just peregrines: New Zealand falcons, a twenty-five-year-old Bateleur eagle, and several owls recovering from gunshot wounds. In the rear of the complex, behind the maintenance garage, there are four small chambers occupied by "tame-hacked," or hand-tamed, falcons: products of crossbreeding between gyrfalcons, the strongest falcon, and peregrines, possibly the fastest flying falcon and certainly the most pleasurable to train. These birds seem to have a genuine fondness for certain humans. I learned this quickly: an eager gyrperegrine ran over from his perch, at shoulder height level, and slipped me a chicken bone, with some meat still attached, through the bars of his chamber. He was delighted to share his meal. Bowing to us, he bent low with his head nearly touching his perch, turning to one side and cooing a soft, chirplike call. The long feathers of his tail were erect and flared high and behind his body.

In the far chamber, a strong beautiful tiercel, having the markings of both arctic and *anatum*, was also eager to share with Donna. As we entered his domain, the bell around his neck tinkled in anticipation and his body quivered. He would not look at us, but rather stared down at his talons and the small indentation he had made in the center of his gravel perch.

"He's made a scrape for you, Donna," Jack Shelley said. "Peregrines don't build nests. Instead, the tiercel clears out a space and shows the female, through nest-scraping displays, that he's ready to mate. Since males are the weaker sex, the only way to attract a possible mate is to find a suitable ledge and use sex appeal to lure her in."[29]

The peregrine chirped his agreement, looked up to the roof of his chamber and then back to us. "If he could, he'd put on an aerial display to show you he's ready to mate," Jack continued. "Probably wants to do a few loop-de-loops right now."

Satisfied with this explanation, the tiercel launched from his perch, landed at Donna's feet, and began to circle as his bell rang with the fever of sex. Crying, he looked up to her plaintively.

Donna smiled, looked down to him and said, "You're gonna have to build a hell of a lot bigger nest than that to fit *me* in there."

Skirting the river road, (my forenoon walk, my rest,)
Skyward in air a sudden muffled sound, the dalliance
of the eagles,
The rushing amorous contact high in space together,
The clinching interlocking claws, a living, fierce, gyrating
wheel,
Four beating wings, two beaks, a swirling mass tight
grappling,
In tumbling turning clustering loops, straight downward
falling,
Till o'er the river pois'd, the twain yet one, a moment's
lull,
A motionless still balance in the air, then parting, talons
loosing,
Upward again on slow-firm pinions slanting, their
separate diverse flight,
She her, he his, pursuing.[30]

Eagles do not mate in the way Whitman describes here, though after reading this, I could suppose to wish they did. The moment of union is not a prolonged act, but rather one of intensity and the violence of whirring, rapidly beating wings. The few times I have seen raptors copulate I was amazed at the speed and efficiency of their performance. The falcon leans forward from her perch, bending forward and down at a forty-five degree angle. Lifting herself on her legs, she lowers her undertail coverts. She stands in a stationary bow. The tiercel, in a flurry of motion, hovers poised, almost frozen in space. His feet lightly balance along the length of her back. Her tail shifts to one side; his tail lowers between one wing and her body. He enters her. And then, in one brief passionate moment, it's over. But they will continue this ritual many times over the next few days.

To be able to watch the moment is extraordinary. It is not, as I stand (or crouch) behind the reverse mirrored glass, an act of prurient voyeurism; rather, it is witness to wonder, creation. What Whitman saw that afternoon was amorous play and engagement. When one mate dives on another, they occasionally lock talons, and sometimes even touch beaks, as they roll together through the air. Raptors are not physically capable of mating in flight.[31] But the aerial kiss and talon-locking in flight are both rituals of courtship.

To say there is love and tenderness between two birds, caught in their passion, would ascribe human characteristics to them and seem foolish. All the more reason to claim myself the fool, then. There *is* tenderness between them; they nuzzle and nudge. They share concern for their brood. There is caring between them. More than once, having climbed to a cliffside nest, the shadow of a parent would fall from the sun. The rush of wings and the hard, incessant cacking were more than warnings: the falcons meant to hurt us as they rushed by, to slap a talon to a face or clip a wing to the head as we held, tenderly and frozen, to the face of the rock. Perhaps what parent raptors share is not love, not in the way we think of it, but compassion; protectiveness. The one false way to describe them is to say, as an early commandant of cadets did, that "falcons have no more personality than a barnyard chicken, and [are] rather dirty when kept in captivity."

For captive breeding to succeed to the point where I could watch falcons mate in a breeding chamber, however, took many years. I was a senior at the Academy before any real successes occurred with the breeding project. In 1974 the first attempts were made with captive breeding. Prior to that, attempts to breed peregrines in captivity resulted in failure. Most of our birds were donated, or we captured them in the wild. Although I never participated in taking chicks from the nest, I did climb up to visit some sites (the locations of which were secret).

Despite receiving official permits and following specific guidelines, there is an inherent and real problem with taking nestlings: it is cruel to steal birds from their parents only to train them to perform as college mascots.[32] Since 1976, though, approximately four new birds have been hatched each year from the breeding projects. Early cooperative attempts between the Peregrine Fund and the Academy produced interesting results. Cross-fostering, the placing of peregrine chicks in prairie falcon nests, failed: peregrine offspring died from infestations of black fly and Mexican bedbug, which had no effect on prairie falcons; prairie falcons often chose nests in vulnerable sites, making predation by great-horned owls, golden eagles, and coyotes a common event.[33]

Double-clutching, however, was more successful. Essentially, double-clutching involves tricking a raptor into producing more eggs than she normally would. The female will lay four to six eggs; both male and female share responsibilities for incubating them. After a period of natural incubation, some eggs are removed and the female will produce more eggs than she normally would to make up for the loss. (The technique of double-clutching has been used successfully in the wild, particularly in eagle nests.) The eggs which have been removed are then "candled," held up to high-intensity light to determine whether they are fertile. Infertile eggs are sometimes saved (I still have an infertile peregrine shell on my desk); fertile eggs are returned to the parents for incubation, or, as the Peregrine Fund does, artificially incubated in machines which have temperature and environmental controls. Double-clutching guarantees a higher production and, ideally, survival rate. When the Peregrine Fund's facilities were located in Colorado, the Academy provided the Fund with double-clutched eggs which supported the recovery project. Sometimes, the recently hatched eggs served as foster babies for peregrine parents. Sometimes, the chicks were returned to the Academy.[34] Presently, there are nearly half a dozen breeders at the Academy and they live in specially built chambers, each approximately ten by ten feet of space. Each chamber contains a gravel nest box, Astroturf perches, natural lighting, and special observation mirrors. Some of the chambers have been used to fledge offspring for training. All of the falcons are fed a diet of Japanese quail (*Coturnix coturnix japonica*) dusted with calcium-phosphorus and vitamin supplement.[35]

In my time, things were not so simple. We did not have the facilities for quail production, nor did we have the equipment to kill our food-supply birds in a relatively humane way with gas. We received one to two thousand cockerel chicks from a local hatchery in both the spring and the fall. They were raised to a specific young stage of development and then they were killed. We put on dust masks, entered a storage shed carrying fifty-gallon garbage cans, and began a festival of slaughter. We took chicks, often two or three in each of our hands, and snapped their necks against a support column. We tried to kill them quickly, to snap them against the metal pillars and then jerk back with our wrists. Those that did not die against the pillars suffocated in the mass of rapidly rising bodies in the garbage cans which bucked and shuffled across the cement floor in response to the writhing death throes of the bodies inside. It was horrible: blood and shit and feathers littered the walls, our masks, faces, our hands. Often we would lean from the open door of the shed and vomit into the dirt. It took as long as three hours each time; it was not an event I remember fondly.

Sometimes, in the short weeks before each season's slaughter, we gave the falcons a treat by feeding them live chicks. It was wrong to do, I realize that now. But there was also a strange fascination in it. Baffin, our arctic gyrfalcon, the official Academy mascot, craved young chicks. Baffin, who seemed to recognize whenever a camera was pointed in her general direction, who then seemed to rise from the perch of a falconer's fist and preen and glisten with the knowledge of how beautiful she was, would, whenever fed a live chicken, become a vicious beast. I remember standing at the entrance to her mews, watching her hold a writhing chick in the grasp of her talon, straining her neck to catch, and then catching, a second live chick which had been tossed to her.

Sometimes in winter, the security police would bring us a deer which had been hit by a car on Academy grounds. Venison was rich, and too much of it could kill a bird. But in the long pull of winter it helped them keep warm and survive as each of them perched by a window, staring through bars and beyond the fall of the snow to the thickly treed woods and the looming shadows from the rising front range of the Rockies.

In those days, our attempts at breeding the birds proved always unsuccessful. Falcons, at best, ignored each other; at worst, they would rather have killed one another than mate. The reasons for this strange relationship between falcon and tiercel (which I first ascribed to the bizarre personality of the *falco mexicanus*) relates to the situation under which falcons, in the wild, mate: when they are ready. As part of their courtship and nesting behavior, the female broods while the male obtains food. A female, stimulated to ask for and expect food, and a male, not particularly excited about offering food, will, naturally, have problems together in a breeding chamber. Although there may be enough provided food for both in the chamber, the sexually motivated falcon may drive the tiercel around the mews, from perch to perch, chitter-screaming in exasperation with the male's sullen behavior. The falcon will take an aggressive posture: she will be motivated to receive food, rather than obtain it herself. Sometimes, a falcon will become so aggressive that she will trap her "mate," and, angered by his failure to respond, kill him.[36]

Now, a decade later, many of those problems have disappeared. The Academy's breeding program continues to produce off-spring; the Peregrine Fund's new facility at Boise, Idaho, has achieved assembly-line efficiency. Recently at Cornell I saw slides of what must be the most wonderful, perverse, bizarre, and effective method yet for collecting samples. Picture this: a bearded man, wearing a slight smile, stands with his arms crossed. He is looking at something beyond the frame of the picture. He is wearing a tall, black top hat. There is a small opening at the hat's back: a thin, coiled line flows from the opening to a reservoir at the base of the hat. A tame-hacked tiercel is caught by the picture in flight as he enters the opening at the back of the hat. He briefly mates with his imprinted human; the coil catches the flow of his semen which is later used for insemination. Unusual, yes, but certainly more fair than the method we used, in those days: laying the tiercel on the flat of a couch, pinning his wings to the blue vinyl with our hands, while a world-renowned raptor biologist essentially masturbated him with tweezers, holding a capillary tube to catch the flow of his sperm. The tiercel fought, screamed, and violently thrashed his head from side to side as though he were possessed. The sharp fork of his tongue protruded; if he could have, he would have spit. I remember looking into the dark of his eyes, and his eyes shooting back: *I'm going to get you for this.*

A popular notion claims that eagles mate for life; if one mate dies before the other, the living mate will remain alone forever. Fortunately, the latter part of this claim is, largely, false. Two eagles recently established a nest in the Montezuma National Wildlife Refuge, which lies at the northern end of Lake Cayuga, thirty-eight miles north of Ithaca. They had not yet produced eggs in their huge nursery, sprawling twenty feet across at the base, carefully built in the high trees of twigs and small branches. Toward the end of the season, when the weather began to turn, when they both would begin their migration south, the male was shot by a hunter.

Many feared that the female would not return, that she would never produce a brood of her own. This year, though, she did return, and with a new mate.

In Baltimore, Rhett and Scarlett, a pair of peregrines who lived on the high ledge of an insurance building, had similar problems. The insurance company had built them a nest of pink, marbled stone which matched the building's façade. The reverse mirrored glass prevented the falcons from seeing inside; but each day, at lunch hour, Rhett and Scarlett drew a large, enthusiastic and appreciative audience. Someone remarked: *Why bother to go out into the country, when all the wildlife you'd ever want to see is three feet in front of you?*

They were a popular couple.

Rhett slammed into a building one day and plummeted down into the Baltimore traffic below, another universe away. For a while, Scarlett seemed to mourn his absence. When it came time to mate, though, she flew off for several days, kidnapped a tiercel and dragged him back to her nest. An employee reported seeing Scarlett drop a live bird in front of her male fledgling on the first day he flew from the nest.[37] Though it's unlikely this happened, parents do actually drop prey to their young. These aerial transfers seem aimed at progressively teaching their fledglings how to take game. During the early stages of the parent and child relationship, the eyass will grab the food from the mouth, or the feet, of the parent. Later, the adult will practice dropping dead prey from above for the eyass to catch; if the young falcon fails to catch it, the adult will often retrieve it. Eventually, parents will practice dropping live prey from above and into the flight path of the eyass.[38] When fledglings are capable of killing prey, parents and young falcons will engage in hunting forays; the parents will often herd prey into the line of a young falcon's attack.

None of these events can happen here. What seems most intriguing, even perplexing, is how these Fire Lake eyasses manage to progress and teach themselves, in the absence of parents. The line between play and practice is never clear. When they tumble together on the wing, they, unknowingly, adjust their bodies to the current of air, prepare for the sensation of hitting game with the full force of their extended toes.[39] When they pick at a branch or a piece of a moss, their plucking becomes more determined: they prepare themselves for killing game.

When they shove and push each other off the cliff, each asserts independence. When they tumble and grab on to each other, bite each other's tails, they are plucking and pulling in the same manner as they would take quarry. (Fledglings have been known to attack parents, sinking their feet into the adult's breast, as a form of aggressive coveting of food.) When these fledglings confront each other angrily, they prepare to defend themselves against other species, as well as for the day when each of them must be, finally, alone.

Eleven years ago I received my first falcon: Oneida. Though I had spent a miserable year as an apprentice, Oneida quickly cured my doubts about the worth of being a licensed falconer. He was a second-year tiercel, taken from the wild. He was quick, precise in flight, and dependable. I had hoped to release him back into the wild after his second season. That never happened.

In late spring, I entered the mews and found Oneida lying at the base of a plate glass window which overlooked Cathedral Rock and the far canyon. An apprentice had entered Oneida's chamber alone, something strictly forbidden. Oneida had flown over his shoulder while he tried to adjust the falcon's jesses to his glove, and then, seeing the open valley outside the window, collided with the glass. My anger with the apprentice was tempered by sorrow for my falcon. Oneida's neck was broken; I fed him by eyedropper every hour. Three nights later, in my room, he died while cradled in my open palms. It was the first time, probably the only time, I wept without concern for who would know or see.

The Colorado Wildlife Department tried to prevent me from taking Oneida to a taxidermist, claiming that although Oneida "belonged" to me alive, he should be allowed to revert to his wild state at death. Foolishly, I had my falcon stuffed anyway. It was a gross mistake. The replica I received was not a falcon; it was a caricature of what another human thought a falcon looked like. I have kept Oneida with me, however, these past eleven years; he is a reminder of all the mistakes I made, and never fixed.

In 1978, when Baffin, the mascot once sought after by a prince, lay in her chamber suffering from the sudden shock of cerebral hemorrhage, I felt the same loss and grief.

*   *   *

When I began training Aragorn, I used every reasonable method I knew. Our first week together, I kept him in total darkness. I played a radio constantly to help him adjust to human voices, and walked in circles though his chamber to make him know my presence. Later, I brought him up to my room, unhooded him, and waited for the transformation: from wild eyass to confident falcon and companion. He responded by looking around the room, and then at me, with perfect terror. He screamed once, a harsh chitter-scream of terror, and then sank the incisor-like claw of his talon into the fleshy part of my hand between thumb and forefinger. I held back my own scream and carefully, not wanting to damage his still very delicate toes, extracted the claw. Aragorn helped by peeling strips of skin from my wrist.

Within a week he was a different bird. Asking him to accept a hood in open daylight, however, took patience and time. But something magical happened one Saturday morning as I sat by a brook, and he perched on my glove, while the rest of the cadet wing marched on the parade ground two miles away. I gave him small lengths of flesh nestled in the open ridge of the hood; occasionally, I'd caress the hard keel of his breast with the hood's soft leather. A female hummingbird, green backed and missing the male's fiery ruby color on her throat, suddenly appeared and hovered inches from my face. She circled us for twenty minutes, puzzled by the falcon on my fist. She moved closer and fell back, the sharp whirl of her invisible wings flooding out the running water's sound. And then she disappeared. Aragorn accepted the hood; I leaned over and grasped the draw behind with my right hand and fastened it with my teeth.

He never noticed the hummingbird.

1400.

An ant struggles by carrying a greenhead fly, more than twenty times her size. Amazed, I watch her haul the massive insect up the granite ledge, pausing every few inches to rest. I consider relieving her of the burden and sacrificing the fly to the goddess Arachne, who lives in the roof of my tent, spinning her proud, delicate web. But the ant disappears in blueberry growth. Heading for her own nest, she drags home the evening meal.

Two months ago I found two newspaper articles in a desk drawer of my study. One article's title is "Air Force Cadet Learns to Toughen Up." It was taken from a Brooklyn newspaper. In the far right corner of the page is a picture of Donna in a military uniform, cradling an M-14 rifle in her arms. In the other article, Donna and I are holding on to each other in the photograph; its title is "Pair's 'Juggling Act' Strengthens Marriage."

I winced painfully when I found these pieces. I was sick inside. Both of them are twisted versions of things we might have said, lives we might wish to lead. I was impressed with Donna's claim that she viewed the Academy "as a peace academy rather than a war academy." I was not so pleased when the article pictured Donna as a trailblazer, "a non-conformist joining the Air Force and placing herself alongside old-fashioned, chauvinistic men." I've no doubt the claim is true; I've no doubt that Donna would never say that while enrolled there.

There were, and are, hostilities against women at the Academy. Sometimes, often, they flood the lip of reasonable behavior and produce fierce reactions. (During Hell Week, Donna was forced to walk the length of a long tunnel of screaming upperclassmen on the marble strips outside our dormitory. She was tough enough to prove she would not break down. But it hurt. Things happened which she would never forget. One upperclassman pulled her off the strip, stared into her eyes from three inches away. His stale breath was on her face. He yelled: *You know, bitch, I think you're the ugliest thing I've seen on this terrazzo.*)

But it wasn't intelligent comments such as that which made her leave; after all, she was strong enough, and grew inured enough, for such comments to inflict only a slight stinging pain. Though she may have looked enthusiastic in the newspaper article she knew that the Academy and the military were institutions she would never understand.

By the time that second article was written, we were almost adversaries. There was almost nothing we could do to stop it. For several years, I could write nothing. She had given up a potential career in theater and dance, which had begun to blossom in Manhattan after she left the Academy, to become a *military* wife. It's difficult, I'm sure, to be anyone's wife; I've often felt uncomfortable about speaking of or introducing Donna as "my wife," as though it were an act of possession. (The official term for the spouse of a military member is *dependent*: as though one could not exist without support.) With my job as a pilot, the problems which come with any relationship grew worse. We rarely saw each other, and when we did, it took time to understand and to trust one another. And then I would be gone again.

We both loved so many things about life, about the very wonder of the natural earth. But we were drifting farther and farther apart. The things we once loved were kept from our lives by the pressures of an intense job, and her own plaguing self-doubt: had she given up something which had been so important to live with someone she hardly ever saw? Once, I read of how Darwin had waited until his final few years to return to reading poetry and lyrical works—things which mattered most in his youth—only to find that he had lost the sense (and the essence) of what he was reading. I thought: *the same thing will happen to me.*

What hurt most then was seeing how drawn and exhausted we looked in the second picture. The article seemed to suggest that we believed North Dakota to be the finest place on earth, and that Donna and I had had very few problems trying to balance interests in the arts with a job in the military.

If only that were true.

I think of that time now, this summer, when I have *volunteered* to leave and work on this project: I should not forgive myself for that absence.

In the past year, with both of us attending Cornell, it has been as though we were meeting each other for the first time. She encouraged me to leave this time; she thought I could help in a worthwhile cause; she wanted me to work with peregrines. Maybe there is a difference: knowing I'll return, knowing we may have a more certain future than before.

I become upset when people talk of my successes. Part of that upset springs from the sad truth that I am married to someone far more artistically sensitive and generous than I am or will ever be. I have given up and lost far less in our relationship.

I remember, in winter, returning from Europe after two months' temporary duty and watching our marriage fall to its final point of erosion. *I don't need you anymore; I've found someone else.*

We did in fact still need each other, but it was as if we had become perfect and complete strangers. In bed we held each other and talked little. We would not have known the right thing to say. Our bodies curled together like a question mark, we stared off at the darkness and the silence: afraid to leave, afraid to stay.

I really believed it was over. I do not know how we survived.

I remember standing at a window, watching the snow pile flake upon flake outside, wanting to scream, or to cry, or to keep silent forever, and then not knowing if that destitute wish to break down was sincere or merely a ploy to keep her from leaving.

I remember one night, coming completely apart: I put my fist through the face of an etching titled "Autumn Sunset"—a small New England cottage by a lake, the leaves exploding in color, the sun dying to the west. It had taken hours of patience, on the artist's part, to score a design on the metal plate and print it on fine paper. Multiple inkings of color and shades had been carefully run on the paper through a press.

In a moment, I destroyed it. The glass shattered and I brought my hand back, covered in blood. The peeled-back skin of my knuckles was crowned with sharp tears of glass.

I brought the etching to an art gallery on consignment. The glass had punctured a tiny scrape a few inches above the idyllic cabin by the lake. It was a beautiful piece, but I could not keep it.

It sold the next day.

I decide to hitchhike into town. I should call the Peregrine Fund with an update. I need supplies; I should do laundry. And shower. I'm beginning to smell "rich."

While packing across the south end of Fire Lake Mountain, I step up high on a sharp incline. The thin rock splinters and I begin to fall. I slam hard with my left leg down and over across the rock shelf, pulling the up weight of my pack and body as I stand. A month ago I could not have done this.

As usual, I am walking and reading. Today, I act out the vicious personalities in Jonson's *Volpone*. And so I smell them first, rather than hear or see: unmistakable scent singing the wind. The wind is in my favor and they do not notice me. Yet.

Our first night on the mountain, Tom and I climbed the north face to receive supplies dropped by helicopter. I found what I'm sure was a lair: a thick grove of spruce covering a triangular entrance which led down into the shadow of a boulder. A damp, musky smell. I thought I heard twigs snap nearby and a low, guttural groan. I wasn't sure.

Now I am. I'm not afraid. Mostly, I'm excited, though I am ready to "beat cheeks" for cover any moment. The male is large, over 300 pounds. The ample girth of his matted belly scrapes in the dirt. The female stops, looks at me quizzically. Her nostrils quiver. The wind does not change. She nudges her cub, barely nine inches long, who stumbles beneath her, and then, because he doesn't move fast enough, she picks him up and flings him into the high grass.

Finding the road, I have a ride within minutes. Dave, the sheriff of Beaverkill, six-gun still strapped to his side, hat cocked, pulls up his pickup and yells: "Haul ya ass in here!" The caretaker's sister told me that he even sleeps with his guns. During a recent camping trip, a raccoon ravaged the food supply. The sheriff stood up, slapped on his hat, reached into his sleeping bag for his pistol and shot once—a clean hole through the scavenger's head—and then fell back to sleep.

The sheriff has missed seeing the bear, though. By the time he stops to pick me up, they are gone. They were under the *Camp Beaverkill and Lumber Co./No Trespassing* sign.

The wind continues a high wail and the rain begins. Through the spotting scope's 20x magnification I am able to read the expression of a falcon's face, decode the source of each bird's cry, watch in fascination as the nictitating membrane slides over an eyelid in sleep. They twist their heads sideways, sometimes almost inverting them, when they fixate on an object. What seems a look of puzzlement or curiosity is actually the falcon overriding the *fovea centralis* in the eye, of seeing *around* to see something in a different way. The eye of a falcon is an intensely complex structure; it occupies a large part of the facial composition. It would be difficult to imagine eyes as large in a human face: the diameter of each cornea would be three inches across; each organ would weigh four pounds.[40]

The rain slaps granite. The falcons lift their wings, begin to dance around each other in a ritual of joy and celebration.

I have been dreaming about Remmler, trainer of hunting eagles. Nothing seemed to make sense. We crossed in a long black skiff over the Ice Sea to a distant island where he had raised and released a family of wolves: "the old bitch and three younger ones; perhaps four or five. Who knows?" They breed and run free on the island; they live in complete isolation.

There were four, perhaps five other men in the boat, but I could not see them clearly. They passed a flask of cognac between them, speaking in whispers of harsh, guttural Finnish. The moon was high and cast its dead light across the silver and even breadth of the water which lay flat, covered with a film of ice. Black, rippling glass sheets of nilas covered the landscape. Seals sometimes broke the surface of ice near us; their heads seemed to pop from the water and stare at us as we glided past. Flashes of lightning struck at the distance. Ahead, the crest of the island rose up, the sharp features of cliffs and stark rock seemed huge, fractured, against the emptiness of water and horizon beyond. Occasionally, the crack of thunder struck. It seemed close, as if it were coming from under us, from under the water. The thunder had little or nothing to do with the lightning. It would boom like a depth charge beneath us, and then suddenly crackle over our heads, and there would be nothing but the moon shining beyond the lip of the sea.

There was a man at the stern of the boat, guiding a motor; the motor seemed to do nothing. It purred and hummed, though we were moving in a skiff with a life of its own, skimming the surface of ice rather than breaking through chunks and cakes of the floe.

I sat near the bow. I was dressed in a jacket of leather, a suit of armor, the same jacket which Remmler had his children wear when he first trained his eagles to hunt wolves. My arms were tied behind. The soft pelt of a wolf covered my back and crept up my spine; fur whispered along the skin of my neck. I could not tell if there was meat strapped to my back, or if I was a human lure. But slightly ahead of me sat Remmler, and over his shoulder, her two talons gripping the lip of the boat, Louhi perched, unhooded. Her dark eyes bore down; at times, her beak clicked together as if it were a salivating human mouth, anticipating a feast. Her eyes gleamed with a dull, yellow glow. Her eyes were her only visible feature. When the lightning flashed, her silhouette filled up the crest of the boat. She seemed like a carrion eagle carried by a Roman Legionnaire into the battle's wake.

"She hates me, you know," Remmler said to the dark. "She has tried to kill me more than once. I remember hunting ravens:

how she flew up from behind a boulder and struck at me. She knocked me from my horse. I ran into the wood, and she followed on foot. Her wings were spread wide, like a mantle of black, as if she were trying to stop me from leaving the trees. She stood at the edge of the woods, pacing, searching for me with her eyes, not willing to release me so easily. I swear I could hear a low groan, a growl rise from her throat.

"One winter, in Kajana, Louhi was set free to train in the yard. Her handlers did not know I was in the area. Immediately, she sensed me and climbed high over the barn as I rode in on horseback. She rose up, making a pitch. I saw her shadow, falling, blocking the sun. She struck my arm, almost breaking it. One of her talons caught my palms as I defended my face. My hands spurted blood. I slipped from the horse and fled for the open door of the barn; I escaped. My horse, though, was not so lucky. Unsated, she gripped at his spine, her beak slashing the poor stud's neck. Within a minute, the horse was dead.

"Yes, it's true. She hates me.

"Which is, I suppose, why she is my finest wolf eagle. She can match the finest Kirghizian berkute. During training, she killed two wolves in less than a minute! *In less than a minute!* If I had not seen it myself, I would not believe it.

"She thirsts for the hunt. Louhi is a killer."

As he spoke, I saw the words lift from the page, lift and cover his face like a shroud, as if he were speaking and writing, and I were reading, all at the same instant:

> The eagle lets loose with the left claw and sinks it into the face. . . . Now he presses with unbelievable force the wolf's head against its flank . . . the eagle lets loose with his right claw and sinks it into the breast . . . using a kneading action of the talons, he shreds the heart and lungs and death also follows in seconds.[41]

He spoke proudly and lovingly of his birds.

We struck the shallow coast of the island. Remmler with one hand lifted Louhi from the edge of the skiff; he grabbed me with the other hand by the collar of my jacket and pulled me to shore. The thunder ignited. Louhi howled; yes, howled. The rarely heard scream of an eagle is a low, bellowing expulsion of air.

"Come. You must see this," Remmler exclaimed, a small trace of encouragement in his voice. Although only my arms were tied, my legs seemed clumsy and unable to balance. I stumbled, rose, then fell again. Behind us, the men slept in the boat. Perhaps they had passed out from the cognac. "Come along, damn you! We don't have much time!" he barked.

Louhi cackled; the two lips of her beak slapped together like grinding teeth. Her stiff feathers lay smooth along the black glow of her body.

The island was a maze of fissures; steep clefts rose up in V's and we squeezed through the clefts. A type of lichen clung to the rock, and stuck to my face as I edged and struggled through the tight, narrow openings. I wanted to run to catch up with Remmler and Louhi. The distance between us increased. My legs refused to speed up.

Finally we reached an open glade, several hundred meters across. Thin, narrow: a slight rise of meadow rose up to a far nest of winter trees which fell into shadow. Around us, small groupings of dwarf birch pushed up from the ground, sprung from the meager outcroppings of rock. To the east, to our left, the earth sloped down to a rocky beach. There, feeding on a seal's fresh carcass, a huge European wolf lifted his head and snarled at us.

"My God!" Remmler expelled in his perfect, clipped English. "He's the largest wolf I've seen!" The sharp grey of the wolf's flank captured the moonlight. Suddenly, as if I were staring into his eyes, I could feel his breath on my mouth, I saw blood painting the length of his aged, yellow teeth. I heard, but could not see, two ravens laughing overhead. They were talking, each to each, taking wagers on what was going to happen.

Louhi went into a frenzy. She tore at her jesses, began rousing her wings. She lifted a talon, spasmodically clutching the air. Her body swayed, pulsing, wanting to be rid of her human perch. Remmler held her away from him. She bent down, tearing pieces of cloth from his coat, and then pieces of flesh from his naked arm. Remmler did not cast her off. She leapt from his hold, dragging him with her. He let go of her.

She climbed into the dark, suddenly in no particular hurry. She waited on above the wolf, who pounded up from the beach and ran for the woods rising above us. His movements were slow, impossibly slow. I could see each elongated muscle of his body strain for escape. His fogged breath startled the clear air. His panting was hard, desperate.

Evenly beating her wings twice, Louhi soared to the open space in front of the forest. She waited for the wolf's slow approach. It seemed she was planning to attack from the front and then turn on the wolf's side, binding his flank, ripping his heart and lungs with one massive swipe of her talon. She had all the time in the world. The wolf moved achingly up into the glade. His pants had become frantic. She held in the still air, playing her game. She was teasing him on, and he did not swerve from her threat.

Suddenly, as he moved into her range, fifteen feet beneath her, she dove. Her wings tucked to a slight sloop. She checked her descent, pulling up slightly. Instead of binding the wolf, she slapped him with the back of her talon. He flew, weightless, into the air and slapped hard against the face of a rock and fell to the earth. Her wings tucked, Louhi flew like a bullet toward the frozen figure of Remmler who stood at the base of the glade. Although Remmler stood several meters in front of me, I could see his mouth opened in a perfect O of shock. Louhi's eyes smiled with hate: revenge, they seemed to say, was going to be hers. Her beak opened to swallow us.

She grabbed Remmler by his head, which cracked like an egg under the force of the blow. She threw his lifeless body to the grass. With one awful, peeling motion, she pulled the hard length of his spine from his back. A crunching, metallic sound: she bit down with her jaws.

I stood helpless. My arms tied behind, the leather jacket embraced me and tightened. I could not breathe. I looked down at my legs: the base of my thighs to the soles of my feet had rooted in earth. I was trapped. Louhi looked back at me, her next victim; she tossed a thin strip of flesh from her bill. Taking her time, she freaked her bill against the edge of a log, preening the blood from her face.

Then, in a confused but perfectly logical moment of dream, I was both locked in the ground and staring in horror, while somehow also becoming the dying body of Remmler in the grasp of her talons. The body quivered and shook in her clutch. The fingers and arms shook in the pain of her pleasure, straining to fight back at the raptor, straining to escape; then they were still. Louhi bent down again and bit hard at the base of our neck. She severed the head from the corpse.

Suddenly, we rose into the air. My, our, eyes were open,

watching her rise from the earth. The hard rush of the air in her flight path tore at our vision. The wind ripped into the sockets; water formed, freezing the field of our sight. Suddenly, we were high in the air. We held in the space between the dark and the daylight, no longer poised in the stillness above an island in the Ice Sea. The sun lifted east, lighting the distance of Whiteface. Louhi, grasping the head in her talons, flew to the peak of Fire Lake Mountain. Then she released her hold on the head; we fell to the rock and slammed onto a ledge of the observation point. We saw the fledglings, rising from sleep, on the ledges beneath. Kathy and Figmo, playing at combat, dodged and tail-chased each other over the woods. Anne, in a calm ruffle of feathers, perched on a ledge by the boxes. Rondeau slept on the prow of the ship, one hundred feet below.

Louhi screamed in delight. Remmler or I, whatever the head that lay on the observation point was, wanted to shout out a warning. But Louhi had ripped out our tongue. The fledglings, seeing the eagle climb into the morning sky, scanning her quarry, suddenly fled from the cliff. All ten together, the fledglings took wing, rising into the space over the valley. Louhi dropped, slashing and screaming. Her howl echoed across the length of the mountain. It happened so quickly. It was if she had struck one target, instead of ten, all at once. What once was a brood of ten helpless fledglings, a few days into the first test of their wings, helpless and ignorant of the kill and their own survival, was now a mass of feather and bone which fell through the air, which littered the landscape.

Another peal of thunder exploded.

Sunday, 6 July

Last night I survived the worst thunderstorm of my life: three and a half hours. This mountain seems to be its own self-conducting lightning rod. Tremors of thunder and electricity flooded the valley with echoes. A bolt hit dead center in camp; its ripple effect ran through the ground. I felt its power as it passed beneath my sleeping bag. My skin was cold, despite my intense sweat a few moments before, and the hair on my scalp and exposed flesh rose. The rain ran straight through the material of my tent, forming tiny reservoirs in my living room.

I was violently ill. Food poisoning. Knowing I'd never get off the mountain, and exposing myself to greater risk if I tried, I opened the flap of my tent and let go of everything I had inside.

Jack Shelley told me of one night last summer, while climbing up to a historic peregrine aërie in Franconia Notch, how a woman hiking nearby had been struck in the head by lightning. Her husband, a medical student, had carried her down the trail. By the time he reached the ranger station, he was in shock; she was long past saving. That sad image, their helplessness, haunted me; I thought of it every few seconds that night, when the sky ignited.

I make two trips for water. The mountain streams are running. They will be dry mud beds by tomorrow. Over Fire Lake, five falcons dogfight. Two of them notice me and head my way; pausing overhead, they gaze down at my strange shape. One of them raises a wing, pitches toward me. I hear his familiar cack. I laugh. "Figmo!" He makes repeated dives and finally, bored with me, flies back to the others. Does he recognize me? Is it anger, or sport, or begging for food which causes his behavior? Would he do this to anyone? I hope not. One day, he might be diving down towards a human who is lining him up in the sights of a rifle.

TUESDAY, 8 JULY

The boxes are empty. Belladonna lands on a near ledge, clasping a clump of dry moss as if it were chicken, greedily ripping into it. She attacks an inanimate object as though alive: perhaps she imagines she is eating game, delicately peeling the skin back from the breast, plucking the red tears from the eyes, the welling blood.

I slide down the cliff and throw two chickens near the boxes; one of them, of course, falls off the edge. There is a flurry of wings and cacks. Four birds fledge from beneath the observation point, head north. Figmo pauses long enough to make his daily attack on me, then flies off to join the others.

I am supposed to place chicken and quail at the feeding station without disturbing the birds, without them even noticing me. So far I have performed miserably.

Yesterday only six birds fed at the boxes. Tahawus, whom I had not seen since 4 July, returns at dusk, 2100. She steals a chicken from Rondeau; they fight, like two angels with bill-hooks for its soul. I thought Tahawus would never return. She has been the most independent eyass.

I have twice spotted a female adult peregrine, without federal ID tag or markings. The grey, mottled back of the adult is unmistakable; it easily contrasts with the dust brown plumage of an immature fledgling. I first saw her three miles south of Clear Lake, six miles east of here. A few days later, she passed south to north on the cliff face, cacking and carefully eyeing our small spectacle. The eyasses ignored her.

Adult falcons have been known to drive off young from attractive nest sites, preferring to let them starve than lose an opportunity for food or a potential roost. Adults have also adopted others' young as if part of their own brood. An adult can teach its young special techniques of hunting and flying. I am sorry this does not happen here. The chance to watch a free, unmarked adult is rare.

This is the second adult peregrine I've seen in the past two months. The first sighting occurred at our home in Enfield in late May. We live on fifty acres of uncultivated land; it's a favorite spot for deer, rabbit, woodchucks, and hawks. A pair of great-horned owls often nests in the apple tree outside our bedroom window; the female sings to her mate with throaty eloquence. Sometimes, Donna and I will wake to hear them dancing on the roof above our heads.

On that day, Shakespeare and I were lolling on the back porch, thinking about nothing and enjoying it. I saw a reflection pass by the glass door; at first I thought it was the outline of a hawk. But the wings arched back sharply from the shoulder, the wing-beats were strong and powerful, and I recognized the dark mask and long sideburns. I turned. She was less than fifty feet from us. Shakespeare groaned, rolled over, and went back to sleep. The falcon rose on a thermal, spiralling up. A few minutes later, I saw her make a kill, diving out of a steep pitch, wings tucked and body streamlined as she fell to earth.

She stayed ten days. Sometimes I would watch her make a tight spiral up until she was over a mile from the earth, finally invisible. Perhaps she left because of the great-horned owls; perhaps she was headed farther north.

*   *   *

While making the week's last trip for water, I stumble onto the female bear. She's moving fast through the brush, pursuing something I catch only a glimpse of: the height of a mid-size dog; it moves like a black leopard, with a cat's tail. Probably a cub, Tom tells me later. Probably. We must have names for the things we can't perceive.

Rondeau sets down on the high perch-pole. His head bobs violently. His beak stretches in a wide yawn; a disgorged pellet pops from his throat. He cocks his head to the side and watches the cast tumble a thousand feet down.

WEDNESDAY, 9 JULY   *Dawn.*

An invisible falcon dives past the observation point. A sudden rush of air, and then nothing. The boxes and the surrounding ledges are empty. There are constant birdcalls, of course, as if we're enclosed in a huge aviary. The caw of a crow a mile off. The echo of barred owls. A woodpecker drilling for breakfast.

The sun rises over the high peaks. For the third straight day the weather will be good, a "first." A chipmunk hurries from beneath a spruce, starts rummaging through my backpack: books, field notes, cameras—not much worthwhile.

Later on I'll exercise: drag my tired thirty years through fifty jumping jacks, fifty twists, fifty leg-lifts, seventy sit-ups, thirty-five push-ups. The weary engine of my body runs down quickly.

The birds spend much of their time away now, returning only briefly to feed. Yesterday, Tahawus was so upset at my presence, at my watching her through the scope, she flew off with her chicken. Shadowfax and Madonna returned at 2100, sunset. They didn't eat. They roosted on the prow of the ship. Kathy returned, starving. She knocked Fuentes off a full chicken he had been savoring. She attacked it, knocking feathers and bones over the rock, and did not stop until there were only small backbones and yellow legs remaining. Her crop was distended, swollen. Fuentes scavenged in the rocks.

Kathy is the largest eyass I have ever seen. She knows her size and uses it, often. And if it concerns food, nothing stops her. She is nearly twice the size of Figmo (the runt). Yet she is the type of mate I frivolously imagine Figmo might find: a huge female who will overpower and dominate him, or who will be forced into submission by his overwhelming cack.

At dusk, Anne and Belladonna delicately nuzzle, cleaning dried blood and meat from each other's beaks. With no one to love him, Figmo freaks and cleans his own beak. He cacks out his sad complaint to the world in general, and to me in particular.

I crawl down to disconnect the food chute. It collapsed permanently during the last thunderstorm. In a clearing I find the perfect ground zero of a lightning strike—trees singed at the base, and broken; ferns tilting away from a neat center. This spot had been our first choice for a campsite. Some decisions, I am grateful for.

The chute disconnects quickly, with a few knife cuts against the tripod. Underneath, a pile of rotting chicken has accumulated. The smell is rank. Maggots infest the flesh. I take two sticks and fling the rotten bodies off the cliff.

Falcons attack from the north face. They drop in high and low, from different angles, speeds, from all directions. They no longer fear me. They are furious with my invasion of their space. Talons barely miss my face; a wing slaps against the rock, just above my head.

Figmo lands on the perch-pole, grasps a rotting length of flesh and flies off with his treat.

THURSDAY, 10 JULY

Shortly after dawn a float plane lifts from Longman's Pond and circles the mountain. Perhaps puzzled by what she or he sees, the pilot continues to circle over the boxes and my solitary figure. I follow its path with my camera.

A few hours later an F-111 flies over the pond; its engines whine as it makes a turning rejoin on the lead aircraft overhead. Figmo launches in their direction, and then turns back to attack me, as if I'm responsible for the violation of airspace.

My brother was an F-111 pilot; he was stationed at Upper Heyford. It could have once been possible for both of us to be involved in the raid on Tripoli. I think of that, find it hard to believe there is another world out there, one we are all finally ignorant of.

Divorce, separation, family breakup: they seem so much a part of the military package. Things one should learn to expect, things one should do everything to avoid. One thing sifts into the other and I sort among them in the rubble. I cannot escape the truth here on Fire Lake Mountain that I may be doing my best to save an endangered species but am likely doing little at all to save an endangered marriage. If it all falls apart, I must take on the blame.

We tried to avoid raising children while I was on active duty flying. Both of us agreed on that. In some ways, I never forgave my father for always being gone while I was growing up, and I resented my mother for her believing she could do as good a job of parenting without him.

The winter I flew home from Alaska (with Shakespeare in my flight jacket), our families met us at the plane. I taxied up to the parking ramp, shut down the engines, and watched as my crew ran down the steps to meet their wives and husbands and children. My squadron commander came on board, shook my hand, and after seeing Shakespeare peek out from under my jacket, said calmly, *How can I say no?*

But what struck me most was watching the child screaming below me on the pavement. A woman was pushing him toward my copilot, and the child, red-faced and bawling, would keep tearing away. He screamed in agony and battered his fists on the side of the blue staff car, pounding and slamming the metal. He refused to believe he had any connection with the man in the green flightsuit.

He was my copilot's son.

Recently I learned that my former copilot divorced. I feel terrible about it, but that loss is tempered by the knowledge that divorce is common among military people: you spend so much time away, you become a stranger to the ones you used to love.

One day in the commissary a young boy, probably no more than two years old, grabbed the leg of my flightsuit and refused to let go. He kept holding on to me, looking up with hopeless eyes, kept murmuring *Daddy . . . Daddy.* For him, I had become another Faceless Wonder: my wearing a flightsuit was all the proof he needed. I thought for a moment I would burst into tears: his face was so desperate, and his need was so great, as if he could wish for, and as if I might be, someone, anyone whom he might call a father.

Noon.

A snake suns on the rock in front of me. When I stand, he slithers off the ledge and falls into the undergrowth. Icelandic poets, in their kennings, had a term for summer: Joy of the Fish of the Valley. The snake represented the Fish of the Valley, as it twisted and swam through tall grass, and Joy was the snake's pleasure at basking in the midday sun.

Figmo, terrified of Kathleen, tries to grab a chicken while she's feeding. He moves in from behind, leans over toward an untouched carcass. Immediately, she turns on him. He flies straight up, screaming, with the chicken in his talons. Four eyasses drop from the sky to attack. Figmo circles, cacking and furiously flapping his wings. He realizes he is trapped. The chicken suddenly drops, a white body falling to the treetops in the valley. "You little shit!" I scream. My anger at this needless waste of food echoes in the valley.

Two tiercels, who have been sky-wrestling for the past twenty minutes, suddenly lock talons. Like a flaring meteor, they cut down and across my line of sight, their bodies fused together as they vanish in the woods, neither willing to let go.

Tuesday, 15 July

Today I returned to the site after spending the weekend with Donna in Brooklyn. At the Museum of Natural History we saw a brief film on the history of flight. There is a scene where a man hang glides; extending his arm from the balance bar, we see he is wearing a falconer's glove. A golden eagle, trailing jesses, lands on his fist. Perhaps, if one image could show the kind of joy a human might share with a raptor in flight, it is this.

We drive to Ithaca in a crippled car. It can no longer handle the Adirondack back roads. I slap saddlebags on my motorcycle, feel like a Yankee cowboy. Six hours later, I am fighting my way through the day's third rainstorm. Often the rain is so intense I am blinded, unable to even find the highway's shoulder. I see clear sky a few miles ahead, raise my visor and ingest an insect. I push the speedometer to 85. My form is a blur. Speed, and the needle sting of raindrops, are the only sensations I feel.

A group of bikers riding Harleys pass on the opposite side

of the road. They wave. Unlike me, they are smart enough to don raingear.

From the highway to the base of the mountain takes two hours, crossing three streams, sliding in mud. On my way in, I stop by an ancient crumbling estate which borders the eastern edge of Horseheads Lake. Once, this estate was beautiful. It formed part of the Adirondacks empire which Augustus Leer controlled. Now, it is crumbling; the outlying cabins smell of decay. In one of these cabins we keep a freezer which the Peregrine Fund transported and installed. When the Fund asked for approval to use a cabin to store frozen chickens, permission was given immediately. Whenever Tom or I leave Fire Lake Mountain, we stop here, on our way back in, to load fifty to a hundred pounds of food for the fledglings, haul their icy-cold bodies in our backpacks up the mountain. Sometimes, leaving the cabin, I see the caretaker, and wave to him across the dark green lawn of the estate which slopes down to the lake. The caretaker is old, stooped from the shoulders. (All caretakers of crumbling, ancient estates must be, by law it seems, old and stooped.) A veteran, he limps slightly from the shrapnel bits never removed from his right hip, souvenirs of victory in the Philippines. He lives on the property with his wife, shaggy dog, and fifteen cats. Sometimes he returns my greeting, waving back slowly as if he had forgotten who I was, or as if he did not know.

Much of the trail has washed away. I reach the summit in time to watch the sun set beyond Blueberry Lake. A single falcon waits on above me. I'd like to think I'm being welcomed back. She hangs motionless on the still air. Her wings are long, slightly tilted. She is silent and confident.

WEDNESDAY, 16 JULY

Tahawus has been absent since last Wednesday. She was fifty-seven days old then; she would be sixty-four today. Neither Tom nor I consider her absence a mishap. Sometimes, after a day's absence, she would return to feed just before dark. Anne, the youngest (sixty days today), often spent time with her before Tahawus began to range; I hope she benefited from their brief companionship.

This morning we tie food to small branches and perch-poles

to prevent the caching of food. Figmo, especially, has been flying off with chicken and returning with an empty crop. His greedy efforts to build his own savings account could mean hunger for another bird returning to feed. If we let this continue, another bird might disperse early, not have enough confidence to hunt prey, and then starve.

We knot the carcasses securely so they will not dangle from the edge, so that a falcon will not fly off with meat in its talons only to be slammed back into the rock face. Stubbornly, they would hang on the cliff, flapping wildly, refusing to let go. They could snap critical primary feathers, or break a wing. Young falcons have hung upside down from a snapped branch, delicately plucking leaves and pine cones as they plummeted to the ground.

Tahawus returns at midday. A rush of wind over me, like air being squeezed through a tunnel. She lands at the feeding station and tears into her meal. She seems angry that the chicken is tied to rock. She flashes her wings, pulls with her talons; she's not going anywhere. She calms herself and feeds. Two barn swallows pass and she pursues them, then returns to her entrée.

Six falcons pulse through the observation point. A female kestrel, half the size of an eyass peregrine, joins their formation. She lands at the feeding station and watches their futile attempts to wrestle the secured chicken. She cacks in ridicule.

I have always had a fondness for kestrels. Legolas, a kestrel I once knew in Colorado, could drive any prairie falcon off the lure with vicious energy and then claim the prize. His favorite behavior, when not in the mood for socializing, was to hide in my bookcase and express his opinion with loud, cacking screams. I responded by playing the bird call of great-horned owls on my stereo to shut him up.

1900.

Figmo and Belladonna feed. Belladonna raises her head to scream, but can't. A face, the size of a bear through the spotting scope, pops from behind the near hack box. It ambles toward the falcons. They fly out, turn, and try to attack from the air. I run through the trees, reach the ledge in time to see it carrying a fat chicken off in its mouth. My shouting is useless.

Next morning there are striated fingers of mist across the valleys and peaks. A downy woodpecker drills a mountain paper birch ten feet away. Loons call from Longman's Pond. The feeding station is a mess of feathers and blood. Only scrawny chicken legs remain, tied to the ropes.

We have a 'coon problem.

FRIDAY, 18 JULY

Tom and I visit the DEC state offices to pick up our last supply of chicken. The wildlife management office is, as usual, empty. I phone the Hawk Barn. Jon Keats, who lives at the barn with eight dogs and over twenty raptors, is furious when I mention the raccoon. "Goddammit, this is the first year we've had this problem at all the sites. . . . I'll get some DEC people up there to get rid of it." I'm not thrilled. Part of the reason for the raccoon showing up is my fault. I have overfed the falcons. I decide now to cut their food supply in half. If the raccoon steals chicken as soon as I set it out, he is interfering with the program's whole purpose.

As I leave the building I overhear two men ask an administrator what type of bird is mounted on the east wall of the main wildlife office. It is an abused, worn specimen; the bird's beak is open in a gesture I assume indicates a violent and fierce nature.

The administrator is puzzled. She stares at the stuffed bird, as though she'd never seen it before. Finally, she shrugs and says, "It's an owl . . . I guess."

"It's a broad-winged hawk," I offer.

"Does it eat fish?"

"No. Why?"

One of the men turns to me. "We saw something on our lake last night that swooped down and pulled a fish from the water. It looked like that." He points to the raptor on the wall. The bird is squeezing a weasel in its talons in the reconstructed perpetual moment of the kill. "But it was much larger, like an eagle."

I suggest they saw an osprey. I pull Peterson's *Field Guide* from the nearby bookshelf, find an illustration and show them. Many people have mistaken ospreys for eagles, particularly mature eagles, and sometimes vultures. Their soaring techniques are different, however: vultures have a dihedral upsweep to the wing; eagles fly with flat, full extension; ospreys fly with a slight crook in the wing as it bends back from the wrist (where the primary feathers begin). The eagle also has a full wingspan of eight feet.

I am excited by their report. I ask about the bird's "fishing," and tell them how on the previous weekend I saw an osprey over Horseheads Lake. The bird circled high, and then dived: legs slowly extending like landing gear and talons splayed. The wings rotated back, acted as air brakes as he hit the water. I thought the bird had gone under in the spray of white which seemed to swallow him; instead, he flew up and away, "double-clutching": holding a bright, squirming fish in each talon. The water closed behind his path and stilled. The raptor settled on some high branches for dinner.

The lake is stocked with two and a half million fish. Some things just can't stay secret.

We stop by the DEC auto shop, strip and shower next to the storage freezer. Afterwards, we load seventy-five pounds of chicken in the trunk of Tom's car and head for Copper Mountain, the second peregrine release site in the Adirondacks. There are six eyasses here, released on 12 June; some of them may already have dispersed by now. We turn off the highway and travel down seven miles of smooth, unpaved road. George Gordon has told us that the attendants have no problem getting to and from their cabin at night; they often take a leisurely meal at the local Pizza Hut. Tom and I marvel at such decadence.

Just short of the road which leads to the trail entrance is a pipe bringing fresh springwater down from the hillside. The water tastes cold, delicious. We drive up to the cabin, an old Adirondack ranger station complete with fieldstone fireplace, screened front porch and two bedrooms. The cabin is empty. We hike up the half-mile trail behind the parking lot. The path over-flows with warning signs, gaily marked in canary yellow and bureaucratic green: WARNING/ENDANGERED SPECIES CRITICAL AREA. If an intruder had any question about where to find pere-grine hack boxes, these signs serve as excellent trail markers, and prevent confusion.

The trail is steep. It rises on an old logging path and leads to an abandoned fire tower. It takes Tom fifteen minutes to reach the peak; it takes me twenty-five. I hate Tom.

"Boy, this is the first trail where I've *really* felt challenged," Tom breathes. His cheeks are flushed, but he is not even winded.

"Yeah, sure . . ." I mumble and breathe out. How easy it would be to shove him off a ledge: send him whistling hundreds of feet down. I struggle for breath; I breathe through my nose and try not to make it obvious how badly I need air. Thirty years old, I am an aged man.

"Are you happy here?" I ask. I am surprised at my question, not even knowing I would ask it.

"Yeah, why not?" Tom instantly replies. "There's not much to do—it's a little boring. But I can take time off . . . makes the routine go quicker."

"I'm happy here," I say. "Not happy in the sense of laughing, going crazy, you know. But I like these woods. I'd be happy if this project never ended, if I never had to go back."

"What about Donna?"

"Maybe she'd be happy if I didn't come back." I laugh. "No, I think she'd want to be here too. She understands. There's not much in the outside worth having.

"Yes," I say, suddenly positive. "She'd want to be here."

After a pause, I offer: "Sounds like I'm talking about a prison, out there, doesn't it?"

Tom shrugs a response of neither agreement nor acknowledgment. He owns a half-smile of acceptance of the world—and of all of us who have fallen into it.

He moves up the path.

The summit is a broad, flat crest. There is a wooded area to the east which would have made a superb camp location. (The cabin, no doubt, is more civilized.) To the west is a wide, sloping rock face stunted with occasional scrub pines twisting their arms back to the sky, the way Joshua trees do in the Sierras, refusing to die in spite of the constant miserable weather, the high winds. The hack box is on a narrow ledge below a boulder. It is tied down with rope onto rocks. A white string runs up through the brush; it's used as a release cord to drop food into the box each morning.

A peregrine soars high above us. She stoops on a turkey vulture, which has been eying her food. We cruise along the perimeter of the cliff. The eyass follows, turning and circling, as if she is our guide. Her wings are wide, motionless. The view gives a magnificent panorama. We overlook a broad, fertile valley of ponds and coniferous forest, a logging area, outcroppings of marsh and high off-road trail, the opposite side of Whiteface. We see the Saint Regis valley to the north. South, across a river, the knolls of two green hills rise to our height.

We leave after the falcon completes her grand tour and flies off. On our way down, Tom leaves a note on a critical species sign: "Hey, what is this, the Garden of Eden? Come see us sometime. . . ."

Figmo does not enjoy a tied-down dinner. He flaps in midair as his talons grip the head of a chicken, its body straining at the knotted plastic laundry cord. A falcon treadmill. Disgusted, worn out, he gives up. He eats his dinner in Madonna's presence, who shares the feeding station with him. Figmo continues to scream as he eats, voice muffled as he gorges on food. He sounds like a muted trumpet.

Gus, meanwhile, wants to diversify his portfolio. He decides to join Madonna. She responds by knocking him over. He stumbles off, perplexed. She returns to the joy of solitary dining.

SATURDAY, 19 JULY

Last night the mountain was attacked. A formation of Marine F-4s, mounted with smokeless engines, circled the mountain, dipping down the back side and streaking over Fire Lake at several hundred knots. I wonder if this performance is in honor of tonight's guest at the lodge, someone of importance, whoever she or he is. Earlier today, a jet helicopter with landing floats hovered over the lake, discharged its passengers, and left, heading east.

The noise is incredible. When I flew low-level missions, I had no idea that engines were this loud. Inside the cockpit, the ground seemed only a function of airspeed, relative to how quickly it passed beneath the aircraft's nose. I am earthbound now, and these planes seem full of fury. But they too are part of the landscape.

Near dawn, two invisible aircraft break the sound barrier. The shock of the sonic wave comes seconds after I feel the formation go through: two engines popping, a few moments of silence as sound flows away from its source, and then two loud WHAMs, like several sticks of dynamite ignited. . . . The birds flush immediately; terrified, they fly off.

At noon, one of the owners of Camp Beaverkill visits. He has left some guests hiding in the trees, and asks permission to see the birds. I welcome their company. He tiptoes back. A few moments later he returns with his flock: two middle-aged men and a woman, two young boys. Furtively, they step out to the observation point. They whisper: "How are you doing?" "Fine," I say, raising my voice. "I'm Pete Liotta." I extend my hand.

One of the boys considers me, then asks haughtily: "Well, where are they?" I reply, calmly: "They aren't here right now. Haven't been for two hours."

The boy looks up to me. His face is an expression of how he's wasted his time hiking up here to see nothing.

My own face, I think, betrays my exasperation with him. In a true sense, I can't blame him: he is, after all, just a child; I shouldn't expect him to understand that Fire Lake Mountain isn't his family's own private zoo, or that these falcons are meant to be his wilderness pets. *I have to control myself*, I think. *Each time I'm around humans, I grow to dislike them more.*

"Don't worry," I say. "They'll be here soon. Intruders interest them."

As if on cue, Figmo and Belladonna appear from the north in the company of a broad-winged hawk, three black stripes on the tail. The falcons dive, stooping over our heads. They have grace and speed, and we listen, awed by the powerful rush of separating as they pass.

All of us are in awe. They rapid-fire questions, about anything: "Is that your big motorcycle down there?"; "How fast are they flying?"; "Why don't they kill the hawk?"

The two boys are cousins. They have devised a unique plan to attract falcons. On their hike up the mountain they collected toads, and tied their legs to blue strings rigged to four corners of a plastic sheet. They drop their toad parachutes off the cliff. They flutter and fall. A father mentions to his son, "Perhaps you shouldn't do that."

But that's it. The father doesn't correct him, doesn't sternly remind the son that he's killing a living creature. He doesn't do a damn thing. I ask myself: *Is this the kind of parent I may one day be?*

I walk to the edge, look down. A toad lies on its back fifteen feet below me. Legs splayed and kicking, it struggles to live as it bakes in the sun.

The vanity of human lives.

SUNDAY, 20 JULY

Tom has been offered a week-long job as a guide on a canoe trek through north country. I encourage him to accept. The site is quiet enough for one person to complete the daily sightings, make notes, and take care of problems. I have noticed recently how frustrated he's become. The hours of waiting to sight one bird no longer appeal to him. Whenever we talk, and it is not that often, he wistfully mentions his planned first trip out west in the fall.

I did not know, when I first came here, how I craved isolation. In the past few weeks, though, I have enjoyed the lack of human contact. Each dawn, I walk out to a nearby rock shelf and sit with a family of deer as they feed. My closest, most intimate companions. Like Gulliver, I am a Yahoo in the presence of Houyhnhnms.

Each day the squirrels wake me with precision bombing, dropping pine cones on the roof of my tent. At night, they ransack my stove and pots, searching for food. Two days ago, they ate my dishwashing pad; yesterday, they kidnapped my lighter.

At dawn, I hear the stove fall over, a metallic crash. I slide up and out of my sleeping bag, open my mouth to yell at squirrels, and freeze. I see the outline of a black bear leaning into my tent, ten inches away. I feel nostrils open and quiver, hear a slight snort. The bear considers my flesh. A thin wall of nylon separates us.

I slide back down in my sleeping bag and hold my breath.

I decide to sleep in late this morning.

LEARNING TO FLY

Eventually, all things merge into one, and a river runs through it. The river was cut by the world's great flood and runs over rocks from the basement of time. On some of the rocks are timeless raindrops. Under the rocks are the words, and some of the words are theirs.
—NORMAN MACLEAN, *A River Runs Through It*

Solstice

I am sitting on the edge
of a thousand-foot cliff
in the central Adirondacks,
watching the hard disk
of the moon, a white
tabula rasa, rise from behind
Blue Mountain, forty-five
miles east. One hundred
and fifty yards to my left
and below: ten peregrine
fledglings are my only
witnesses, and they have
no tongue to tell you how
we see the last of the sun's
dying, how the light flares back
across the shagged carpet
of green in the valley, how
the pocked craters of moon
swell and magnify, seem more
dead than ever in this
empty light.

        Now the falcons
begin to cack at a tandem
formation of F-111's which
stream over the peaks at eight-
hundred knots, terrain radar
making their shapes trace
the rough outline of landscape.
The lead aircraft breaks, arcs
up into black: "flicking his
Bic," a short burst of fuel
dumped between lit after-
burners, a tongue of flame
which reaches three, four
ship lengths.

                    In the meadow
beneath, fireflies rise in a
constellation of activity:
tachistoscopic, confused, they
flash like a misaligned path
of runway markers or a field
of living stars. Five miles west
on Horseheads Lake, a pair
of loons reel each other in
as if they both were lost.
A vein of cold delight runs

through me. I feel the way a
drowned man might, with eyes
that see long after death, inside
a body turning and turning in
the dark murk of lake, wound
in fish-line and reeds. But now
the grappling hooks arrest my
gyre and I am returned to moonlight coiled on the surface
of breathable air.

                    Why
has it taken me so long to see
my life evolve in this third world
from the sun? The earth, this lake,
these woods need no occasion
to celebrate themselves. They've
done just fine these million years
without me. Why have I not known
that the shortest space between
two points is the Great Circle:
to make allowance for magnetic
variance and drift? If I see where
I am I can't see where I'm going.

Tonight the only voice I hear
is my own; and that knowing,
even if I don't believe it, is still
my greatest sin. I can only
wonder at the bright declination
of the stars, can only touch
this world which I have only half-
created, where everything changes
and does not change, even
as I write these words to undo
the things I cannot alter.

MONDAY, 21 JULY

The moon rises through pines outside my tent. I sleep now at night with only the mosquito netting zipped. I wake each morning at first light.

I read by flashlight. I have spent the last few hours with Donald Knowler's *The Falconer of Central Park*, which is not a book about falconry, but rather a consideration of how humans and animals survive in that wooded preserve nestled in the center of a concrete forest. While considering Mr. Knowler's descriptions of the peregrine and gyrfalcon, my foam mattress stirs beneath me. The small head of a mouse pops out. Six inches from my nose, he stares down the tractile beam of my flashlight. He crawls up onto the right half of the book, curious to know what I'm reading.

"Come on," I say. "Give me some peace. Leave me alone." But the mouse isn't listening. He runs for my soft pack and hides. I search for him in the tent with my spotlight. I open a flap of the mosquito netting, politely ask him to leave. It's no use.

In the morning, I wake and find him sleeping next to my pillow. Content and sated, after feasting on an abundant supply of almond-cheddar soup mix. There's no escape: bear, raccoon, squirrel, deer, mouse. I'm not alone up here. The only ones leaving are these falcons, my surrogate children.

TUESDAY, 22 JULY

Mr. Knowler mentions briefly in his book that peregrines, "reared in captivity," have been released in New York City.[42] Ostensibly, that is true, or was. Yet I hope anyone reading these notes realizes that the release process is more involved than merely flinging a bird into the air like a carrier pigeon and tearfully waving good-bye as the young raptor flies off in pursuit of prey.

The oldest of these Fire Lake birds is now seventy days. At ten weeks of age, a wild eyass would still probably be fed by parents. These ten falcons, larger than any normal brood, have made tremendous progress. They have taught each other how to fly; in the next few days each will make a first kill. And luck will help some survive this next winter.

Belladonna, Fuentes, Figmo, and Kathleen have not returned these past four days. Despite my affection for them, I hope never to see them again. It is already a miracle that all the eyasses are still alive. No attacks from great-horned owls. The raccoon has disappeared. (I joked to Tom that the DEC would be here with a trap in September or October, when even the boxes are gone.) Yesterday, Anne repulsed an attack by a broad-winged hawk as she was feeding.

I am a witness. I have had little or nothing to do with their growth. I wonder, at times, if hacking is the best possible method. It is now used throughout the world, with some miserable failures and some remarkable successes. Success brings the most publicity. Hacking fervor has taken hold: peregrine, bald eagle, osprey, elf owl, Aplomado falcon. Let's hack 'em.[43]

Extinction, I suppose, is a natural process. We can't prevent some of the changes the earth demands. We can, however, alter the celerity with which humanity has unnaturally altered the life cycle of certain species. The regulation of DDT, and its dangerous byproduct DDE, has, since 1970, helped prevent the final destruction of osprey and peregrine in America. But it took years of study to understand the raptors' disappearance. Meanwhile, DDE, concentrated in the aquatic chain of many species which were prey for the "duck hawk" peregrine, caused thinning in eggshells and complete mortality in offspring. The process by which this happened was insidious, simple: peregrines were at the top of a food chain directly affected by pesticide use. When agricultural areas were sprayed, insects living off the plants carried the poison inside their tissues; birds, which were eventual quarry for the falcon, consumed these insects. Ducks, especially, devoured poisoned insects which clustered over open ponds and lakes. The duck hawk, in taking her favorite game, was killing herself. East of the Mississippi, where nearly 400 pairs once bred, the nesting population was completely extirpated.

I have never seen falcons suffering from pesticide poisoning; I've read of its horror, the "seizures, trembling, thrashing wildly, and foaming . . . as the poisons destroy their central nervous system,"[44] ". . . clutching insanely at the sky in their last convulsions."[45] DDE, formed in the breakdown process of DDT, enters a falcon's body and produces disastrous effects. In the 1950's, David Ratcliffe discovered that pesticides had produced as much as a 19 percent weight decrease in comparison to peregrine eggshells measured in the previous decade. Because calcium flow for egg production had been disrupted, the walls of the shells had grown thinner; some researchers gave evidence that shell strength was reduced by 60 percent. Because peregrines do not build nests, but rather brood on their eggs on the scrapes of rough rock ledges, mortality soared. An eggshell of normal strength and weight would be able to resist the harsh treatment from parents; often, the new shell would break under the weight of an incubating tiercel. The pesticide also produced bizarre and erratic behavior in adults. In 1969, T. J. Cade found that a significant number of Alaskan peregrine chicks were dying from exposure and starvation.[46] The normally instinctive responses of the parents to brood over, care for, feed, and teach their young were missing. Pesticides appeared to have controlled the production of estrogen levels in falcons which directly affected courtship, mating, and reproductive cycles. Although parents lived with nestlings at an aërie, they ignored their offspring, and let them starve. DDE had destroyed instinct.

Five decades ago, a janitor in a Montreal insurance building noticed a female peregrine eating her own egg. What she had done, actually, was consume a cracked shell. He considered her behavior abnormal and did not tell anyone of it until years later, when the causal relationship between chemical use and wildlife mortality became apparent. By then it was too late, almost: pesticides had begun their horrible effects.

The return of the falcon has been helped by the efforts of dedicated people; and I must admit, despite my poor relations with them, how much the New York DEC staff have helped this program. Since the early 1970's, the Peregrine Fund has successfully released over 850 peregrine falcons and observed over sixty-five documented nestings. The goal is to establish twenty to thirty breeding pairs in the northeast. That goal is very near completion.

Admirably, the recovery program in the east will breed itself out of existence. The breeding facilities at Cornell were closed last year and the breeding parents now live and reproduce at the World Center for Birds of Prey.

The recovery program has cost several million dollars, minimal compared to the tens of millions that will be spent to try to save the California condor. Money often isn't enough. Success with falcons cannot guarantee success with condors. The fierce debate to collect condors from the wild was intense, and sad.

(I recall seeing a film of a condor fledgling being fed in an incubator by a hand puppet, a mock-up of a parent. The chick ate greedily and responded tenderly to the "parent's" caressing touch.)

Now, there is no such thing as a "wild" California condor.

New efforts and strategies appear. No one knows if they are right. In America and Europe, pesticide use is regulated. Yet, each year, raptors which migrate to Central and South America return north with high concentrations of DDT, the residues of their wintering roost. (DDT is one of the cheapest—and most effective—pesticides available there. Although banned in the U.S., the pesticide is freely sold and used elsewhere.)[47] Greenland peregrine eggs have been contaminated. In Africa, the fish eagle and the Teita falcon are succumbing to DDT. The Bateleur eagle, most majestic and regal of raptors, has vanished from much of her range. In the Indian Ocean, the island of Mauritius, one of the most densely human populated areas in the world, is sole habitat for the Mauritius kestrel. Only fifty square kilometers of this bird's boreal environment remain.

No one has been able to successfully predict how peregrine introduction will affect other species, or how the presence of new peregrines will alter the natural environment. I recently learned of a problem with peregrines successfully released on Cape Cod: the roseate tern colony on Rock Island (where 30 percent of the roseates nest in the United States) is being threatened by these peregrines.[48] The roseate tern is endangered; the peregrine is endangered. Which population do you then protect? A conundrum, by any measure.

Peregrines have had their problems adapting. Fifteen years ago, when recovery efforts first began, some suggested crossbreeding peregrine and prairie falcons. The experiment failed. Although peregrines have shown extraordinary reintroduction success at constructed tower locations (most often in New Jersey), the most publicized releases have been urban sites. Traditionally, falcons have shown a preference for insurance buildings, though the gothic Saint Regis Hotel in New York was also a historical roost. Peregrines have been hacked in Baltimore, Atlanta, Boston, and on the castle tower of the Smithsonian. New York City is no longer a release site. Despite the attractions of Central Park, and several other abundant areas, the success rate was poor, while costs and falcon mortality were high. There are still active nests, however, on the Verrazano and Throgs Neck bridges. These new locations have proved immensely successful; peregrines have adapted to the urban wilderness, and by so doing have almost guaranteed their own survival. Their most common (and it seems most favorite) prey are feral pigeons. Pigeons are largely grain-eating; they hold far less poisonous residue than insect-eating birds. Faithful bird-watchers at many city sites, skyscraper or bridge, keep copious notes and remain enthusiastic falcon fans.

Human interaction has not always been so positive. A short while ago, a woman in Brooklyn trapped an adult, or haggard, peregrine. Confined in a wire mesh cage, the bird was fed a diet of chicken fat; he soon destroyed his primary feathers while flailing to escape. The woman called her publisher before anyone else to tell of her discovery. The bird died two days later.

>   This
> has been the time of the finishing off of the animals.
> They are going away—their fur and their wild eyes,
> their voices. Deer leap and leap in front
> of the screaming snowmobiles until they leap
> out of existence. Hawks circle once or twice
> around their shattered nests and then they climb
> to the stars. I have lived with them fifty years,
> we have lived with them fifty million years,
> and now they are going, almost gone. I don't know
> if the animals are capable of reproach.
> But clearly they do not bother to say good-bye.[49]

WEDNESDAY, 23 JULY

A ruby-throated hummingbird hovers by the spotting scope. The bright crest of his neck shimmers. His long bill tilts up. "Hovers" is the wrong verb: he is perfectly still. His wings, which beat more than sixty times a second, are invisible. I have missed seeing both him and his mate this past week. I have not been near their nest by the hammock, on the opposite side of the observation point.

Belladonna appears briefly to feed, and then leaves. Madonna unknots a chicken and flies off. She will not be able to consume the entire body; another falcon will not have food. My fault. There is only a limited amount of food I'll supply: my failure to tie a simple knot will foster greed on their part.

Belladonna is unable to take food from Shadowfax. Unlike Figmo in his daily bouts with Kathy, Shadowfax will not yield to another bird, not even a larger female. Yesterday, with a full crop, he wrestled Tahawus over a torn and ripped carcass. Eventually, he sank his talons in and clung to the meat. Each time Tahawus ripped a piece of flesh, she bore the weight of falcon and chicken on her neck.

Today, Tahawus roosts on the upper perch-pole and waits for food. All the chicken is gone. Occasionally, she cries out with hunger. Her vocalized begging is an attitude of misery. Her feathers fluff around her puffed-out body, as if she is going to rouse. Her wings droop. She sends out a sad chitter-scream, and then a long pronounced note of anguish. She traces all her problems back to me.

During the early seventies, the Air Force asked the Academy falconry program to help erase a bird problem, specifically the prairie chicken problem, at one of its bases in Missouri. The birds that lived alongside the edge and at the ends of the runways had lost much of their hearing because of the constant churn of jumbo jets taking off. Because of their loss of hearing, they had also lost the ability to detect and avoid approaching aircraft. Not hearing a huge jet overhead, they would fly up, often in a huge flock, only to be swallowed by jet intakes and churned out by rotating turbines, or slam into fuselages and cockpit windows, causing severe damage. Previous attempts at controlling the birdstrike threat consisted of constant harassment: the grass around the runways was continually clipped to shorter than nesting height and higher than the height birds favored for taking seeds, insects, and worms; trapping attempts were made in conjunction with artificial bird calls to attract threats; flight schedules were changed to times of the day when birds were expected to be least active; shotguns were fired into the air from moving pickup trucks to frighten the birds off. All of the attempts failed.

The crash of a B-1B in 1987 strengthens the irony that a bird has the power to destroy a $280,000,000 airplane: the sophisticated bomber, which carries two and a half tons of electronic warfare equipment designed to escape enemy detection, hit an

American white pelican during a low-level training flight on a strategic range in Colorado; one crew member died during ejection, and two others were killed because they could not open the bottom escape hatch. No windscreen can resist the force of impact at high—often just barely below supersonic—speeds during penetration attacks.[50] A bird of only a few pounds—prairie chicken, pigeon, Siberian crane—can take an aircraft from the sky instantly. And though new systems are in design, whether they be high-sound irritators, metal deflectors under the wing, or synthetic Kevlar material to cover sensitive areas, nothing has proven effective. A bird can whip though a cockpit like a bullet.

The Missouri project was not a new or unique endeavor. Previous pilot programs have been used with hawks and falcons at runways in Canada, England, Holland, Scotland, and Spain. During the Second World War, the Royal Air Force established falconry squadrons to control small birds near runways. (Prince Albert decided to build the Crystal Palace around a tree for the Great Exhibition. Queen Victoria, shocked by the abundance of sparrows in the tree, however, and acting on the counsel of the Duke of Wellington, used sparrowhawks to quickly solve the problem.)

Four hawks and one falcon were used at the runway in Missouri, but the results were questionable. There were simply too many birds roosting in the grass along the runway. Predation had little or no effect; often the raptors would simply scare off and not kill the prairie chickens. Not surprisingly, the most successful and threatening of the five hunting birds was a goshawk: the prairie chickens dispersed immediately whenever he was in the air. Although the raptors effectively threatened the population, the odds proved overwhelming. There were, simply, too many chickens. Raptors actually kill very little of any population, and at this particular base the prairie chickens would return every night. Although owls were released in the hope of controlling a nighttime threat to aircraft, no substantial results were ever obtained. Eventually, the program died. In the early eighties the Academy gave seventeen falcons to a project to control birdstrikes at a fighter base in Nevada. This, too, failed.

Recently I read that the Air Force has developed skinny metal scarecrows, with painted frowns, and placed them at the end of runways to frighten off birds. I think of Diogenes who asked his friends not to bury him but to dress him as a scarecrow and hang his body in the fields, to let the jackdaws take their pleasure of his heart.

Shortly before sunset I see a shape move on the ledge above the boxes. I hope Tahawus has returned. Through the scope I make out something much larger. It slinks through the brush—a huge cat? It moves into the open: a fisher. It is the same animal I saw running from the female bear. I realize why the cooler was open this morning.

Fishers are rarely seen. Almost nothing is known of their social patterns or territorial behavior. They inhabit northern woods and feed on hare, porcupine, and, this evening, have an interest in chicken. They are members of the weasel family, *Mustelidae*, yet are larger and thinner than weasel. This fisher's eyes are quick, attentive. The ears are pointed like a black fox. A catlike tail.

Near a fissure of rock, I see a long arm reach out and, like a domestic Siamese, rapidly paw a white mass of feathers hidden in scrub pine. There was chicken there all along! It's still attached to its line. Falcons aren't the only ones upset about food being tied down.

Walking briskly, but not at the insane speed I used to chase our raccoon, I reach the upper ledges and stumble on two fisher cubs who head for the trees and their mother. Low branches snap as they race off.

I am doubly guilty. I cannot just run down and toss food to Tahawus. That would make her realize my reason for being here, and that she can depend on me to feed her. But food was there, though hidden, and I never saw it. She doesn't have to be hungry. I take three more carcasses from the cooler and start a vigil to make sure that a falcon will eat at least something tonight.

At dusk, a large brown bat swoops up the cliff and past me. He is hawking insects. A few minutes later, the mysterious adult peregrine flies over the observation point. She circles once. Confident that everything seems in order, she heads east. A guardian raptor.

*   *   *

A full moon.

The unmistakable outline of a falcon crosses in the light, lands on the ledge and begins to feed.

Thursday, 24 July

Reviewing notes from the past two days, I see how pessimistic, even cynical, I seem about human consideration for wildlife. One happy exception occurs every spring in Tokyo: children prepare for it in schools; thousands line the street, and millions more around the country wait in anticipation; police boundaries are established to insure safe passage. For what?—the annual procession of a mother and her young ducklings, as they cross from the gates of the Imperial Palace to a small pond in the city park to take their first swimming lesson. The chicks follow in single file, oblivious to the cheers and flashing camera shutters.

In Western Europe, falconry became popular about the time of the Norman conquest in 1066. Every schoolboy knew about falconry. Dame Juliana Berners wrote *The Boke of Saint Albans* as a primer for students in her grammar school, and falconry achieved a significant rank in the social structure after publication of the book, in 1486. It was even a punishable crime for those of a lower order to be caught with a bird above their station. The social hierarchy she gives to human and raptor is:

Emperor	Eagle
King	Gerfalcon and tiercil of gerfalcon
Prince	Falcon gentle and tiercil gentle
Duke	Rock
Erle	Peregrine
Baron	Bastard
Knight	Sacre and sacret
Squire	Lanare and lanret
Lady	Mezylon [Merlin]
Young Man	Hobby
Yeoman	Goshawk
Poorman	Tezcett
Priest	Sparrowhark [European Sparrowhawk, similar to the Goshawk]
Holywater Clerk	Muskayte [tiercel Sparrowhawk]

Falconry was once a measure of social position. (I wonder if now it is as much a statement of social isolation?) The gauntlet, creánces, jesses, bells, and lures were all carefully crafted. The often ornate hoods bore tufted plumes from various exotic birds. Anne Boleyn possessed a pure white falcon (either albino or gyrfalcon in the Arctic phase), and Mary, Queen of Scots, daily flew her merlin from the Tower of London while awaiting execution. *Sir Orfeo*, an anonymous Middle English epic (which borrowed from the legend of Orpheus), illustrates the pleasures of the sport:

> And on a day he seigh biside
> Sixty ladies on horse ride,
> Gentil and jolif as brid on ris—
> Nought oo man amonges hem nis.
> And eech a faucon on hond beer,
> And riden on hawking by river.
> Of game they founde wel good haunt,
> Maulaurdes, hairoun, and cormeraunt.
> The fowles of the water ariseth;
> The faucons hem wel deviseth.
> [Lines 303–12]

In the 1600s, there were three important works on falconry: Turbervile's *The Booke of Falconrie and Hawking*, a treatise on falconry by Latham, and *Bert's Treatise of Hawks and Hawking*. The basic training methods have not changed significantly, although treatments for health disorders and disease (much to the benefit of raptors) have.

It was startling, though, to read Shakespeare again as a cadet, after my experience with falconry. It seemed as if I had never *read* Shakespeare: the images I recognized were lines ignored in high school classes. I was seeing something I had seen a hundred times before, and yet never knew existed. The Bard consistently used the most eloquent phrases regarding hawks, eagles, falcons, owls, and vultures. He made several hundred falconry allusions in his plays, and many have received crude critical interpretations. In *The Riverside Shakespeare*, for example, an explanation of the following lines from Act IV, Scene 1 of *Henry V* is offered simply as ". . . the rising of desires":

> And though his affections higher mounted
> than ours yet, when they stoop, they stoop
> with like wing.

The allusion carries much more than this: "mount" is synony-
mous with the "pitch" of a raptor rising on a thermal; "stoop"
is her blinding, swift dive.

For an Elizabethan audience, the allusion made perfect sense.
They recognized the aspects of falconry in the way an American
audience would absorb the statistics and individual averages of
each member of a World Series baseball team. Now, the allusions
to the hunt have receded into the Shakespearean past. Now
when we look back, we can glimpse but small moments of this
richness.

In *Henry VI*, Act II, for example, references to "point" and
"pitch" would have had rich layers of meaning to Elizabethans
that are lost to the modern sensibility:

> But what a point, my lord, your falcon made,
> And what a pitch she flew above the rest!—
> To see how God in all his creatures works!
> Yea, man and birds are fain of climbing high.

Another term for the "point," or "pitch," is the "tower" (sometimes called "ringing up"). From *Macbeth*, Act II, Scene 4:

> On Tuesday last,
> A falcon, tow'ring in her pride of place,
> Was by a mousing owl hawked at and killed.

Again, the portent of this omen, following the death of Dun-
can, is obvious for an Elizabethan audience: it is normally impossible for an owl to rise above the "pitch" of the falcon and
stoop upon her.

Shakespeare plays continually, in his allusions to falconry, on
the confusions and attractions of the sexes in the human (and
the raptor) species. In *Othello*, Act III, Scene 3:

> If I do prove her haggard,
> Though that her jesses, were my dear heartstrings,
> I'd whistle her off, and let her down the wind,
> To prey at fortune.

Hawks are always flown upwind. If flown "down the wind,"
the falconer is almost certain to lose the bird—as Othello came
to lose his love and, finally, his sanity.

T. H. White claimed that Shakespeare used a subtle knowledge
of austringers and hawks when he described how Petruchio tamed
his Kate (". . . very like Kite to me") in *The Taming of the Shrew*:[51]

Thus have I politely begun my reign,
And 'tis my hope to end successfully.
My falcon now is sharp and passing empty;
And, till she stoop, she must not be full-gorged,
For then she never looks upon her lure.
Another way I have to man my haggard,
To make her come, and know her keeper's call,
That is, to watch her, as we watch those kites
That bate, and beat, and will not be obedient.
She ate no meat today, nor none shall eat:
Last night she slept not, nor tonight she shall not.

I wonder. "Falcon," "sharp-set," "stoop," "full-gorged," "lure," "haggard," "watch," "man," and "bate": all terms with definite meaning. But, as Petruchio struts about and blows hot air through his rapidly expanding lungs, does he see, in his un- bounded pride, that Kate herself may play her role for only a short while—there has never been a tiercel yet to man his falcon? And does Juliet know this as clearly? In *Romeo and Juliet*, Act II, Scene 2:

O for a falconer's voice
To lure this tassel-gentle back again!

Shakespeare's sharpest bird imagery, though, is found in *Hamlet* (Act II, Scene 2):

I am mad but north-north-west: when the wind
is southerly, I know a hawk from a handshaw.

Handshaw was originally written hernshaw, the old name for a heron. Although it is obviously not difficult to distinguish between species, perhaps Hamlet suggests that he is feigning madness only when it serves his purpose:

Among the ancient Aegyptians, the hawk signified the
Etresian, or northerly wind, in the beginning of summer
. . . that bird follows the direction of that wind (Job
xxxix, 26). The heron, hern, or hernshaw signified the
southerly wind . . . because it follows the course of the
Nile. . . . Now Hamlet, though feigning madness, yet
claims sufficient sanity to distinguish hawk from hernshaw when the wind is southerly; that is, on the time
of the migration of the latter to the north, and when the
former is not to be seen.[52]

Perhaps Touchstone, the clown, speaks the most famous lines of all, in *As You Like It*, Act III, Scene 3:

As the ox hath his bow, sir, the horse his curb,
the falcon her bells, so man hath his desires.

I dismantle the supply tent. My time here is running out.
I empty the cooler of chicken and, to my disgust, find that flies
have broken through the lid and consumed what's left. Maggots
feed beneath the skin, which slowly boils. I have learned to
accept their presence; I leave the chickens in the open for small
birds to feed on the larvae. Within an hour, the chicken is gone.

While dragging the supply tent down the trail, I meet Sandy,
the caretaker, and Dave, the sheriff. They tell me that the F-4
fire power demonstration Friday evening was put on by a Marine
commander for the benefit of his ex-wife, a visitor at the lodge.
Dave and Sandy do not explain if the pilot and his wife are still
on good terms, or if he was delivering a message that he's not
too happy about alimony payments.

When I mention the raccoon and fisher, they respond with
interest, wanting especially to know how large I think the fisher
family is. They do not seem enthusiastic when I mention that
the DEC has not shown up to trap the raccoon. Sandy's senti-
ment is exact: "Nobody traps on this goddamned land, 'less it's
me." I curse myself for my stupidity. I realize game wardens
would not even consider crossing the border of private property.

I bike down to the old estate which overlooks Horseheads Lake
where we keep our freezer. The caretaker stops to chat while I
unplug the freezer, shut off the generator, make arrangements
for returning the key. He tells me he is "damn proud to help in
this wildlife program." I laugh, shake his hand, and thank him,
sincerely, for his help.

I load a hundred pounds of chicken in my pack, straddle the
motorcycle, and take off. As I ride away, I turn over my shoulder
and see him still there, watching me. He is withered, stooped from
the shoulders, most of his teeth missing, a NY Yankees cap
pulled low over his eyes. I wave good-bye. He returns my salute.

Near an inlet to the lake, the water cascades in waterfalls,
pulsing underneath the road and fanning in several directions,
forming creeks which flow down to the reservoir. The sound of
moving water is mesmerizing. I pull over and watch a great blue
heron fish. The heron freezes, transfixed by something below
the surface.

Imperceptibly, his long stilted legs move less than a yard in
five minutes. To a fish, perhaps they seem like reeds moving in

the wind. The heron's face is white, with a black streak running through the crest, a sharp plume which forms behind the head. The perfect S of his neck uncoils like a snapped whip and his bill hits the surface. He spears a frog and pulls it from the water, its legs kicking and swimming through air.

I am not done with this wonder. I am not ready to leave.

FRIDAY, 25 JULY

I tie six chickens to a ledge shortly after dawn. I am unsure how many birds are still feeding. Only four falcons showed yesterday: Anne, Shadowfax, Tahawus, Fuentes. Three turkey vultures fly overhead, their wings uplifted in a shallow V, elongated fingers of their primaries each separately testing the wind. They are adults, distinguished by their red, suppurated heads. They glide motionless over the cliff. A fledgling vulture, black and grey, scabby scalp, follows behind. His wings rock and tilt unsteadily on the air.

I lug another load of supplies down the cliff. I look like a vagrant, my entire fortune in my hands and on my back: a cooler, a propane stove, camera gear, and books. The haze deepens from yesterday; it covers the valley. Visibility is around six miles. It is not hot, though the air is humid and muggy. Several hundred deer flies and mosquitoes feed on my dwindling blood supply. With my hands and arms full, I can do nothing to stop them.

I sweat and their hunger increases. I fall several times on the slick, muddy trail and lie in a swarm of sound. They seem agitated by my clumsiness. At times, I am a difficult target.

I return to camp, strip off my clothes, and leave them on the rocks to dry. I drink two quarts of water; this past week, I have drunk nearly two gallons a day. On the observation point, to my dismay, the food is gone. A few legs, some meat-stripped bone. One hundred feet below, on the ship prow, Anne suns herself in postprandial pleasure.

We used to have a parrot named Aristotle, a red-breasted Amazon with a bald yellowish pate which reminded us of Gerald Ford. I always wondered how much he knew, how much he realized what it was he was saying in his mimicking characters of speech. One night, shortly after Donna and I had brought him home, I closed the living room curtains and threw a blanket

over his cage. Donna innocently asked if the blanket was necessary, since the curtains were closed—why not give him room to
look around, to get accustomed to his new surroundings? My
reply was that it was foolish to take off the blanket—he was
a bird; what did it matter whether he could see or not? Aristotle's immediate and muffled response, from under his blue felt
canopy, was: *Fuck off*. . . .

Shocked, Donna and I broke into laughter. Parrots, of course,
cannot really talk. Parrots parrot the action of speech: that's
what they are supposed to do. They don't have the ability to
think. But I wonder. It seemed clear that he intended to have a
say in the affairs of his life. An even stranger response, another
phrase we never taught him to say, flew from his beak whenever
guests visited our home: *I can talk. Can you fly?* He was always
the perfect conversation piece who perched in his cage in our
living room and impartially threw seeds and screamed through
the course of a dinner. People were always delighted; how clever,
they said, that we could teach a bird to say something so wonderful. Donna and I smiled. We never admitted to our bewilderment.

Aristotle and his uncanny manners of speech are gone now.
He has, to use the euphemism, passed on to the heaven for
animals. But I still think of him, perched on the low branch of
a tree, asserting his place in the hierarchy of things by greeting
each new arrival with *I can talk. Can you fly?*

It's a tough thing, really. It takes time, equal parcels of patience
and love or understanding, humility and humiliation: learning
to fly. I think I've found that this summer, pulled it from the
pool of experience as if it were the most significant truth I should
have known all along. But, of course, I didn't. It took, finally,
my being a passive witness to ten peregrine fledglings who
struggled and refused to give in. It took realizing how little
I knew of how difficult it is to simply survive. I've had an easy
time of it, most of my life. I thought, as part of my time spent
here, I could make some grand and definitive statement about
my being a pilot and falconer, about how close I came to understanding my life. "To write something significant which was of
enduring beauty. . . . It was not the beauty but the endurance,
for endurance was beautiful."[53]

The truth is I've found nothing grand and significant. And
I'm rather glad of it. The truth is that life is fairly simple, simple,

that is, beyond the huge task of staying alive.

It's easy to be, like Antoine de Saint-Exupéry, a stranger to the earth and a child in the upper layers of atmosphere. We read greedily his accounts of the lonely sentinel, hovering over the tiny oases of civilization which glisten like tiny stars on the planet's surface, ready to do anything to save those he lives to protect. We vicariously see through his beautiful, breathtaking accounts and want to be, like him, a saint of the sky. And it's easy to be like a monk on the mountaintop, or a hermit: to write of one's solitude and awareness and damnation of the suffering world below. But the hard part is life, and reality, the drudge of existence.

I have thought, too, of how since the turn of this century, when humans finally strayed from the ground, there has been the constant demand to associate human flying with the flight of a bird. But the truth, again, is that we have little or nothing to do with their innate ability, and by our final escape into the air we have merely intruded. We fly because of technology; they fly out of their nature. On 14 December 1903, as the result of a coin toss, Wilbur Wright became the first man to break free from the bonds of earth over the sands near Kitty Hawk: the flight would last 3.5 seconds before he would stall the aircraft and cover a distance the length of a KC-135's wingspan. In 1914, the Spad aircraft, with 15 metering instruments on a panel for the pilot's information, would enter into aerial combat. In World War II the P-51 Mustang had 53 gauges gracing the cockpit. Today, in an F-15 fighter, a pilot is responsible for more than 450 individual design systems: he must be intimately familiar with each gauge and measurement, be able to instantly read what he is being told. The task of flying is immensely difficult now: it is a labor of knowledge and stress.

As I think of the warplanes which have decorated and lit up this valley, I realize how little they have to do with the natural earth. They are fierce, fast, deadly accurate. Special missile systems can track and shoot down targets from a hundred miles away; radar can identify airspace intruders from an incredible distance; Gatling guns can rotate an aircraft with the force of their spitting tongues; laser bombs can perfectly ignite on mark. Our systems are precise, purposeful, definite. We have given names and identifiers to our constructed birds of the sky:

the Grumman F-6F Hellcat; the Curtiss Goshawk; the P-51 Mustang; the P-38 Lightning (and a dual cockpit version known as "the Widowmaker"); the C-47 Gooney Bird; the C-9 Nightingale; the C-7 Caribou; the OV-10 Bronco; the UV-18 Twin Otter; the VSTOL Hawker Harrier; the Sepecat Jaguar; the Tu-16 Badger; the Tu-95 Bear; the Mya-4 Bison; the T-38 Talon; the SR-71 Blackbird; the A-37 Dragonfly; the F-4 Phantom; the F-15 Eagle; the F-16 Falcon; the F-18 Hornet. We have done the same with our missiles and weapons systems: the Phoenix; the ADM-20 Quail; the AGM-28 Hounddog; the AGM-45 Shrike; the AGM-62 Walleye; the AGM-65 Maverick; the AIM-4 Falcon; the AIM-7 Sparrow; the AIM-9 Sidewinder. In a few short decades, we have created marvels of technology and achievement. How long, I wonder, did it take for a raptor to evolve into her perfected state? Now I think I understand why Figmo so viciously attacked the warplanes which entered his airspace: he was asserting his right to remain there and be free, to show *his* dominion over the air.

I wonder, too, how long these planes which have occupied our dreams and ambitions for hundreds, perhaps thousands of years, will remain. Certainly, fighter aircraft will soon be a thing of the past. One need only examine the kill ratios of the two World Wars, Korea, and South Vietnam to see how radically the place of the fighter, and, for that matter, aerial combat, have changed. In World War I, Manfred Von Richtofen earned 80 kills in the air; when he was finally shot down, his plane somehow landed successfully on an open field; astonishingly, Richtofen was already dead by the time his aircraft touched down. Eddie Rickenbacker's 75 official (and as many as 125 unofficial) shootdowns of enemy pilots placed him first among American pilots; his aircraft suffered a single bullet hit during his time in the air. The British Edward "Mick" Mannock had 73 confirmed kills. In World War II, Major Erich Hartmann achieved an incredible 352 air victories, all but 9 against Russian aircraft. Luftwaffe Captain Hans Joachim Marseille shot down 17 planes in 3 missions over North Africa. Ninety-nine pilots in the Luftwaffe each earned over 100 kills in the air, flying such "birds" as the Me-109, the FW-190, and, the first jet fighter of the air, the Me-262. The infamous British pilot, Douglas Bader, who lost both legs during an accident in 1931, was one of the heroes of the Battle of Britain: he achieved 23 German kills in the air. (When finally brought down in 1941, he made so many escape attempts from the prison camp, the German commandant took his artificial legs from him and locked them in his office.) The highest scoring British Ace— one who has shot down five or more enemy craft in the air—was Group Captain "Johnnie" Johnson, with a mere 38 credits. The leading Japanese Ace was not a commissioned officer: Chief Warrant Officer Hiroyashi Nishizawa had 87 kills. (And it is an irony that he was never touched during aerial combat; he was shot down while flying a transport plane back to Japan.) The highest scoring woman Ace of all time was the Russian Lieutenant Lilya Litvak, with 13 kills. The most successful Russian, however, was General Ivan Kohzedub, with 62 air victories. Major Richard Bong was the highest scoring American Ace, with 40. (Bong was the definitive insane American: Before being shipped overseas, he took a P-38 Lightning from his field, flew a loop-the-loop over the Golden Gate Bridge, and then buzzed Market Street, waving at the secretaries; after the war, he died as a test pilot in the XP-80 Shooting Star—a trapped fuel system caused complete engine malfunction, and the plane exploded in flames.) Major Thomas McGuire had 38; Lieutenant Colonel "Gabby" Gabreski had 31; Navy Captain David McCampbell had 9 record kills in a single mission known as the Marianas Turkey Shoot; Lieutenant "Pappy" Boyington earned 28 kills over the Pacific.

On 8 November 1950, things began to change: in the skies over Korea, Lieutenant Russell Brown, in his F-80, went into aerial combat against a Russian Mig-15. With modesty and diffidence, Brown remarked: "I had superior skill and courage, and in the true spirit of the Air Force, I shot his ass down!" Such is the ego of the fighter jock. America's first jet Ace was Captain James Jabara, with fifteen air victories. Captain Joseph McConnell became the highest jet Ace with a total of sixteen kills. Yet, despite an F-86–to–Mig-15 kill ratio of 14.7 to 1 in Korea, aerial combat in Korea began to dwindle. Indeed, the very notion of aerial combat was becoming a thing of the past. In Vietnam there were only three Aces, two of them Academy graduates. (It is interesting to note that the highest-scoring Ace of the war with six kills, Captain Jeff Feinstein, was not a pilot but rather an F-4 navigator.)[54] Why did the actual number of aerial confrontations drop? Certainly it was not because these new warbirds were less sophisticated than their predecessors. They had accurate radar tracking systems, sophisticated missiles and guns, could climb higher and faster than ever before. The pilots were better trained. (In World War II a combat pilot received as little as eight hours' time in the cockpit before being shipped off to war; today, an undergraduate pilot receives almost two hundred hours actual flight, as many hours of practice in simulators, and several hundred more hours in classroom academics.) Today pilots are even more eager to fight. The legend of the fighter jock was born even as the myth became more and more obvious. In the skies over Verdun, pilots had engaged in a chivalric code (saluting their fallen comrades who plummeted back to earth), a code which no longer had meaning for those in the trenches below, who died, sometimes hundreds at a time, who advanced on the battlefield less than a hundred yards in the space of a year, victims to mustard gas and the early refinements of modern chemical warfare.

Somewhere and sometime over the South China Sea, the role of the warbird became a practical role of brutal engagement, from the early failures of *Rolling Thunder* to the final annihilation of the *Linebacker* campaigns. The true warbird of Southeast Asia (and any real fighter pilot would cringe at this notion) was the B-52, the stark, overwhelming machine of death from above: unseen as it emptied its immense payloads from the high wealth of the air and peeled back the landscape with scars that even now show the immense cost of destruction.

It is not unfair, nor is it wrong, to compare the fighter pilot to the chivalric, medieval knight. Impressive to be, impressive to see. But the advent of technology, the advance of the applications of warfare, made the image fade: one bullet, after all, could pierce a knight's thickest armor. Is it any wonder that the planes of the future, the Stealth fighters and bombers, are planned to be most successful when they are most invisible, to avoid detection by enemy radar, to fly low and fast to penetrate the lines of adversary defense, to erase any final consideration that the skies over the land are the last realm to *fight the good fight?* In the future, there will be no battlefields of the air. "Shut up and die like an aviator!"—How many times has that radio call been cast on the airwaves over the land and above the surface of the sea in Europe, the Pacific, Korea, Southeast Asia?

"Lance and plume! *I'm a knight!* Come on up and fight! Why hold back! Knights of the Right Stuff!"[55]

Is it any wonder that the most common fear among military pilots is acrophobia, a fear of height?

The days of one man: one bullet/two fighters: one dogfight are gone. The rules of engagement now dictate expanding theories of *Massive Retaliation, Mutual Assured Destruction, Windows of Vulnerability, First and Second Strike Capability, Escalation of Conflict.* Technology has eclipsed the role of the fighter. We expand into new realms in the science of warfare.

"I go to nature because man is scary," A. R. Ammons writes. He's right, of course, as much as he is wrong. As with almost all of Archie's poems, what is left out is just as precise and important as what fills up the line. Man *is* scary. Nature is pretty damned scary, too. I hope and wonder each day that these tiny explosions of fury and speed and death live long enough to take their place in a mysterious order which is anything but *natural.* It is, I think, just in nature: It, She, He (which identifier shall I use to lay the blame back on the earth?) has the power for pure, overwhelming destruction, and man has finally gained that power, too. In nature, though, that power is more predictable, more honest and real.

There is a peak named Eagleshead which looms above the southwest borders of the Academy. It dominates the landscape. Once, it was a historical peregrine aërie; once, decades ago, an EC-121 Warning Star slammed into its face during a winter storm. The plane buried itself in the naked rock of the mountain. Even today, on afternoons when the sun is at a perfect declination, light from the silver carcass glints and sparkles on the face of the peak. One afternoon I hiked up to Eagleshead in hopes of finding what little remained of the falcon nest. It remained hidden. My hiking companion and I came into a hollow space beneath the cliff face where the Warning Star had impacted. Pieces of engine and wing littered the ground. My companion reached down and picked up a piston—an almost living thing which once had hummed with its own small fury and had done its best to lift this impossible metal thing into the air—and tossed it into his backpack. Later, I learned he had fashioned it into an ashtray. I was not pleased with his action. Nor was I pleased with how pleased he had seemed with his theft. He had taken an object from the sacred floor of the forest, and made it both artifact and conversation piece. But it was meant to remain an object, perhaps forever, an object as real and as permanent as a tree, or a stone, or a man when he is dead.

My first raptor was a barn owl. I was home for spring break from the Academy, when a neighbor knocked on the back porch screen, asking if it was true that I had an interest in birds. The tiny owl lay in the corner of a cardboard box, looking up to us: an expression like a sad-faced monkey or a smiling human child. I took the owl on the next day to a local veterinarian, who refused to do anything for him (. . . *let the damn thing die*, he said). I didn't take his advice. Apparently, he had been shot in the wing. I say apparently because whatever had happened had happened weeks before; the bird had hobbled around for weeks before my neighbor picked him up. His greatest threat then was starvation. Some of the long fingers had snapped on his rust-colored wing and it was almost impossible to repair. I considered, for a short while, imping some of the feathers from his tail and shaping them to fit his wing. (The process of imping involves trimming the broken feather at the fracture, taking a triangular-shaped imping needle sharpened at both ends and gluing the pieces of feather together again.) Fortunately, I chose not to do this. The main reason was that I had never seen this grafting process performed; I had only read about it. The second, and probably wiser, reason why I chose not to imp his wing was because imping should be done with the same type of feather, preferably taken from the same bird from a previous year's molt. Grafting a tail feather onto a wing would have been idiotic: I didn't want to play hobby shop with the bird. So I spent twelve days in his company. After I returned to the Academy, I left him with a friend who lived on a huge sprawling ranch in the western desert of Texas and raised pigeons. For a while, I thought the owl would either think himself a pigeon, or end up killing one. Neither happened. By that summer, he was released into the air, flew happily away, and I never saw him again.

I made my first pair of jesses for him, thin strips of leather, one for each leg. At the trailing end of each jess, I used a falconer's knot through a swivel to prevent the owl from flying off the fist. We had a hard time getting used to each other. I, for the first few days at least, was uncomfortable with a tiny bird (for a raptor) perched constantly on my fist. He, clicking his beak in a strange metallic way, was uncomfortable with me. After our first day, we were still uneasy. He suddenly cacked, opened his mouth, and for a moment emitted only a sharp hiss of air, and then *it* came: a cry of inhuman agony and terror. I have never heard anything like it since; I was terrified. But the owl suddenly roused and ruffled his feathers, relaxed on my fist. He'd had his say and now was ready to get down to the business of association. During the days of that short spring break, we were constantly in each other's company. We took long walks through the streets and the dust and the Texas emptiness. Sometimes people would slow their cars to stare. No one stopped to talk. The amazement of humans, though, was minor compared to the frustration of birds. Small birds, finches and swallows, fled at our sight. Jackdaws would scream overhead, and flock suddenly together. I remember one day hearing the incessant howls and cacking of the crows, turning to see hundreds of them filling the trees in the wake of our path. The trees had turned black. Their cries and jeering laughter took hold of the air. The tiny barn owl turned his head to one side, puzzled and looking back to the trees, and then back at me as if to say: *What's wrong with them?* We hid, quietly, in a neighbor's garage for over an hour. The crows heckled and jeered.

The barn owl never had a name.

My first close experience with feeding a raptor came with the most imposing raptor of all. A bald eagle had been shot, recovered by the Department of Wildlife, and given to the Academy for care. She recovered quickly, and was released a few weeks later. I was an apprentice. An upperclassman, a falconer, practicing a new variation on the concept of hazing, told me to cut up some chicken *and feed the eagle.* He handed me a fencing mask. I donned it like a helmet, ready for combat; the caged wire mesh limited my sight. I slid open the door of her chamber. She perched on a high bar ledge. (She was far too large to roost on a shelf perch.) I slid the door closed behind me, and held the chicken behind my back. I extended my hand and proffered the chicken to her. Her imperious gaze said, *So?* I set the meat gently down on the bar on the opposite side of her perch. She stared at me, at the chicken. She gave a slight hop. Extending one long talon, she pulled the food into her range, delicately began ripping and tearing at flesh. I heard the soft crunching of bone.

My first flight in a military jet was in a T-33 T-Bird. I was a basic cadet in training at the Academy. It was intended for motivation: an *incentive flight*. The cockpit was tight and cramped, cluttered with instruments and dials. I sat in the back, feeling the bubble of the canopy slide over my head, engulfing me. The engine rumbled and groaned. The asthmatic air system coughed. I never believed we would leave the ground. But we did, and as we heaved and struggled into the Colorado air at 7,000 feet above the level sea, I heard the pilot call on the intercom: *Here— come on the controls with me. . . .* I gripped the stick, muscles tensing, as if I was trying to choke it. *No, no*, came the response. *This way. Follow me through.* I felt the ghostly, invisible presence of hands on the stick, felt the slightest pressures of rudder correction, trained response and ease at flight. I moved with his hands and his feet, thinking I could learn how to fly simply by tactile sense. We cakewalked into the sky, step by step climbing the stairs of the atmosphere. We barrel-rolled over the Rockies, using Pike's Peak as our aim point. We chandelled, floated in the precise falling of a lazy eight. *So this*, I thought, *is what it's all about.* Flying is a series of still moments, frozen photographs, like Zeno's paradox of the arrow singing from its bow: if a line is made up of points, and a point has no length, how can a line have length? If motion is a straight line over distance, motion must not exist, and nothing truly gets you from one point to another along the spatial segments which eventually suppose a line.

All things will be unhoused by time.

But getting "the right picture" is what it's all about, as if the brain were an Instamatic camera snapping off moments and images. I first learned to fly in a sailplane, and it will be the closest I'll ever come to what it feels like to fly on the breath of the air, without the support of motor or engine. My first solo, reaching altitude, I gripped at the instrument panel and pulled the release cable. No sound but the rush of air, no rhythm but the pulse of your blood as you move stick and rudder. The wind grazing your canopy.

For days, I lived to be in the still air; each time as I was lifted into the sky, I was unwilling to admit I belonged to earth. But gravity and the laws of flight were against me. The longest I could "make wing" was forty minutes. Each time I came down I wanted to go up; each time I was up I didn't want to come down. One day, I almost didn't. Caught under a thundercloud, I felt myself being pulled up into the swirling mass of violence. Ten, twelve, thirteen thousand feet. I entered a spin, trying to lose altitude. I came out of the spin at five hundred feet higher than when I had entered.

My first falcon was Oneida. We trained together for a few short months, established a friendship, and then he was dead. Then I was given the great grey gyrfalcon Gandalf to train: the reckless flyer, ready to test your courage at a moment's pass to the lure. Snapping a wing to the head, a talon to the face, he seemed to laugh as he rushed by in the enveloping wind, the air moving in to fill the spaces of his wake. One winter I entered his chamber and found him frozen, lying on his shelf perch. No one knew why he had died, or even that he was ill. His grey, unmoving body slumped by the window; his lifeless eyes caved in on themselves.

There is a time in any human's life to realize limits. In flying, the best skills and sharpest maneuvers come by knowing the strength of those limitations, and using them. For me, these past weeks have been a coming to terms with my limits: my failures as much as my hopes. The training of falcons affected the tenor of my existence; it left an indelible impression. So much was sunk and hoped and poured into the falcon that the truest falconer would come to realize that, if she or he believes in the independence of the raptor, the time must surely come when she or he can no longer practice falconry, must finally recognize an independent way of life.

When you cast a falcon into air, when she rises on the swirling thermals, a part of you rises, too, something shared between human and raptor. You try to explain this to others, and they do not understand; you try to explain this to yourself, this joy which you helped create, and it becomes a moment of sadness because you know that you are greedily, hungrily, selfishly holding this joy captive.

The best falcon I ever trained, and perhaps the last falcon I will ever train, was Aragorn. It strikes me now how much his name sounds like *arrogance*. Arrogant he was; he'd make the boasting of any modern fighter jock seem modest. But he lived up to his self-belief: he flew stronger, faster, sharper than any falcon I saw before or since the short year we spent together.

He sometimes waited on above me for thirty minutes, patiently waiting for my whistling call to bring him down to attack the lure. Sometimes, I would release him, cast him off, and watch him fly over the rising hills to the north of Cathedral Rock. I would wait, underneath a tree or in a field, and then an hour later call him. He'd return across the distance, zooming toward me at a hundred miles per hour, a sure look in his eyes, his beak open to the waiting lure. For a year we were each other's best companions. I began by "manning" him, patiently waiting for him to sit quietly on my gloved fist, while he impatiently refused to cooperate. Trying to stop him from bating, from hanging clumsily by his jesses from my fist, squawking and fluttering his wings, turning in circles with the breeze, I would walk with him for hours underneath the pines near the mews, or sit by a stream as I tried to taunt him with chicken. Sometimes, stroking his breast with a feather, I tried to put some of the calmness that I so badly needed, into him. For a long while, he resisted every approach with effective and purposeful deterrence. I continued to smooth his breast, soothe him with the feather, teach him how to accept a hood. His defiance turned to distrust; he would open his beak in surprise at me, thinking me the fool if I thought I was *ever* going to get him to wear that piece of leather over his eyes. But distrust faded; time won out. He eventually, grudgingly, accepted the hood. Each day, he stepped onto my fist when I entered his mews to feed him. Then I set him outside on a block perch, tied by a swivel to the end of a long leash now joined to his jesses. For the next few days, he hopped and then flew to my fist from the perch: two feet; five feet; ten; twenty.

Soon he was ready to fly with a creänce, a long elastic line of twenty-five yards. I stood one hundred feet away, held out the dangling lure from behind my back. Aragorn bobbed once, twice, and flicked his wings and then flew toward me. A small flight for the tiercel; I, however, was ready to burst with pride, to run, scream, and shout. Instead, I merely hopped around in place, Aragorn feeding on the lure now held in my fist, and hopping with me. Normally, it takes a falcon four weeks to adjust to the creänce. Aragorn had adjusted in one week, and was ready for free flight. In the first weeks of flying free, Aragorn did not have the radar-tracking telemetry band attached to his leg. (The small, thimble-sized transmitter was not attached until he started flying exhibitions.) Some of the falconers used bells, made in Pakistan, to hear the approach of the birds. Aragorn, though, flew free. After a few days of practice at flying "straight-in" approaches, he was ready to fly a sustained game of catch with the flying lure. What takes normally ten to twelve weeks of training, Aragorn did in four. The rest is memory.

I remember, in winter, when football season had long ended with the roar of stadiums and stories of his escapes and escapades, setting Aragorn down on a block perch. It was dusk; the winter pines loomed over us, their shadows were longer now, a time soon after the solstice. I was teasing Aragorn with the lure, flopping it in the snow, telling him to come fetch it. Aragorn did his best to ignore me. I walked over to him, my huge figure blocking his sight, mock scolding him. He looked at me, his head tilted straight back and up. He feigned fright; he opened his beak in an O of surprise.

Behind me, a rustle of wings. I turned and saw a red-tailed hawk, shoulders forward and down, his wings now mantling the lure, his talons clutching the meat as he bent down and hungrily swallowed. Aragorn seemed perfectly calm, as if it were the most natural thing that a bird should fall from the branches to take his food. Silently, we formed a small triangle, each of us watching the other. When the hawk was finished, I crouched down and duck-waddled my way through the snow. (Exactly what a raptor does while on the ground: she waddles and stumbles once back on earth.) The hawk's wings moved back to his torso with measured purpose; the two eyes in his regal head, though calm, fixed on me like headlights. I extended my fist and he stepped onto my glove. I took him inside the mews, leaving Aragorn outside to pout in the snow. Fifteen minutes later, I had fashioned crude jesses for him. He seemed perfectly comfortable with them. It was a mystery where he came from. But it was certain he had been around humans before.

I called him Winterhawk. I gave him to a falconer who lived in the mountains. I visited him three times after he left the Academy. By the time of my last visit, he had become a quick, reliable hunter. By autumn he would take rabbits and even one small fox. He seemed to remember me. As I bent down in the dark of my friend's backyard which opened to miles of open field and forest, I saw the soft glitter of Winterhawk's eyes. Over our eyes, the stars gleamed in the atmosphere of ten thousand feet. I reached out my hand, and Winterhawk unfurled his dun-colored wings, breaking the still outline of his body against the stars as his thighs lifted and bent and he flew to my fist. It seemed we were saying good-bye.

A few weeks later, I was playing the same game in the snow with Aragorn. He, as usual, couldn't care less about training. It was winter: he wanted to eat, sleep, eat, sleep. As I bent over his perch, I again heard a rustle of wings. *What now?* I thought. A great-horned owl was the answer. She clutched the lure, and looked defiantly back at us. The devilish peak of her crown flared; she seemed eager to rip us apart for the sake of the lure. I was eager to stay where we were for the sake of our health. A massive shuddering of wings, she rose into the air clutching the lure with her talons. The line of the lure flared like a streamer behind her as she climbed over the trees and her shadow folded itself into the gathering dark.

And then there are these peregrines. I do not belong to them, nor they to me.

Seven birds appear before sunset. Madonna aggressively challenges Belladonna at the feeding station, clasping her by the neck and ripping with her beak. They fight over a few remaining chicken wings. Shadowfax stares down the barrel of my spotting scope. His cries are sharp, accusing; he lets me know that I am responsible for his hunger.

Tahawus lands beside him on the ledge, joins Shadowfax in a chorus of misery. Both of them have empty crops. I expect the activity of potential prey to increase near dusk. Belladonna and Madonna move to a ledge which is mostly hidden from view as it angles north. They seem to share food which I can't see. Tahawus flies away, returns later with a full crop. Fuentes joins Shadowfax on the rock. Two barn swallows sail past, taunting them.

One of them turns back, peaks up the north face. Shadowfax does not notice. But Fuentes rises up, drops a wing and falls.

Watching through the scope, I see him strike. He flies to a nearby ledge, carrying the struggling and still very much alive bird, and kills it.

This is the first kill. I am lucky: most hack site attendants will never see a falcon taking prey. These eyasses are now birds of prey; I am no longer needed. He kills, and makes this blood his own. He's learned what I can't teach.

Through the scope I try to focus on Fuentes, but cannot define the expression on his face. His eyes are alive with the terror and his victory over death. He seems to consider my hostile human figure. But he is staring beyond me, as if searching for something from which he cannot look away.

Shadowfax begins a characteristic head-bob and drops to join Fuentes 500 feet below. Hungry cries are replaced by something more intense: Fuentes' shrieks.

It is not a moment of beauty, but of brutal joy.

The woods, which were alive with songbirds, are suddenly quiet.

SATURDAY, 26 JULY   0730.

Belladonna and Madonna fly south, circle high over Panther Peak. They scan the woods for prey. Last night, together, they shared their own first kill. Now they search again.

Over Fire Lake they see a blue jay wheeling above the water, chased by two smaller birds. Belladonna rises high and stoops a thousand feet, falling at more than a hundred miles per hour, her beak open, her body streamlined. She hits the jay and drives his flailing body to the water. He breaks away, flies up and off, shaking himself, confused. Madonna grabs him from behind, instantly breaks his neck.

The sheriff of Beaverkill stands on the main landing dock of the lake. He drinks his morning coffee. Dumbfounded, he looks up, cannot believe what he sees. Thirty seconds later, the falcons disappear, vanishing in mist at the west end of the lake.

SUNDAY, 27 JULY

I feed the birds every other day now. They are ready to disperse. Tom, back for the day, helps take down the boxes, wrap the

plywood in tarp and store it under some pines in the forest.
Six falcons chase each other above. The cliff looks naked and empty.

Monday, 28 July

A thick fog settles. The five chickens which I tied down remain untouched. Occasionally, I hear Shadowfax's scream roll across the valley.

There is a Zen legend which claims that before she will mate, the female raptor will fly for three days, with the most eager males in pursuit. Only the strongest males will be able to match the strength of the larger female, and at the end of the third day only one male, the perfectly chosen mate, will remain.

The legend, as far as anyone may know, is apocryphal, but there is a certain beauty in the truth of its lie. As with almost all legends, there is a small essential grain of knowledge which falls aside; certainly, for the peregrine falcon, the image of aloneness unfolds with an existence which brought near-extinction, as equally as the tenacity to endure explains a refusal to disappear. If I were to finally observe these ten fledglings in a dispassionate way, I would see nothing more than ten killing machines, whose survival depends on nothing more or less than how well they're able to snap their prey's neck on the wing. I, of course, have been unable to remain dispassionate. I have refused it.

Tom, several long weeks ago, finally decided that there was nothing much really happening up here, nothing more than daily observations, constant routine. But he disappeared too quickly; I rarely spoke with him, because he has not seen what I have discovered, known why I invest every sense of my self into the daily lives of these birds. I feel, simply, a constant wonder at why I see so little of the life around me. I do not mean physical observation, though looking across the vast expanse of this 6-million-acre wilderness, I know it's true that finally there is very little my eye can take in, my brain can hold or form into some recognizable image that memory will ever know. I mean observation in the sense that I could finally explain some perfect reason for existence. There is, of course, none. Yet why do I say "of course"? What course, other than aimlessness, is any of us following? In my days as a pilot, the military spent several million dollars to ensure I could reasonably react to unpredictable events: I knew hundreds of checklists by heart, knew hundreds of pages of technical manuals, spent hundreds of hours in simulators preparing for any type of emergency. But when it happened, when each unpredictable event occurred, the hours of preparation meant nothing. They had to be taken for certain, held deep in the back of every conscious reaction. I could not say, *I recall a similar emergency procedure on page 16-dash-4 of the technical manual—why don't we reference that?* When an outboard engine exploded inflight, I knew what to do. When I saw my copilot's face turn white with horror, after two engines ignited in flames when the cartridge explosives misfired during an emergency ground start, I knew what to do. I sent the rest of my crew scrambling for the rescue trucks, while the copilot and I did whatever we could to save the engines, to save the plane, to save the rest of the planes around us.

Was it simply reaction? Was it simply a response of, *We must do something and do it now?* I believe so, but I don't know. These fledglings, I do know, are reacting to forces, to natural controls which each has no control over. There is a sad humor that only a few days ago the fledglings sat on a cliff ledge with jays and wrens, socializing, sharing their food. A few days from now, those tiny birds will become the surest food source. Nineteenth-century theologians and scientists (and often there was no difference between the two) did their best to show how nature mirrors humanity's conception of good and evil. This notion is, as perplexed observers came to realize, not true. It is a fallacy. Take the example of the ichneumon wasp, which survives by ruthless determination, which plagued and perplexed naturalists who wished to see a natural order that matched their own deeply held spiritual beliefs about how the earth *should* be. For the ichneumon, there is no possibility other than to act as predator, to survive by predation. The female lays her eggs on her host's, or her victim's, body. She then paralyzes it for her offspring; they consume the body, seeming to inflict as much pain as possible, yet careful to keep the host alive until the last possible moment.

Nearly a decade ago I felt ice chips scatter up my spine when I saw a creature swimming in an innocuous, tiny tank at the

San Francisco Aquarium in Golden Gate Park: the Pacific hag-fish, a particularly nasty creation, with a circular sucking mouth and rows of horny teeth. The male and female each bear the vestigial sex organs of the other inside. The hagfish is from the first order of primitive fish, *Myxine,* jawless descendants of the ostracoderms. It is well adapted: it lives by boring into the bodies of larger fish, consuming internal organs and flesh, leaving only skin and skeleton.

There is nothing anthropomorphic about the animals which inhabit our earth. We cannot take an anthropocentric view when we see them. But we do, we always do. Even now, the only beings capable of articulate thought in an indifferent universe, we remain largely dumb, inarticulate, incapable of sight. Yet I won-der if there may be some value in such blindness. Arthur M. Young has suggested that it is necessary to view nature in human terms, as a process of translation. To deal appropriately in meta-phor may be the only way to understand our own humanness.

Recently, I have learned that the Gaea hypothesis (taken from the Greek γαια, the original earth goddess and mother and nourisher of all things) is receiving serious attention. What seems so surprising about this, to me, is that much of what springs from the notions of adaptability in Darwin (grossly translated later as "survival of the fittest") takes on a more graceful and mutable character in the Gaea hypothesis: all living organisms act cooperatively to manipulate the planet, to make their mutual existence more hospitable. Oxygen, one of our four biophil elements (carbon, nitrogen, oxygen, and phosphorous), may have been created by plants to induce and nurture other life forms; it is possible that all life grew from a bacterium of a sulfur-based atmosphere. Even the planet itself is a living organism, sleeved in the delicate and fragile biosphere which holds us.

The notion of creation takes on various identities in different myths, which may be the only way to acknowledge our past, or our temporal presence: we see it in Osiris, in the Rig Veda, in the Persian *Shánáma,* in the *Popul Vuh* of the Quechua. But there is something supremely attractive about the Gaea hypo-thesis. If it is true that I might be able to see most clearly through metaphor (and it seems, for quantum physics at least, to be the *only* way to see), even knowing that such limitations may blind me to another way of knowledge, I accept it. I believe it because I need to believe it. Metaphor may be the basic measuring instrument of the imagination. There may be no way to bring myself close to these fledglings other than through comparison: it may be the only way my mind invents, through "that parallelism we finally call narrative."[56] Finally, there is one metaphor I cannot escape: Gaea, the first earth mother and creator, in Greek mythology is also the daughter of Chaos.

Now I am aware of the caution with which I must approach the notes of this journal: the struggle of these words are at best a palimpsest, the images are pentimenti. A narrative cannot stand entirely for experience; I cannot make my experience represent the entire progression of what has happened here on Fire Lake Mountain. I hope not to have exaggerated the risks of my life; nor have I wanted to seem complacent. But I can stare at the outline of a peregrine fledgling, who floats on the currents of warm thermal air, and feel nothing but envy, and love. It is their lives about to begin. And the nature of life is risk. They have no time or ability to consider the odds. I wishfully hope for such determination: "The impeccable and indisputable integrity I want in myself."[57]

I have survived while so many others, so many I have been close to, have not.

I ask myself why, and I have no answer.

"When you are ready," Buddhists claim, "the teacher will appear."[58] When you are ready to understand, you will. I see now that the human who has taught me the most is the human I have been most close to. It was the simple act of her faith: a willingness not to let go, an unswerving belief in each of us.

Donna and I were married twenty months after we met. I have never regretted our relationship, though I cannot, of course, make similar claims on her behalf. Nearly every weekend, she and King and Shakespeare have followed the six-hour trail north from Ithaca to enter this different world. Each week she continues her work and study on a summer anthropology fellowship from Cornell. There is something strange and ironic in that: she studies the peculiarities of man, perhaps trying to understand the man she lives with, while I study the habits of fledgling peregrines and try to reason with what I have become.

Last year she visited the Soviet Union for four weeks. One

night in Leningrad, after too much vodka and dancing and celebration, members of her group lifted their glasses to make
a last, rousing chorus of toasts. "To the people of the Soviet
Union!" they shouted. "To the people of the United States!" their
hosts replied. "To the President!" "To the General Secretary!"

Donna lifted her glass and called out—"To world peace!" The
room went suddenly quiet. She was met with the shocked ex-
pressions of Soviets and Americans alike.

No one raised a glass to echo her.

Something about this will always astonish me. Not the fact of
their silence, but their submission to the world outside. Those
eyes staring at her: *How could you say such a thing?* What she
said had not been wrong, but only too right. She had echoed
their most fervent hopes, and touched their most secret fears.
If I had been there, and not known Donna as I do, would I,
too, have remained numb and silent and frozen, while knowing
inside of me that what she was saying was what each of us
needs so badly to know?

The vast measure of the world engulfs us, and we cling to
small pockets of hope. The flood rushes past, and we keep cling-
ing until we can no longer: abandonment as way of life. And
even in such desperate moments must come the notion of challenging the torrent: *when the earth has lost your name, still
whisper to the earth* I'm flowing, *to the flashing waters say,
I am.*

I am afraid to dream of the things I want most.

And yet, why not? If I had come to be as honest as Donna,
and if those stunned citizens had too, perhaps we could perceive
things in a way detached from our particular attachments. I
need to perceive my life in the way that she lives hers. She is
the teacher I have found.

A simple act of faith, which is anything but simple.

TUESDAY, 29 JULY

A few falcons soar in the distance. I think of Figmo eloping with
Kathleen. Perhaps they're honeymooning in Niagara Falls, bliss-
fully killing feral pigeons and mooning together over the lulling
sounds of the waterfall's cascade each night.

In the light of the afternoon the thick haze casts a permanent
stillness to the air. No bird sings.

Tom is returning today because I must leave. I received a scholarship from the Frost Place in Franconia, New Hampshire, two months ago. The Peregrine Fund agreed to let me leave at the end of July. That time has come.

All morning the sun hangs frozen on the sky. I begin to laugh. So much of this summer has been spent in rain, in lousy weather, it seems strange and wonderfully bizarre to finally witness the sun. When the white light of that not-so-distant star appears, it withholds its radiance. But the song of birds is welcome. The days remain long; the nights are brief periods of sleep and dream. I sit at the edge of the observation point, and wait.

The wilderness was born in my refusal to listen to the silence. Now I believe that every human, if only once in a life, should turn back to whatever she or he can take up of the remembered earth. Every human should stare into the distance of whatever landscapes reveal themselves—the endless horizons of Dakota sunrise, where the million acres of sleeping sunflowers stir and waken to the sudden brilliance; should pause and let the singleness of sight fly up to the star which no one else on the face of the planet sees at this particular moment, this particular night or day; should wonder as the footsteps take away the mountain path, how many stepped there before, how many would forget themselves, moments away, years from now or then. To forget whatever small and precious things one has learned, to believe they are foolish things really, only the beginnings of understanding or the remnants of some acquired education, to discard one's particular way of sight as surely as Picasso did in his first flight in an aircraft, when he looked down to the earth unfolding beneath his starboard window, and muttered absently to himself, *Cubism.* Everyone should see the earth from such fractured angles, to be so uncertain of the certainty of one's existence. Everyone should imagine existence without the presence of the self, to remove every thought of one's own life from the equation; and only by doing that can one begin to believe the sureness and the truth of one's own life. Everyone should feel the faintest motions of the wind and realize its stillness, see the iridescence of distance in the colors of light, look up into the fractured surface of the oval moon and see how the sudden grey-blue pieces of icebergs have fallen from the arctic poles of this planet and recollected themselves on the now no-longer-dead surface of our neighbor satellite.

I can say this because no one will believe it. Everyone should wander in that strange territory outside the self. I am no exception. There is a part of me which longs to return: to drink and be stupid, to make love, to say among friends idiotic things which we might pretend are grand, to scrape the layers of dirt from my skin, to see my home again. But I am sad thinking about each of these things; each of them has a different meaning and importance; each is not the same. Part of me remains here, in these woods, stubborn and refusing to leave. Perhaps I should abandon the beauty of this solitary place, forget its existence. To think of the continual *now* is to lose the permanence of this moment. I hold it, and then it's gone. My head feels light at this altitude, which is by no means a mountain's elevation. I have the qualities of distance, meditation, thought. No one could possibly ask for more; there is nothing more.

I pull back into stillness; the wind and the light and this mountain withdraw into their selves, and describe the body of time. Looking across this distance, I could believe this landscape might exist forever. The perfect vein of Whiteface challenges my illusion of permanence. I am the transient here. These fledglings belong to the landscape, but I do not. I have, throughout my life, sought after, perhaps attacked experience, while I may have been searching most for the still center of my own being. I, like any normal human being (and what exactly does "normal" mean?), am consumed by, and consume desire. I seem to thrive on the shock of memory, as if this could be the thing to finally shock me into love. I want to fall into a sense of presence which, for me, most always exists only in the present tense. Eternity means nothing if its awe is not surviving in the here or now—the now/here of nowhere.

A falcon rushes by, the slight unfolding pull of air and rustling wings. I look up in the light, but see nothing. My awareness and my awe suspend themselves in the instant. I breathe: a long, sustained exhalation of the instant's presence. If there is such a thing as enlightenment, I have found it. I hold it for however long it stays with me, and, thus, I do not hold it. I should exist, and not think about existence, or the present, because if I do—think or try to realize them—they are already gone. I should, simply, know what I may have lost. But will I remember?

Will I?

I strike my tent and load my backpack. I walk to the observation point, take a last look at the empty ledges. A few scattered chicken feathers. Hiking down the mountain, the woods seem quiet.

The motorcycle feels each rock and rut in the long road out. The trail from Beaverkill has been freshly graded by a tractor. Near Horseheads Lake I wave as Tom drives up. We say good-bye. Partners—yet we remain strangers. I promise to submit my final report to the Peregrine Fund by Thursday.

At the inlet to the lake I stop to watch the heron fish. I kill the motor, unstrap my pack, and wait. The heron ignores me; he continues with routine.

Across the lake I see our mountain rise above the surrounding forest, against the cerulean sky. I take out the camera, expose one frame, and stow it, knowing the picture will almost certainly be an unrecognizable mass of rock and fog. The tall cliffs seem tiny scratchings on a palette, and so far away, hardly distinguishable. The sharp features, crags and fissures, are smoothed and the outline of the peak is leveled by distance.

I don my helmet. I start the engine, gun the throttle, and accelerate through the narrow trail of pine which snakes down to the highway. The motorcycle is a gyroscope; it lists with me as I lean into turns. My response is automatic, without thought. Suddenly, without forcing or trying to imagine it, I think of Aragorn, hooded, on the edge of a perch: we are seated together in the cargo section of an old, battered and camouflaged C-130 transport, and he leans and moves with the struggling aircraft as it groans and lifts from the runway into the heaving mass of the air. Something inside—maybe what we used to call the human heart—drifts on the summit of Fire Lake Mountain.

I am haunted by the cries of falcons overhead.

However long it takes for reality to intrude, I do not know. But when it does, I see how the road unfurls before me, taking me south towards Blue Mountain and back into the oblivion of this world, and since nothing stops the road from moving on, I let it go.

EPILOGUE

*Animals confound us not because they are
deceptively simple but because they are
finally inseparable from the complexities
of life.*
—BARRY LOPEZ, *Arctic Dreams*

We are standing at the edge of a thousand-foot cliff. Donna and I look out across the valley which once seemed so familiar. It is late April, yet even now small pockets of snow cling to the terrain, defying the change of seasons. The outlines of Horseheads Lake, the Snake River, Triangle Pond seem more perfectly described, precise, than ever.

Two days ago Jack Shelley called me from the Peregrine Fund. He asked us to travel back to the Adirondacks, to Fire Lake Mountain, to see if the site would still be usable for the coming summer. Nothing much has changed here. We are glad of it.

The boxes that we covered with tarp and stored under scrub pine remain; some plywood corners have been nibbled at and chewed on, but the boxes will survive. The wind is calm, though storm clouds tumble overhead.

Jack Shelley also asked another question: would I serve as assistant reintroduction specialist for the northeast United States? The Peregrine Fund could use my help to oversee hack locations; as a pilot, I could also transport fledglings to new sites. It was difficult to say, but I said no. I, of course, did not have a choice: I had a previous commitment to the Air Force. During the coming summer, I would be returning to Colorado, teaching, or trying to teach, Academy cadets about literature and about what it's like to be an officer. Though I had no option, part of me still wondered if I could live in both worlds at once.

We are ready to leave, though I try hard to remain. But Donna takes my hand, and we turn back from the cliff and the valley beneath us, knowing that in our present incarnation this will be the last time we stand at this height. We smile, and, hand in hand, take our few, wandering steps back down the solitary path of the mountain.

We know that we are leaving Eden.

*   *   *

Tom headed west in the fall. I have not heard from him since, though I hope all goes the way he wants.

Hope is a common notion these days. Hope, and the idea of survival. Within two days of my departure, all of the eyasses had dispersed. An accurate record of their range is not possible. The color-ID anklet markings have disintegrated; the federal number bands will prove useful only if they decide to return. Unlike other species which can be tracked with radio collars over territory of a few hundred square miles, the peregrine roams freely over the globe. With the exception of Antarctica, they inhabit every major continent. Her scientific name, *Falco peregrinus*, signifies her nature: the traveler, or, more appropriately, the wanderer.

As the seasons change, they will migrate. I think of ten eyasses spending their first winter south of the equator, lazily sunning in the warm climes of South America, or circling high over Tierra del Fuego. And then, months later, their mysterious genetic tapes will unreel and they will fly north, perhaps to find mates and establish nests.

I think of them often, and wish them well; and when I do, I am happy to know they never think of me.

APPENDIX I:
Peregrine Fund Summary Report

1. *Description of Site.*
Fire Lake, five miles west of Horseheads Lake and one mile northwest (300°) of Triangle Pond, St. Andrews County, New York: a cliff site located on Fire Lake Mountain, elevation 2519'. This is the first year the site has been used. It is located on private property under the auspices of Camp Beaverkill, and is patrolled by two caretakers, providing protection from human intrusion. The observation point is 150 yards west of the hack boxes. The site overlooks densely forested area, consisting of American beech (*Fagus grandifolia*), mountain paper birch (*Betula papyrifera*), red spruce (*Picea rubens*), red maple (*Acer rubrum*), an amalgam of fern and an abundance of blueberry (*Vaccinium* spp.) vegetation. Significant avian life included: barn swallow (*Hirundo rustica*); hermit thrush (*Cathartus guttatus*); chimney swift (*Chaetura pelagica*); blue jay (*Cyanocitta cristata*); blackpoll warbler (*Dendroica striata*); junco (*Junco hyemalis*); cedar waxwing (*Bombycilla cedrorum*); ruby-throated hummingbird (*Archilochus colubris*); ruffed grouse (*Bonasa umbellus*); great blue heron (*Ardea herodias*); red-headed woodpecker (*Melanerpes erythrocephalus*); white-throated sparrow (*Zonotrichia albicollis*); Eastern bluebird (*Sialia sialis*).

Raptors in the vicinity included: barred owl (*Strix varia*); osprey (*Pandion haliaetus*); red-tailed hawk (*Buteo jamaicensis*); broad-winged hawk (*Buteo platypterus*); turkey vulture (*Cathartes aura*—Cf. "Hunting Behavior"); American kestrel (*Falco sparverius*); adult peregrine (*Falco peregrinus*—Cf. "Unusual Incidents").

2. *History and Details of Young.*

Name	Sex	Federal Band Number/Leg	Color Band Number/Leg	Date and Age Placed in Box
Rondeau	M	619-27534/R	A43A/L	12 June, 30 Days
Augustus	M	619-27535/L	A44A/R	12 June, 27 Days
Figmo	M	619-27536/L	A45A/R	12 June, 27 Days
Fuentes	M	619-27537/L	A46A/R	12 June, 28 Days
Shadowfax	M	619-27538/R	A47A/L	12 June, 31 Days
Madonna	F	897-23283/L	B51B/R	12 June, 29 Days
Anne	F	897-23284/L	B52B/R	12 June, 27 Days
Belladonna	F	897-23285/R	B54B/L	12 June, 32 Days
Kathleen	F	897-23286/R	B55B/L	12 June, 31 Days
Tahawus	F	897-23287/R	B56B/L	12 June, 30 Days

3. *Pre-release Details.*

The fledglings were placed in the hack boxes on 12 June under conditions of heavy fog and rain and moderately heavy updraft wind conditions. Release was delayed until 25 June due to inclement weather. Anne and Rondeau remained in the hide almost continually until four days prior to release.

4. *Release Details.*

Name	Sex	Date and Time Released	Age at Release	Time to First Flight	Time to Return to Box after Flight
Rondeau	M	25 June, 1058	43 Days	3:44 hrs.	19:56 hrs.
Augustus	M	25 June, 1058	40 Days	23:42 hrs.	1:13 hrs.
Figmo	M	25 June, 1058	40 Days	20:12 hrs.	2:54 hrs.
Fuentes	M	25 June, 1058	41 Days	6:47 hrs.	5 min.
Shadowfax	M	25 June, 1058	44 Days	2 min.	6:26 hrs.
Madonna	F	25 June, 1058	42 Days	32:01 hrs.	immediate
Anne	F	25 June, 1058	40 Days	32:57 hrs.	immediate
Belladonna	F	25 June, 1058	45 Days	27:43 hrs.	2:25 hrs.
Kathleen	F	25 June, 1058	44 Days	19:02 hrs.	immediate
Tahawus	F	25 June, 1058	43 Days	27:44 hrs.	1:18 hrs.

The release was attended by Jack Shelley and Kathleen O'Heir. Belladonna remained in the hack boxes the first evening. Rondeau did not return to the boxes on his first evening of flight.

Although Anne was the last to fly, she was also the youngest female, and progressed rapidly in skills.

5. *Hunting Behavior.*

On 30 June, 1000, Rondeau (48 days; 5 days after release) drove a turkey vulture from the area, on occasion flying through the scavenger's tail feathers. On 9 July, 1937, Shadowfax (59 days; 14 days after release), pursued by Fuentes, was seen carrying the head of a small unidentified bird. On 16 July, Tahawus (64 days; 21 days from release), after a week's absence, appeared at the feed station and immediately began chasing prey. On 25 July, 1955, Fuentes (71 days; 30 days from release) captured a small bird, probably a barn swallow, flew to a ledge and killed it. On 26 July, 0730, Belladonna (76 days) and Madonna (73 days) took prey over Fire Lake. On 27 July, 2025, an unidentified falcon hawked prey near the northeast face of the mountain and was pursued by four other falcons.

6. *Roosting Behavior.*

Postprandial periods were spent on ledges below the feed station; a particular favorite spot was a flat, triangulated ledge shaped like the prow of a ship. The eyasses, after the first week, spent their evenings away from observation.

7. *Dispersal.*

Name	Sex	Date Last Seen Eating at Box	Date Last Seen at Site	Age When Last Seen	# of Days after Release
Rondeau	M	28 July	28 July	76 Days	35 Days
Augustus	M	23 July	23 July	68 Days	29 Days
Figmo	M	18 July	19 July	64 Days	24 Days
Fuentes	M	27 July	27 July	73 Days	32 Days
Shadowfax	M	30 July	30 July	79 Days	35 Days
Madonna	F	28 July	29 July	76 Days	34 Days
Anne	F	30 July	30 July	75 Days	35 Days
Belladonna	F	27 July	27 July	77 Days	32 Days
Kathleen	F	18 July	19 July	68 Days	24 Days
Tahawus	F	30 July	30 July	78 Days	35 Days

8. *General Evaluation of Falcons.*

Kathleen, the largest of the eyasses, and Figmo, the smallest, proved aggressive towards the attendants, often practicing stoops on the observation point. Shadowfax and Fuentes were the most agile fliers; however, Belladonna was able to consistently dominate them during intraspecific play. All birds were independent and were not commonly seen together, except during feeding periods. Anne associated with Tahawus up to the point of the latter's week-long absence.

9. *Unusual Incidents.*

On 21 June, 1309, an adult female peregrine was observed crossing Highway 30, three miles south of the village of Clear Lake and six miles east of Fire Lake Mountain. She bore no federal identification bands. On 30 June, 1200, an adult female peregrine without identification bands flew by the east face of the mountain. She did not disturb the eyasses or the hack boxes; she was sighted again on 19 and 23 July. On 21 July, a broadwinged hawk dove on Madonna while she was feeding. The hawk spent several days thermalling with the eyasses. A female American kestrel occasionally visited the site to socialize but did not eat. A raccoon (*Procyon lotor*) stole chicken from the feed station before being driven off. A family of fishers (*Martes pennanti*) visited the site but did not steal food.

10. *General Evaluation of Site.*

Fire Lake # 2 is a superb site for hacking peregrines. It offers complete isolation and far greater visibility for observation than the Copper Mountain hack site. The use of a nearby estate on Horseheads Lake for storing frozen food was a logical choice. Use of color leg band markings was also an innovative idea. With the happy exception of Kathleen O'Heir of the Endangered Species Unit, the Department of Environmental Conservation provided no meaningful or material support. The burden for logistical problems and solutions were left to the already undermanned and overtaxed personnel of the Peregrine Fund. A number of problems should be dealt with, or at least considered, for the future. Despite the injury liability release clause signed by attendants, both the Peregrine Fund and the DEC may be subject to major litigation in the event of an accident, because an adequate safety margin has not been provided. Suggestions:

a. Use of Army or Air Force helicopter for airlift to the sites. A planned DEC airlift for our location was cancelled; George Gordon contracted a private pilot for the job.

b. Use of a two-way emergency radio. During June the property is uninhabited, and the village of Clear Lake is twenty miles away. An emergency signal to the state police at Clear Lake can prevent a serious accident from becoming fatal. A request for an emergency radio was denied.

c. Use of a climbing rope. No technical knowledge is necessary to maneuver on the rock face above and to the side of the hack boxes. With the food chute installed, however, maneuvering is difficult. The rock is slick after a strong rain.

d. Obtaining potable water is a problem and food supplies, for falcons and humans, must be packed in. A running stream was eventually found five miles from the peak. *We recommend a person of slight physical stature not be selected for this site.*

e. Use of a vehicle. Both attendants suffered vehicle damage: two cracked mufflers and a flattened shock absorber. A request made to Bethany Goose for a DEC vehicle was denied on the grounds that we were not state employees. When necessary to pack supplies, the round trip hike to Horseheads Lake was 16 miles.

With more consideration for attendants, Fire Lake will prove an extraordinary location. This year's 100 percent dispersal rate speaks for itself.

11. *Equipment.*
Returned to the Peregrine Fund: supply tent, cooler, freezer, tripod. Returned to state offices at Inferno: hand radios, garbage can, warning signs, spotting scope.

12. *Acknowledgments.*
Jack Shelley and George Gordon, the Peregrine Fund; Sandy Stone and Dave Angeles, caretakers of Beaverkill; Lieutenant Colonel James H. Parsons, AFIT/CIS, and Colonel Edwin Gleason, for allowing Captain Liotta to participate in this research project.

APPENDIX II:
These Common Words

. . . spring from medieval and ancient falconry, as well as from the jargon of military flight. It is not a comprehensive list, and reflects mostly personal meanings. I apologize to those falconers, and to those pilots, who would disagree.

Ace—a combat pilot who has shot down five or more enemy aircraft.

Accipiter—the scientific designation for a genus of short-winged hawks with long tails able to fly in great bursts of speed over a short distance, such as the goshawk and Cooper's hawk.

Active—the runway in use.

Aërie—a raptor's nest.

Aileron—the movable control surface on an aircraft's wing which partially controls turn rate, bank, and direction by creating opposite lift forces.

Air brakes—deflecting control surfaces (sometimes called "spoilers") which, when directed into the slipstream, slow (or spoil) forward motion. On the KC-135, the air brakes are on top of the wing; on the T-38, they are on the underbody. Once, when I saw an osprey fish, I noticed his use of wings as air brakes to retard his sudden fall from the air.

Altimeter—a flight instrument which displays altitude.

Alula (sometimes called the "bastard" wing)—a set of quill-like feathers above the middle coverts of a falcon's wing which controls a falcon's stoop.

Artificial horizon—the indicator at the center of an ADI, which shows the actual position of the aircraft. During instrument flight, the artificial horizon is critically important.

Attitude Direction Indicator (ADI)—a gyro-operated flight instrument which displays an aircraft's position relative to the horizon. The instrument also displays pitch and bank attitude. On the KC-135, a bright orange delta rests at the center of the ADI and is meant to represent the aircraft.

Austringer—a handler of short-winged hawks (accipiters).

Base leg—the point where an aircraft turns from downwind to fly perpendicular to the landing runway in the traffic pattern.

Bate—a falcon's attempt to fly off the glove while still restrained by jesses.

Break—the pitchout for landing from an overhead pattern.

Buteo—scientific designation for a genus of raptors, which includes, for example, the common red-tailed hawk.

Cack—the harsh, staccato banter of a falcon, used as a warning or fear response.

Cast—the launching of a hawk from the fist; also, a small pellet regularly created and discharged in the digestion process, often a mixture of feather and bone from the prey.

Chandelle—an abrupt climbing turn in which the aircraft dissipates energy, almost to the point of stalling, and reverses direction.

Chitter-scream—I have taken this term from Steve K. Sherrod's definition of a high-pitched chitter used by fledglings in cases of extreme alarm. There are actually quite a number of different voice modulations which eyasses use, ranging from a contented burping chirp to the rapid fire of the cack.

Compass north—the direction which the compass needle shows to be north. At certain latitudes, compass north can be grossly inaccurate.

Crab—an aerial dogfight between falcons. In aircraft, to crab means to tack into the wind (in the same way a sailboat does) to make correction for wind effect.

Creance—a tethered line used to secure a falcon during her first training flights.

Crop—a sac, located above the sternum, where a falcon stores food before passing it down to the stomach.

Cross-fostering—within the same genus, substituting a chick of one species into the nest of a bird of another species; for example, placing a peregrine chick in a prairie falcon's congeneric nest.

Dead reckoning—prediction of one's position without reference to the sun or stars, based on the last previous known position, present direction, and speed data.

Declination—the angular distance of a star or other heavenly body from the celestial equator.

Dispersal—the point where the eyass successfully kills prey and permanently leaves the hack site (the surrogate nest). Dispersal is a natural part of the migration process; it is the final goal of any reintroduction program. Normally, fledglings are fed until the sixth week of the hack, or until they have demonstrated an ability to hunt and kill prey.

Double-clutching—the removal of eggs during the early stages of incubation, causing the falcon to produce a second nest of eggs.

Downwind—the point where the aircraft flies parallel to the active landing runway while approaching the perch to turn base leg. On downwind, the aircraft is opposite the direction of landing: for runway 30 (300°), for example, the aircraft's downwind is approximately (with allowance for drift) 120°.

Drift—the rate of lateral displacement of an aircraft, or other body, by wind effect.

Envelope—the point of an aircraft's, and a pilot's, limits, commonly referred to in the sense of "pushing the edge of the envelope." If you exceed the envelope's limitations, you die.

Eyass—the nestling; young fledgling.

Falcon—may often apply to only the female of any of the long-winged hawks (*See also* "Tiercel"). Females are larger and stronger than males.

Falconer—a handler of long-winged hawks.

Foot—to clutch prey or other objects with the talons.

Freak (sometimes called "feak")—the falcon's wiping of her beak against a perch after feeding.

Full stop—final touchdown of an aircraft. (*See also* "Touch and go").

G's—the unit force exerted on a body by the pull of gravity. Gravitational acceleration is approximately 9.7956 meters per second per second (m/sec^2) at 44° latitude. The force on the body at rest on the earth's surface is 1 g. This is somewhat misleading, however. One is always in a state of flux, and the body is subject to constant forces and acceleration. Merely walking down the street results in varying g forces. Tests indicate the human body is capable of surviving forces in excess of 40 g's for very brief periods.

Great circle—the route between two points on the earth's surface measured along the shorter segment of the circumference of the great circle (whose plane passes through the center of the earth). In the air, flying a great circle course is the shortest distance between two points: it is a line which bends to match the earth's curvature.

Gyroscope—a self-erecting instrument which powers critical flight gauges (the ADI, for example) and resists changes in the direction of its axis no matter how it is manipulated.

Hack boxes—plywood boxes constructed for the hack period.

Hacking—allowing fledglings to roam after release from the hack boxes. Food is provided until the falcons successfully take prey for themselves. Ancient falconers, at the completion of the hack, would trap a falcon that had learned to kill, in the belief that the falcon was a stronger, more confident hunter. Hacking is a vital part of the reintroduction process; in this case, however, the falcons remain free after the hack.

Haggard—an adult raptor.

Head-bob—characteristic response by a falcon, which usually means a focused interest on a distant object. T. J. Cade has suggested that the head-bob may both sharpen and improve the falcon's depth perception by parallax view.

Headwind—a wind blowing from the front of the craft. In flight, a headwind will decrease an aircraft's groundspeed; during final approach for landing, however, a headwind helps smooth out the landing phase.

Hide—a vertical piece of plywood placed in a back corner of the hack box (often used as a sleeping quarters). The fledglings run to the hide whenever they feel threatened.

Hood—a leather covering or helmet, often with ornamental plumage, for the falcon's head; used to quiet the bird before release toward prey or during travel.

Hot brakes—exceeding the maximum kinetic energy of an aircraft's braking system, resulting in fire and probable explosion of the tires.

Immelmann—a sudden climbing change of direction by performing a half loop and a half roll. Hauptmann Max Immelmann, a German Ace, developed this maneuver in World War I, and it was very effective: pursued by an adversary he was able to suddenly turn and confront his pursuer. Herr Immelmann was also the first pilot to successfully use a machine gun and interrupter device on an airplane, allowing his bullets to fire through the propeller arc.

Imping—a method for repairing broken feathers with a needle and glue.

Intercom—part of the radio system on board aircraft, allowing communication between crew members.

Jesses—leather straps attached to the tarsi of the raptor; a falconer's swivel is used with jesses to help keep the bird from bating.

KC-135—the military version of the Boeing 707 commercial carrier, often called the "tanker." Primarily used for inflight refueling (capable of offloading 185,000 pounds of fuel), it is also a cargo and passenger aircraft.

Kevlar—a lightweight synthetic material found in bulletproof vests, recently suggested for use by aircraft manufacturers as a protection against birdstrikes.

Lazy eight—a precise aerobatic maneuver which describes a sideways figure eight in the sky; difficult to perform well.

Lure—a winged effigy, often made of leather, which represents quarry; a falconer uses the lure to train the falcon for the hunt.

Magnetic north—the direction from one's position to the north magnetic pole.

Mews—chambers where raptors are kept.

Mute—the excrement of a bird.

Overhead pattern—a hard-breaking, fighter-type pattern, usually performed before reaching mid-field on a runway. Overheads allow for rapid sequencing and landing; they are also the only practical landing approach to use for formation flights (unless the pilot chooses to make a sequenced, straight-in approach). Sometimes fighter aircraft will break "over the numbers" (at the end of the runway) and, in essence, fall out of the sky to make their landing. Sometimes people are killed doing this.

Passager—a raptor caught (trapped) during the autumn migration.

Perch—the resting spot, often branch or ledge, of a falcon; also, the point at which an aircraft turns from downwind to base leg.

Pitch—the height a falcon attains while "waiting on." I also use the term to describe the climb toward height. In jet aircraft, this is the point where the pilot makes a hard turn to enter the overhead pattern. (*See also* "Break").

Pitot-Static System—instruments which measure the difference between impact and static pressure, as well as drive altimeter, airspeed, and vertical velocity indicators.

Punch—to eject from an aircraft.

Quarry—game sought during the hunt.

Radome—the bubble-type cover for a radar antenna.

Rouse—lifting the feathers (which makes the falcon's body seem to expand), shaking, and then relaxing the feathers.

Soar—to float on thermal air.

Solstice—the point on the ecliptic where the sun reaches its greatest declination from the celestial equator. In the southern and northern hemispheres, solstices are reversed because of the earth's tilt. This partly explains why on Christmas day it may be eighty degrees below zero in North Dakota, and a hundred and twenty above in New South Wales.

Stoop—the head-first dive in which a streamlined falcon achieves incredible speed.

Straight-in—a long final approach from outside the traffic pattern aligned with the active runway.

T-38—an advanced, supersonic trainer jet. At one time, the T-38 was the demonstration plane for the Air Force Thunderbirds; a catastrophic accident in the desert near Las Vegas (which killed lead and all wing airmen) ended the aircraft's use.

Tail-chasing—characteristic play by fledglings, which prepares them to eventually hunt prey.

Tailwind—in flight, wind blowing from the rear and thus increasing an aircraft's groundspeed; during final approach for landing, however, a tailwind can be disastrous.

Tarsus—the shank of a bird's leg; tarsometatarsus.

Telemetry—the tracking of a released falcon by means of a radar transmitter attached to the falcon's tarsus.

Tiercel (tarcel, tassel)—a male falcon, generally one-third smaller than the female. It was once believed that every third egg found in a nest would be a male. In the strictest usage, tiercel refers only to the male goshawk, while the male peregrine is called a "tiercel-gentle" or the "light-tiercel."

Touch and go—practice landings in which an aircraft touches down but does not stop before making another takeoff.

Traffic pattern—the normal rectangular pattern for sequencing and landing aircraft. A traffic pattern includes crosswind, downwind, base, and final.

True north—the direction from one's position to the geographic North Pole.

Variation—the difference between true and magnetic north, expressed in degrees.

VASI—visual approach slope indicator. VASI lights are keyed to a specific visual glide path, usually between 2.5° and 3.0°. If the VASI's indicate red over white during final approach, the pilot is on glide path; white over white, the pilot is too high; red over red, the pilot is too low. VASI's are references only: a pilot does not use them as a primary visual indicator for touchdown.

Wait on—the falcon's flight above the falconer, which lasts for an indefinite period of time.

Wake (sometimes called "manning")—breaking in a falcon by keeping her from sleep. Aragorn's wake involved remaining in total darkness and constant exposure to rock and roll radio.

Yawn (sometimes called "gape")—a behavior with no known explanation. Steve K. Sherrod has suggested that falcons may yawn to clear feathers trapped in the throat, or perhaps to equalize barometric pressure because of high-altitude flight or the presence of a changing weather front.

APPENDIX III:
Influences

This list is eclectic. Some of these books I never referred to during the writing of this work. But their presence was there: many writers, poets, and inquisitive and curious humans have contributed to my understanding, and I am grateful.

Abrams, M. H., ed. *The Norton Anthology of English Literature,* Vol. I, 4th ed. New York: Norton, 1979.

Adams, G. D. *Winged Thunderbolt: The Story of a Peregrine Falcon.* London: Constable & Company, Ltd., 1954.

Ammons, A. R. *Selected Poems: 1951–1977.* New York: Norton, 1977.

———. *Sumerian Vistas.* New York: Norton, 1987.

Andrić, Ivo. *Gospodica—The Woman from Sarajevo.* Translated by Jospeh Hitrec. New York: Alfred A. Knopf, 1965.

Baker, J. A. *The Peregrine.* New York: Harper & Row, 1967.

Beebe, Frank Lyman, and Webster, Harold Melvin. *North American Falconry and Hunting Hawks.* Denver: privately printed, 1964.

Bert's Treatise of Hawks and Hawking. London: Bernard Quaritch, 1891.

Bishop, Elizabeth. *Collected Poems.* New York: Farrar Straus Giroux, 1984.

———. *Collected Prose.* New York: Farrar Straus Giroux, 1984.

Blaine, Gilbert. *Falconry.* London: Neville Spearman, 1936.

Brodsky, Joseph. *Less than One.* New York: Farrar Straus Giroux, 1986.

Broun, Maurice. *Hawks Aloft.* Kutztown, Pa.: Kutztown Pub. Co., 1949.

Cade, Tom J. *The Falcons of the World.* Ithaca: Cornell University Press, 1982.

Carlson, Renee P. *Fenwick Falcon at the Air Academy.* Denver: The Golden Bell Press, 1964.

Carpenter, William. *The Hours of Morning.* Charlottesville: University Press of Virginia, 1981.

———. *Rain.* Boston: Northeastern University Press, 1985.

Carruth, Hayden. *Brothers, I Loved You All.* New York: Sheep Meadows Press, 1978.

Carson, Rachel Louise. *Silent Spring.* Boston: Houghton Mifflin, 1962.

Church, Peggy P. *The House at Otowi Bridge: The Story of Edith Warner and Los Alamos.* Albuquerque: University of New Mexico Press, 1973.

Conroy, Frank. *Stop-Time.* New York: Penguin, 1977.

Dementev, Georgiĭ, Petrovich. *Der Gerfalke.* Originalarbeit aus dem Russischen übersetzt von Erich Meyer. Wittenberg Lutherstadt: A Ziemsen, 1960.

Dillard, Annie. *Pilgrim at Tinker Creek.* New York: Harper's Magazine Press, 1974.

Dinesen, Isak. *Out of Africa.* New York: Random House, 1937.

Dobyns, Stephen. *Black Dog, Red Dog.* New York: Holt, Rinehart and Winston, 1984.

———. *Cemetery Nights.* New York: Viking, 1987.

Driscoll, Jack. *Fishing the Backwash.* Ithaca: Ithaca House, 1984.

Friedrich II of Hohenstaufen. *Arte della Falconeria.* Florence: Editoriale Olimpia, 1980.

———. *De Arte Venandi cum Avibus.* Translated by Casey A. Woodt and F. Marjorie Fyfe. London: Oxford University Press, 1943.

Fuertes, Louis Agassiz. "Falconry, the Sport of Kings: Once the Means of Supplying Man's Necessities, It has Survived the Centuries as One of the Most Romantic Pastimes of History." *National Geographic Magazine* 38, no. 6 (1920), pp. 429–67.

Graves, Robert. *Good-bye to All That.* New York: Doubleday, 1957.

Harting, James Edmund. *The Birds of Shakespeare Critically Examined, Explained, and Illustrated.* London: John Van Voorst, Paternoster Row, 1876.

Hill, Robin. "Trying to master the not so gentle art of Falconry." *Washington Post,* 15 July 1976.

Janowitz, Phyllis. *Visiting Rites.* Princeton: Princeton University Press, 1982.

Kaufmann, John, and Heinz Meng. *Falcons Return.* New York: William Morrow and Company, 1975.

Kerouac, Jack. *The Dharma Bums.* New York: Viking, 1958.

Kinnell, Galway. *Black Light.* San Francisco: North Point Press, 1980.

Klaeber, Frederick, ed. *Beowulf and The Fight at Finnsburg.* Lexington, Massachusetts: D. C. Heath and Company, 1950.

Knowler, Donald. *The Falconer of Central Park.* New York: Bantam, 1986.

Kosinski, Jerzy. *The Painted Bird.* 2d ed. Boston: Houghton Mifflin, 1976.

Kühnert, Gerd. *Falknerei in Afghanistan.* Bonn: Rudolf Habelt Verlag GmbH, 1980.

Kundera, Milan. *Nesnesitelná lehkost bytí—The Unbearable Lightness of Being.* Translated by Michael Henry Heim. New York: Harper & Row, 1984.

Latham, S. *Latham's Falconry, or the Faulcons Lure and Cure.* London: Roger Jackson, 1615.

Lawrence, R. D. *In Praise of Wolves.* New York: Henry Holt & Company, 1986.

Levine, Philip. *Selected Poems.* New York: Atheneum, 1984.

Lopez, Barry. *Arctic Dreams: Imagination and Desire in a Northern Landscape.* New York: Bantam, 1987.

——. *Of Wolves and Men.* New York: Charles Scribner's Sons, 1978.

Lowry, Malcolm. *Under the Volcano.* New York: New American Library, 1984.

McDonald, Walter. *After the Noise of Saigon.* Amherst: University of Massachusetts Press, 1988.

Maclean, Norman. *A River Runs through It.* Chicago: University of Chicago Press, 1976.

Markham, Beryl. *West with the Night.* San Francisco: North Point Press, 1983.

Márquez, Gabriel García. *El otoño del patriarca.* Buenos Aires: Editorial Sudamericana, 1975.

——. *One Hundred Years of Solitude.* Translated by Gregory Rabassa. New York: Harper and Row, 1970.

Matthiessen, Peter. *The Snow Leopard.* New York: The Viking Press, 1978.

——. *The Tree Where Man Was Born.* New York: E. P. Dutton, 1972.

Michell, E. B. *The Art and Practice of Hawking.* London: Holland Press, 1900.

Milosz, Czeslaw. *Bells in Winter.* Translated by Czeslaw Milosz and Lillian Vallee. New York: Ecco Press, 1978.

Morgan, Robert. *At the Edge of the Orchard Country.* Middletown: Wesleyan University Press, 1987.

Mowat, Farley. *And No Birds Sang.* Boston: Atlantic–Little, Brown, 1981.

——. *A Whale for the Killing.* Boston: Atlantic–Little, Brown, 1972.

——. *Never Cry Wolf.* Boston: Atlantic–Little, Brown, 1963.

——. *People of the Deer.* Boston: Atlantic–Little, Brown, 1952.

——. *Sea of Slaughter.* Boston: Atlantic–Little, Brown, 1984.

——. *The World of Farley Mowat.* Boston: Atlantic–Little, Brown, 1980.

Nabokov, Vladimir. *Speak, Memory: An Autobiography Revisited.* New York: G. P. Putnam's Sons, 1966.

Newby, Eric. *A Short Walk in the Hindu Kush: A Preposterous Adventure.* New York: Doubleday, 1958.

Nichols, John. *On the Mesa.* Layton, Utah: Peregrine Smith Books, 1986.

———. *The Last Beautiful Days of Autumn.* New York: Holt, Rinehart and Winston, 1982.

Pavese, Cesare. *Lavorare Stanca—Hard Labor.* Translated by William Arrowsmith. Baltimore: Johns Hopkins University Press, 1979.

Peterson, Roger Tory. *A Field Guide to the Birds of Eastern and Central North America.* Text and illustrations by Roger Tory Peterson; maps by Virginia Marie Peterson. 4th ed. Boston: Houghton Mifflin, 1980.

Peterson, Roger Tory, and Peterson, Virginia Marie. *Audubon's Birds of America: The Audubon Society Baby Elephant Folio.* New York: Abbeville Press, 1981.

Pirsig, Robert M. *Zen and the Art of Motorcycle Maintenance.* Toronto: Bantam, 1975.

Randall, Francis. "Lost at Sea." *Amherst,* Winter (1987), pp. 16–24.

Remmler, F. W. "Reminiscences from My Life with Eagles." Translated by Terry Killion. *Journal of the North American Falconers' Association,* 9 (1970), pp. 26–44.

Rilke, Rainer Maria. *Die Sonnette an Orpheus.* Various Editions.

Saint-Exupéry, Antoine de. *Flight to Arras.* Translated by Lewis Galantière. New York: Reynal and Hitchcock, 1942.

———. *Night Flight.* Translated by Stuart Gilbert. New York: The Century Co., 1932.

Salter, James. *Solo Faces.* Boston: Little, Brown and Company, 1979.

Schaller, George B. *Stones of Silence: Journeys in the Himalaya.* New York: Viking, 1980.

Schley, Jim, ed. "Writers in the Nuclear Age" (special edition). *New England Review/Bread Loaf Quarterly,* 5, no. 4 (1983).

Sherrod, Steve K. *Behavior of Fledgling Peregrines.* Ithaca: The Peregrine Fund, 1983.

Sherrod, Steve K.; Heinrich, William R.; Burnham, William A.; Barclay, Jack; and Cade, Tom J. *Hacking: A Method for Releasing Peregrine Falcons and Other Birds of Prey.* Ithaca: The Peregrine Fund, 1982.

Simic, Charles, and Strand, Mark, eds. *Another Republic.* New York: Ecco Press, 1976.

Stevens, R. *The Taming of Genghis.* London: Faber and Faber, 1956.

Turbervile, George. *The Booke of Falconrie and Hawking: For the onely delight and pleasure of all Noblemen and Gentlemen.* London: George Purfoot, 1611.

Ure, Stellanie. *Hawk Lady.* New York: Doubleday, 1980.

USAF Academy. *Contrails: The Cadet Mandatory Book of Knowledge.* USAF Academy: various editions.

Waters, Frank. *The Woman at Otowi Crossing: A Novel.* Denver: A. Swallow, 1966.

Webb, James. *A Sense of Honour.* London: Panther Books, 1984.

White, T. H. *The Goshawk.* New York: G. P. Putnam's Sons, 1951.

Zimmerman, David R. "Death Comes to the Peregrine Falcon." *The New York Times Magazine,* August 9, 1970.

NOTES

THE BOXES

1. Though most claim that the bottom of an auroral curtain rarely comes closer to the earth's surface than a hundred miles, what we saw that night was around, rather than above us.

2. Most likely, the aurora is created by the instability of electrons and ions in the Van Allen radiation belt.

3. Barry Lopez, *Arctic Dreams: Imagination and Desire in a Northern Landscape* (New York: Bantam, 1987), p. 209.

4. *Beowulf*, lines 1357–67. The translation is mine.

5. Henry David Thoreau, "Where I Lived, and What I Lived For," from *Walden: or, Life in the Woods* (New York: Collier Books, 1962), p. 75.

6. The instructions from George Turbervile's *The Booke of Falconrie and Hawking: For the onely delight and pleasure of all Noblemen and Gentlemen* (London: Thomas Purfoot, 1611) are: "Take a needle threded with untwisted threed, and casting your hawke [holding the wings] take her by the beake, and put the needle through her eye-lidde, not right against the sight of the eye, but somewhat nearer to the beake, because she may see backwards. And you must take good heede that you hurt not the webbe, which is under the eye-lidde, or on the inside thereof. Then put your needle also through that other eye-lidde, drawing the endes of the threed together, tye them over the beake, not with a straight knotte, but cut off the threedes endes in such sorte, that the eye-liddes may be raysed so upwards, that the hawke may not see at all, and when the threede shall

ware loose or untyed, then the hawke may see somewhat back-wardes, which is the cause that the threed is put nearer to the beake."

7. James Wright, "Lying in a Hammock at William Duffy's Farm in Pine Island, Minnesota," from *Collected Poems* (Middletown: Wesleyan University Press, 1971).

RELEASE

8. Steve K. Sherrod, W. R. Heinrich, W. A. Burnham, J. H. Bar-clay, and T. J. Cade, *Hacking: A Method for Releasing Peregrine Falcons and Other Birds of Prey* (Ithaca: The Peregrine Fund, 1982), p. 34.

9. William Carpenter, unpublished poem.

10. Louis Agassiz Fuertes, "Falconry, the Sport of Kings," *National Geographic Magazine*, Vol. 38, No. 6 (1920), p. 459.

11. Fuertes, "Falconry, the Sport of Kings," p. 429, and artist's plate III.

12. During World War II, the British Air Ministry killed over 600 peregrines nesting on the cliffs of Dover. The falcons had been hunting homing pigeons released as location markers by downed pilots.

13. Recently, Donald Duck visited the Academy and had a publicity picture taken with a peregrine falcon (which Cornell had donated to the Academy ten months before). I took a strange delight in this: I imagined the peregrine—whose common name is "duck hawk"—ripping into Donald. The peregrine would leave only wings, the sharp keel of a breast-bone, and a tail. This, of course, didn't happen—the only carnage was in my imagination. In the photograph, the cold and emotionless mask of Donald Duck curves upward into a frozen smile. At the corner of the frame, the peregrine sits on the falconer's fist, looking bewildered.

14. Cade is a Cornell professor who deserves much of the credit for the reintroduction of the peregrine species to the wild.

15. First published in *Esprit*, spring 1988.

16. Barry Lopez, *Of Wolves and Men* (New York: Charles Scribner's Sons, 1978), p. 156.

17. F. W. Remmler, "Reminiscences from My Life with Eagles,"

Journal of the North American Falconers' Association, Vol. 9 (1970), p. 35.

18. T. J. Cade, *The Falcons of the World* (Ithaca: Cornell University Press, 1982), p. 20.

19. Ibid., p. 12.

20. Ibid., p. 26.

21. The highest recorded peregrine nest is 13,000 feet.

22. Steve K. Sherrod, *Behavior of Fledgling Peregrines* (Ithaca: The Peregrine Fund, 1983), pp. 36–37.

23. Cade, *The Falcons of the World*, pp. 62–63.

24. Fuertes, "Falconry, the Sport of Kings," p. 439.

25. The military term for boom operator is "inflight refueling technician," a formal title for a very unusual job. The boom operator, stationed in the rear of the aircraft, is responsible for flying the boom (a cylindrical refueling nozzle, equipped with tiny wings) into a stationary envelope from which the receiver aircraft can refuel. My boom operator, Glen, was eighteen years old.

26. Terrence Des Pres, "Self/Landscape/Grid," *New England Review/Bread Loaf Quarterly*, 5, No. 4 (1983), pp. 441–50.

27. T. H. White, *The Goshawk* (New York: G. P. Putnam's Sons, 1951), pp. 66–67.

28. G. D. Adams, *Winged Thunderbolt: The Story of a Peregrine Falcon* (London: Constable and Co., Ltd., 1954), p. 79.

29. Perhaps a minor chord: I recently read, in a report written by the director of the Academy falconry program, that the official mascot, Mach I, was female. Unaware that female falcons are stronger, more aggressive, more dominant than male tiercels, the publicity director—afraid that the cadet wing faced ridicule for having a female mascot—asked that Mach I be replaced with a male.

30. Walt Whitman, "The Dalliance of the Eagles," *Complete Poetry and Collected Prose* (New York: Library of America, 1982), p. 412.

31. Cade, *The Falcons of the World*, p. 44.

32. The reason for flying prairie falcons, the most irascible and uncooperative of raptors, at hundreds of demonstrations each

year is also evident: peregrines, the most pleasurable falcons to train, are endangered. Flying them at demonstrations is bad publicity and bad practice.

33. Sherrod et al., *Hacking*, p. 2.

34. It is wrong to assume the Academy and the Peregrine Fund had a mutually cooperative and beneficial relationship. I recall several trips to the peregrine breeding chambers at Fort Collins, and some work with the Fund's program. But the Peregrine Fund did far more for us than we for them. They were always willing to help, whether it meant giving advice on training or supplying quail.

35. Some of this information comes from a report written by Colonel Lawrence Schaad, "USAFA Falcon Mascot Program," 7-2.

36. Sherrod, *Behavior of Fledgling Peregrines*, p. 125.

37. Ibid., p. 109.

38. Ibid., pp. 98–101.

39. Slow-motion cinematography has shown that when falcons strike they have all four toes fully extended, and not a half-closed fist—as Louis Agassiz Fuertes claimed—although it is still a mystery how they keep from snapping their toes with the tremendous force of their strike. (Cade, *Falcons of the World*, p. 21.)

40. J. A. Baker, *The Peregrine* (New York: Harper and Row, 1967), p. 35.

41. Remmler, "Reminiscences," p. 27.

LEARNING TO FLY

42. Donald Knowler, *The Falconer of Central Park* (New York: Bantam Books, 1986), p. 37.

43. The Peregrine Fund and the Colorado Wildlife Federation have been using a unique method, as an alternative to hacking, over the past decade: specialists rappel down cliff faces to recover peregrine eggs from a nest while replacing them with dummy eggs. The peregrine eggs are then placed in an incubator and hatched. The chicks are returned to the nest three weeks later. Although the adults rarely reject their new brood, they often seem confused at the sudden appearance of chicks on the cliff ledge and will attempt to incubate the nest. But the loud, squawking "teenagers" demand to be fed, and life in the wild returns to normal.

44. John Kaufmann and Heinz Meng, *Falcons Return* (New York: William Morrow, 1975), p. 35.

45. Baker, *The Peregrine*, pp. 14–15.

46. Kaufmann and Meng, *Falcons Return*, p. 43.

47. It is intriguing, and sad, to note that the discovery of the properties of DDT by Swiss scientist Paul Müller (who received the 1948 Nobel prize in physiology and medicine for his work) led to significant advancements in insecticides and chemical warfare.

48. My thanks to David Godine for this information.

49. Hayden Carruth, "Essay," from *Brothers, I Love You All* (New York: Sheep Meadows Press, 1978), p. 7.

50. The infamous "chicken cannon" used in laboratory tests has shown this clearly: Frozen chickens (sometimes weighing several pounds) are fired at high speeds at the windscreen of an F-111. Though it sounds incredible—and it is—tests have shown that for a windscreen to effectively deflect the force of the bird's impact, the glass would have to be so thick that it would prevent pilots from seeing out of the cockpit.

51. White, *The Goshawk*, p. 158.

52. James Edmund Harting, *The Birds of Shakespeare* (London: John Van Voorst, Paternoster Row, 1876), pp. 75–76. Much of this information is drawn from a paper I wrote as a cadet, "A Portrait of the Bard as an Ardent Falconer." To my knowledge, there is no evidence to prove that Shakespeare actively practiced hawking.

53. White, *The Goshawk*, p. 155.

54. Much of this information comes from *Contrails: The Cadet Mandatory Book of Knowledge*, published in various volumes by the United States Air Force Academy.

55. Tom Wolfe, *The Right Stuff* (New York: Bantam Books, 1980), p. 33.

56. Lopez, *Arctic Dreams*, p. 224.

57. Ibid., p. 362.

58. Peter Matthiessen, *The Snow Leopard* (New York: Viking, 1978), p. 316.